ETHICS AND POWER IN MEDIEVAL ENGLISH REFORMIST WRITING

The late medieval Church obliged all Christians to rebuke the sins of others, especially those who had power to discipline in Church and state: priests, confessors, bishops, judges, the Pope. This practice, in which the injured party had to confront the wrongdoer directly and privately, was known as fraternal correction. Edwin Craun examines how pastoral writing instructed Christians to make this corrective process effective by avoiding slander, insult, and hypocrisy. He explores how John Wyclif and his followers expanded this established practice to authorize their own polemics against mendicants and clerical wealth. Finally, he traces how major English reformist writing – *Piers Plowman*, *Mum and the Sothsegger*, and *The Book of Margery Kempe* – expanded the practice to justify their protests, to protect themselves from repressive elements in the late Ricardian and Lancastrian Church and state, and to urge their readers to mount effective protests against religious, social, and political abuses.

EDWIN D. CRAUN is Henry S. Fox, Jr. Professor of English at Washington and Lee University.

CAMBRIDGE STUDIES IN MEDIEVAL LITERATURE

GENERAL EDITOR
Alastair Minnis, Yale University

EDITORIAL BOARD
Zygmunt G. Barański, University of Cambridge
Christopher C. Baswell, University of California, Los Angeles
John Burrow, University of Bristol
Mary Carruthers, New York University
Rita Copeland, University of Pennsylvania
Simon Gaunt, King's College London
Steven Kruger, City University of New York
Nigel Palmer, University of Oxford
Winthrop Wetherbee, Cornell University
Jocelyn Wogan-Browne, Fordham University

This series of critical books seeks to cover the whole area of literature written in
the major medieval languages – the main European vernaculars, and medieval
Latin and Greek – during the period *c.* 1100–1500. Its chief aim is to publish and
stimulate fresh scholarship and criticism on medieval literature, special emphasis
being placed on understanding major works of poetry, prose, and drama in relation to the contemporary culture and learning which fostered them.

A complete list of titles in the series can be found at the end of the volume.

ETHICS AND POWER IN MEDIEVAL ENGLISH REFORMIST WRITING

EDWIN D. CRAUN

CAMBRIDGE
UNIVERSITY PRESS

CAMBRIDGE UNIVERSITY PRESS
Cambridge, New York, Melbourne, Madrid, Cape Town, Singapore
São Paulo, Delhi, Dubai, Tokyo

Cambridge University Press
The Edinburgh Building, Cambridge CB2 8RU, UK

Published in the United States of America by Cambridge University Press, New York

www.cambridge.org
Information on this title: www.cambridge.org/9780521199322

First published 2010

Printed in the United Kingdom at the University Press, Cambridge

A catalogue record for this publication is available from the British Library

Library of Congress Cataloguing in Publication data

Craun, Edwin D.
Ethics and power in medieval English reformist writing /
Edwin D. Craun.
p. cm.
(Cambridge studies in medieval literature ; 76)
ISBN 978-0-521-19932-2 (Hardback)
1. Admonition–History–To 1500. 2. England–Church history–1066–1485.
3. Church renewal–England–History–To 1500. 4. Church discipline–England–
History–To 1500. 5. Christian literature, English (Middle)–History
and criticism. I. Title.
BR747.C73 2010
241.0942′09023–dc22
2009044696

ISBN 978-0-521-19932-2 Hardback

For Marlys, Lad, and Harlan

Contents

Acknowledgments

The final research for this project and the early stages of writing were supported by a series of grants. In 2002–3 I held a Jessie Ball duPont Fellowship at the National Humanities Center, made possible by the Jessie Ball duPont Religious, Charitable and Educational Fund; my fellowship was supplemented by the Duke Endowment. The Center staff, not least of all the librarians and Kent Mulliken, the Deputy Director at a time of transition, were unstintingly helpful, while the Fellows that year provided intellectual companionship for which I was starved. I was spoiled for life. During the fall of 2002 a Huntington Library and British Academy Fellowship enabled me to extend my research in manuscripts in British collections. In 2003 I held a Fellowship for College Teachers from the National Endowment for the Humanities, while Washington and Lee University supported the project from its inception to its end with a series of John M. Glenn grants during summers and with one Robert E. Lee grant, which gave me a second resourceful student assistant, Katie Destiny Compton. The first, equally resourceful, was Jennifer Fisher.

Few teachers at a liberal arts college have been luckier in their colleagues than I. Lad Sessions in philosophy and David Peterson in medieval and Renaissance Italian history persistently asked searching questions about the earliest draft of the first two chapters that shaped the entire course of this book, while Genelle Gertz has shared ideas about women's religious speech and writing ever since she arrived in my department five years ago. The direction of the whole book – indeed, its very brand of history – was set in part by generous comments by the members of the Medieval/Early Modern Writing Group at the National Humanities Center in 2003: Kathryn Burns, Paulina Kewes, Joanne Rappaport, Moshe Sluhovsky, Helen Solterer, and, over several more years, Kalman Bland, Annabel Wharton, and Gail Gibson. I received shrewd comments on individual chapters or the papers that preceded them from Larry Clopper, Thelma Fenster, the late David Fowler, Andy Galloway, Mike

Kuczynski, Susan Phillips, Derrick Pitard, Dan Smail, Jan Ziolkowski, and the members of the Cultural Studies Colloquium at Washington and Lee. Three editors at Cambridge University Press – Linda Bree, Elizabeth Hanlon, and Rosina Di Marzo – moved my typescripts resourcefully through publication, and Damian Love proved to be the inquisitive and imaginative copy-editor a scholar longs for.

I am indebted to these institutions and people for access to manuscripts in their keeping: the Bodleian Library (chiefly); the British Library; Cambridge University Library; the Master and Fellows of Balliol College, Oxford; the President and Fellows of Magdalen College, Oxford; the Warden and Fellows of Merton College, Oxford; the Provost and Fellows of Oriel College, Oxford; the Master and Fellows of Sidney Sussex College, Cambridge; the Master and Fellows of University College, Oxford; and the Marquess of Bath. Siegfried Wenzel generously shared with me material from several sermons. The librarians at Washington and Lee have been a constant resource, especially the unbeatable Elizabeth Teaffe in interlibrary loans. "'3e, by Peter and by Poul': Lewte and the Practice of Fraternal Correction," an early version of the middle of chapter 3, appeared in *The Yearbook of Langland Studies* 15 (2001), while part of chapter 6, "*Fama* and Pastoral Constraints on Rebuking Sinners: *The Book of Margery Kempe*," was published by Cornell University Press in 2003 in *"Fama": The Politics of Talk and Reputation in Medieval Europe*, edited by Thelma Fenster and Daniel L. Smail.

The dedication of this book records what may seem an unusual debt for an academic. My engagement in the ethics of social and institutional reform has been vivified over the years by three extraordinary people: my wife, Marlys, who devoted twenty-five years to administering public programs for the chronically mentally ill in the face of declining financial support and increasing mandates; my friend Lad Sessions, who dared, as a dean, to imagine that resources for the humanities and social sciences should not be eclipsed by commerce and law; and my friend Harlan Beckley, who founded and runs the innovative Shepherd Program for the Study of Poverty and Human Capability at Washington and Lee University. In the United States of the end of the twentieth and beginning of the twenty-first centuries, only the brave can be fair.

Oxford, Oxon., and Timber Ridge, Virginia

Editorial practices, translations, abbreviations

I modernize Middle English thorn, yogh, and *i-y-u-v* placements, whether in my transcriptions from manuscripts, in early printed books, or in modern editions. In Latin passages, I use *i* for the vowel, *j* for the consonant; *u* for the vowel, *v* for the consonant. I use modern punctuation and capitalization, and I expand contractions. I give all names in the person's vernacular, not Latin for some and English for others. I slightly modernize verses from the Douai translation of the Bible, using it throughout and occasionally modifying it to reflect how my sources read the Vulgate. Save for the Douai, all translations are mine. I use the following abbreviations:

CCCM   Corpus Christianorum: Continuatio Mediaevalis (Turnhout: Brepols, 1966–)

CCSL   Corpus Christianorum Scriptorum Latinorum (Turnhout: Brepols, 1953–)

CSEL   Corpus Scriptorum Ecclesiasticorum Latinorum (Vienna/Leipzig, Prague: Kommission zur Herausgabe des Corpus der lateinischen Kirchenväter, 1866–)

DML   *Dictionary of Medieval Latin from British Sources* (London: Oxford University Press, 1975–)

EETS   Early English Text Society (o.s. for original series and e.s. for extra series)

MED   *Middle English Dictionary* (Ann Arbor: University of Michigan Press, 1956–2001)

OED   *Oxford English Dictionary*, 2nd edn (Oxford University Press, 1989)

PL   Patrologia Latina (Paris: Jacques-Paul Migne, 1844–65)

Introduction

> I see my friends take discounts for which they're not really eligible, buy and wear clothes they later return, stiff waiters, and in many ways cheat the system. I find this deplorable. Then again, when I was young, I used to do many of the same things. How can I justify my righteous attitude when I've been just as guilty? And what do I say when my friends brag about these dubious achievements?

Randy Cohen's answer to this query, submitted to the *New York Times* Sunday column "The Ethicist" a decade ago, could have come from a late medieval sermon or pastoral text on fraternal correction of sin, save for its references to "Oprah" and Dr. Johnson. You have reformed years ago, Cohen advises Allegreta Behar-Blau of Woodland Hills, California, so you are not being inconsistent. Anyhow, you "needn't be completely virtuous to encourage virtue in others." You can tell your friends what you think "if you speak directly, quietly, and without chastising them."[1]

Fraternal correction of sin, the late medieval practice of admonishing others charitably for their evil conduct in order to reform them, is almost as invisible to medievalists as to most other readers of the Sunday *New York Times*. Even though the movement to expand pastoral care from the early thirteenth century on enjoined all Christians – lay and clerical – to reprove sin as an act of charity whenever they encountered it in a fellow Christian, especially clerics in positions of disciplinary power (confessors, bishops, the Pope), no scholar has examined how fraternal correction was constructed in pastoral writing, let alone how it was seized upon and adapted resourcefully by writers intent on widespread reform. Fraternal correction is absent from, for example, André Vauchez's *The Laity in the Middle Ages*, Anne Hudson's exhaustive study of Wycliffite texts, *The Premature Reformation*, and scholarship on those potent English correctors of sin, Margery Kempe and William Langland. Dropped from the Roman Catholic code of canon law in the revision promulgated in 1917, it ceased by 1950 even to be a topic for dissertations in theology (at least published ones).[2] Only Takashi Shogimen has taken up discourse on fraternal correction: He sets forth briefly how thirteenth-century canonists and theologians wrote about correction of superiors so that he can explain how William of Ockham developed from their discourse "a radical theory of legitimate disobedience to papal authority."[3]

This study of fraternal correction is fundamentally historical. It opens access to materials outside the ken of medievalists: the pastoral writing on fraternal correction, largely in manuscript form, produced by clerics engaged in reforming the conduct of Western Christians over the two centuries from just after the Fourth Lateran Council (1215) to the 1440s. Entries labeled "correctio fraterna" and/or general entries on "correctio" or "correptio"[4] that include fraternal correction appear in thirteen general collections of pastoral materials circulating in England before 1440. All four confessional *summae* from the late thirteenth and early fourteenth centuries that survive in British libraries contain a longish entry on "fraterna correctio," rich sources of catechetical and homiletic material. The entries in both genres are complex mini-treatises on fraternal correction, full of biblical exegesis, patristic authorities, scholastic moral theology (often in large chunks), biblical *exempla*, and canon law, often giving a fully dialectical play to a controverted question about correction – and there are many.[5] Usually built out of these materials, sermons advocating fraternal correction were preached on two set occasions in the liturgical year, the Tuesday after the third Sunday in the great preaching season of Lent and the fourth Sunday after Trinity.[6] Not surprisingly bishops preached about fraternal correction when they carried out official visitations of parishes or larger communities, as did monastic visitors.[7]

Studying these main (and other) sources on fraternal correction enables us to redraw the relations between clergy and laity in these two centuries in England. Far from only circumscribing religious speech and writing, as most current scholarship would have it,[8] the clergy licensed and nourished lay reformist criticism of individual clerics. Clerical culture not only prescribed fraternal correction as one of the many duties its prescriptive literature laid out for the laity in the centuries of Gregorian and later reform, but it used the practice to regulate clerical conduct both internally (subordinate clerics reproving superiors) and externally (lay people reproving clerics). In the process, pastoral writing portrayed lay people, including women, and clerical subordinates as ethical agents who could resourcefully negotiate both existing power relations and ethical perplexities in carrying out correction of sin. Constructed as an obligatory practice, fraternal correction became a fluid cultural resource for reformist writers from just before the Uprising of 1381 to the late stages of Lancastrian suppression of religious speech and writing. Reformist writers and the literary figures some of them imagine in visionary literature and lives, like Will in *Piers Plowman* and the Margery Kempe of "her" book, practice fraternal correction as a clerically sanctioned form of writing and speech, a somewhat safe vehicle for reformist thought, as were the apocalyptic prophecies of Hildegard of Bingen, in Kathryn Kerby-Fulton's recent discoveries from careful manuscript work.[9] No matter what the genre or the writer's place on the spectrum from traditional religious thought to radical dissent and heresy, these reformist texts all move to extend fraternal correction to groups, even institutions, and to rethink what is involved in actually bringing about reform. Thus fraternal correction became a resource provided by the institutional Church that promoted vigorous criticism of the forms of English ecclesiastical, social, and political life – political because pastoral texts allow for political authorities, as well as clerical ones, to be the subjects of corrective speech. To steal a term from one of the readers for Cambridge University Press, it could lead to a "critical ecclesiology" – and, less frequently in writing, a critical politics.

To make these claims for what we can learn from studying fraternal correction in these sources is to point to the kinds of history this study practices and writes. Initially and at times throughout, it is a chapter in the history of medieval normative ethics as a branch of intellectual history: I trace how moral theologians and those who disseminated their ideas explored obligations and seemingly contrary goods, texts, and claims, especially as they worked to prevent correction from slipping into deviant speech, like slander and insult. Because fraternal correction is a social practice constructed by a clerical elite (moral theologians and the University-educated clergy), because it must be carried out within existing power relations, and because it deals, in David Gary Shaw's words, with the "*meanings* that guided people as they lived and altered their worlds," this study traverses some of the territory of social history.[10] In its last four chapters, I study social agents who imagine themselves practicing correction as presented in pastoral writing, managing and modifying it according to historical conditions and other social values, especially good repute and truth. However, I do not write fully realized social history. While I labor to place texts and manuscripts in specific locales at specific times, this kind of work is incomplete because we know the exact dates and ownership of very few manuscripts of pastoral texts and sermon collections.[11] Despite much scholarly detective work, the dating and even the authorship of many texts are still uncertain – let alone specific communities for which they were written. Moreover, I do not examine, as a social historian would, sources like the records of episcopal visits or of ecclesiastical courts, attempting to determine how much and among whom writing on correction mobilized action (if such evidence exists). Instead, this book works within the world of discursive and fictional texts – their construction, their rhetoric, their mutual influence, the uses writers imagine that their audiences will make of them. It is a broadly narrative literary and intellectual history of fraternal correction as a social practice, rather than social history in a strict sense. It is akin to David Aers's and Lynn Staley's *The Powers of the Holy,* in which (to take just the first chapter and a half) Aers explains how the humanity of Christ was represented differently and used for different religious purposes by writers like Nicholas Love (the crucified body that fosters Eucharistic devotion) and John Wyclif (the itinerant preacher challenging religious authorities).[12]

This study demands such historical hybridity because fraternal correction is a practice. The study of practices, as Paul Strohm conceives of it, "draws textuality, its occasions, its uses, and the events it describes into a socially performative totality."[13] As I situate fraternal correction as a practice in the communities that constructed and used it, I draw below on Alasdair MacIntyre's concept of practice as a socially constructed activity in which individuals pursue goods internal to the practice itself but also rooted in particular communities (including institutions) and in the individuals' lives. Like the anthropologist Talal Asad's work on medieval monastic practices, MacIntyre's writing considers how people's morality, their practice of virtues, is bound up with participating in practices within social settings.[14] Moreover, MacIntyre, like many social theorists, recognizes the open-endedness of practices, the possibility of extending or altering them, especially through what two of his feminist readers describe as "participants' conscious efforts and arguments about what the practice, and the tradition, *is* – that is, by what we might call a process of interpretive criticism or critique." I depart from MacIntyre's account of historically embedded practices where the two feminist readers do: in paying attention to the differential power of social agents, their relative power to participate in a practice and to alter it, and in spelling out the political grounding of the various "critical understandings and struggles over practices."[15] MacIntyre writes as if individuals played their social games on a level field under the same rules, whereas I believe that we need to study the workings of power – especially in institutions, class relations, and gender relations – in structuring agency.

Attending to power relations is essential in examining not only how people negotiated the practice of correction but how the practice was constructed and disseminated by academic theologians and highly educated priests, and how it served the interests of clerics from popes to parish priests. But to do so is not to see fraternal correction as an instrument that simply advanced the power of the higher clergy, the clergy as a whole, or any other dominant social group. The clergy was far too diverse for that, far too subject to conflicts of interest and interpretation, some of which will emerge in chapter 1. And to return to participants, what Andrew Brown writes of religious rituals could be said of fraternal correction: "the interplay in ritualized activity, between agents [for Brown, authorities who promoted rituals] and participants is often more dynamic than simple imposition of 'social control' by the one over the other."[16]

Such a multidimensional and extended historical narrative demands substantial chapter sketches – inelegant forms, to be sure, but necessary to set forth what this book attempts. These summaries will focus on the central questions about any reform movement. Who were the reformers? What kinds of texts did they write? What conduct – and whose – was to be corrected, "set straight" (to translate literally)? On the grounds of what authority and with what arguments? By what kind of speech – speech that might move offenders to reform while shielding correctors from dismissal, or even harm, as transgressive speakers? For reformers and their opponents alike recognized the "volatile status" of correction, to take a phrase from another reader's report: that the boundaries between efficacious reproof and speech that maliciously injured individuals and groups could be both difficult to discern and contestable.

The first chapter unfolds how pastoral writing, given impetus by scholastic theologians and canonists as well as by conciliar legislation, uses ethical reasoning to construct fraternal correction of sin within existing power relations. Although the high medieval Western movement to promote pastoral care consolidated clerical authority and power, it also enlisted lay people in combating sin, especially the sins of authorities, mainly clerical but also civil. Its texts enjoin all Christians, out of charity, to reprove individual sinners they encounter in order to reform their lives. The practice is firmly (but not always consistently) distinguished from prelatical or disciplinary correction, in which institutional authorities – like bishops, confessors, and judges – wield punishment and act for the common good. By making fraternal correction a universal precept, the clergy conferred pastoral power on the laity: the power to direct others' consciences, to persuade them to hew to religious norms, and to move them toward salvation. Yet pastoral texts also insist that reprovers acknowledge and negotiate existing power relations in certain ways if they are to practice correction ethically and successfully. So fraternal correction could reinforce social, political, and ecclesiastical hierarchies, even as it made lay people and other disciplinary subjects agents for reforming the lives of authorities.

To carry out, even to contemplate, an act of fraternal correction in specific situations was to face perplexity, difficulties, and even threats. "Negotiating contrary things," the second chapter, takes up the central questions explored by pastoral writers on fraternal correction as they struggle with competing claims about what people owe each other, and with seeming contradictions and ambiguities in authoritative texts. Whose sins are people bound to correct, given that they live in a world full of sin? Is it ever justifiable, let alone efficacious, for a known sinner to correct a fellow sinner? Are people ever justified, even required, to divulge someone's sins publicly in the process of reproof? Are harsh words ever acceptable in a practice to be governed by charity? The competing claims of universalizing charity and privacy, of acting for others' benefit and avoiding hypocrisy, of the common good and individuals' reputations, of verbal force and charitable speech drive pastoral writers and preachers to complex ethical reasoning, even to sacrificing one good to another in some circumstances. By these means the writers establish norms, especially constraints, governing how reproof can by practiced with moral authority, avoiding the appearance (or reality) of intrusiveness, hypocrisy, slander, and chiding. In this very process, however, they make the competing claims, the apparently contradictory authorities, and the different modes of ethical reasoning available to readers and listeners. They provide the very means by which their own norms can be contested.

The sources for these first two chapters were all written and circulating before the mid 1370s, when the Oxford theologian John Wyclif and the clerically educated author of *Piers Plowman* (probably William Langland), both outraged by the wealth of many ecclesiastical institutions and by the mercenary abuses of pastoral care, deftly altered dominant pastoral norms in order to extend the practice to correction of groups, communities, and institutions. So, pastoral writing before the mid 1370s serves as a benchmark against which to gauge how reformist writers, later ones as well as Wyclif and Langland, transformed fraternal correction into a tool for ecclesiastical and social reform.

The third chapter explores how Langland builds pastoral discourse on fraternal correction into his vernacular visionary satire by creating allegorical figures who take different stances toward reformist speech as they collide with each other. *Piers Plowman* first develops the strategies by which the corrupt resist correction: They shrewdly turn the ethical worries of traditional pastoral discourse against their reprovers, who are accused of malice and anger, of disclosing sins in public, of spreading falsehoods, and of complicity in what they denounce – in sum, of being deviant speakers, especially slanderers and chiders. Langland's task then becomes to persuade his reform-minded readers – managers of clerical and lay institutions in a time of ecclesiastical and economic unrest – that fraternal correction can survive such discrediting, emerging as a valuable resource for personal and institutional reform. Social exchanges between the dreamer (Will) and other figures develop how reprovers can use traditional clerically created norms and constraints to make their reproofs efficacious, preventing corrective speech from slipping into deviant speech (or being labeled so). But *Piers* does much more than popularize pastoral teaching in a vernacular poem with a wide imagined (and actual) readership. By deploying pastoral authorities deftly, it extends correction from individuals to the social groups they are part of, making readers aware of the institutional dimensions, even origins, of sin. In this and other ways, its vernacular fiction critiques the limits of, and exposes the fissures in, the general pastoral consensus on how to practice correction.

In contrast to *Piers Plowman*'s concern with the corrector's authority and efficacy, Wyclif's theological treatises and sermons boldly advocate fraternal correction as a means to accomplish large-scale reforms in the institutional Church. In *De civili dominio* and in his defenses against papal censure of his teaching on fraternal correction, Wyclif converts it into a disciplinary process involving not only admonition but also punishment, and performed not only for the soul of the cleric but also for the good of the Church. Then he advocates that the laity, especially lords, use correction to remove obstinately sinful clerics from office and so deprive them of their control over the Church's temporal goods. Since any cleric sins habitually if he exercises control of property, Wyclif envisions his melded fraternal/disciplinary correction as returning the whole English clergy to apostolic poverty and depriving it of disciplinary power. Several years later, Wyclif applies his recast fraternal correction specifically to the papacy: All Christians living in charity should not only admonish a sinning Roman pontiff but also refuse to acknowledge his authority, including his excommunications. Thus, Wyclif re-imagines fraternal correction as a tool to redistribute power and control of wealth in religious institutions at every level.

After Wyclif's teaching on fraternal correction (and much else) was condemned by the Blackfriars Council of 1382, ecclesiastical and civil edicts began to make reformist speech and writing more dangerous in England. The fifth chapter examines how Wyclif's followers embraced fraternal correction as a way of defining themselves and of defending themselves against oppression. Dismissed as slanderous and viciously insulting by those attacked, their polemical tracts and visionary narratives (in the *Piers Plowman* tradition) from 1381 until just after 1400 respond that Wycliffites hew strictly to the speech of Jesus, whose harsh rebukes of the Pharisees (never an element in pastoral teaching on correction) now become their model. So armed, they toss aside many, sometimes all, earlier constraints on reproof: concern for the sinners' response, fear of committing mortal Sins of the Tongue, reverence for social superiors, the social value of reputation. What validates their jeremiads against clerical groups, witnessing to their pastoral power and moral authority, is their conviction that they, followers of evangelical law and of Jesus, have direct, ecstatic access to God. Wycliffite polemics then go for the institutional jugular: the clergy's practice of pastoral care. All clerics who take tithes or set fees for pastoral acts are hypocrites because they correct others while practicing avarice. Pastoral power has passed to the Wycliffite, who alone knows the truth, alone lives in charity, and so alone can judge what is necessary for the salvation of others.

Wycliffism continued to unleash ecclesiastical reaction, notably in the form of Archbishop Thomas Arundel's Constitutions (1409), designed to extirpate heresy by regulating religious speech and writing in sweeping ways. To what extent did the Constitutions inhibit discourse on fraternal correction and corrective speech itself? After exploring that question, the last chapter takes up two reformist lives, *Mum and the Sothsegger* and *The Book of Margery Kempe*, which employ similar strategies for conveying boldly the need to practice fraternal correction in this repressive age. They take the practice into somewhat new reformist arenas: political counsel of King Henry IV and a woman's encounter with ecclesiastical authorities. *Mum* defines the good life as a life of truth-telling, of conveying the grievances of the commons to those in power, a life contrasted with that of Mum, who practices self-interested silence and flattery to amass goods and influence. The *Book* depicts a lay woman, shaped by the movement of pastoral reform, who ostentatiously hews to pastoral norms and constraints for corrective speech, while subtly directing pastoral rhetoric to reveal clerical sins and the institutional practices that feed them. In the process, she neatly escapes being judged a slanderer and uncharitable reprover of clerics, an offence now closely associated with Wycliffism. Looking back over the whole study, a postscript then addresses a pressing question in literary and historical studies: What effects did the movement for pastoral reform have on English society?

Three historiated initials mark three entries on correction in *Omne bonum*, a vast (and unfinished) encyclopedia of religious knowledge compiled largely of extracts from the Bible, moral theology, canon law commentaries, history, and hagiography, probably by James le Palmer (before 1327–1375), a scribe of the Exchequer and a native Londoner. In the initial before the first entry, on prelatical/disciplinary correction, a group of errant clerics in belted tunics, one with a sword between his legs, is being set straight by a figure pointing his finger at them, whom Lucy Freeman Sandler sees as a scholar or a judge (perhaps lay). A second initial is similar, save that two of the clerics are crouching, huddled, at the scholar's feet; it introduces a short entry on who should correct and a list of topics for the third entry. The third initial, reproduced on the front cover of this book (as the second initial is on the back), prefaces an entry entirely on fraternal correction. In it, two laymen embrace, a gesture of the reconciliation between sinner and corrector that fraternal correction was designed to accomplish.[17] This third initial clearly marks fraternal correction as speech open to lay people. The artist, probably James, himself a cleric, does not choose to represent the more socially leveling kind of fraternal correction: a lay person reproving a cleric, setting him straight, and intending to amend his life. This kind largely engages the reformist writers of this study, lay and clerical alike, who find in the clerics' pastoral movement of reform a practice and a rhetoric that can achieve what lay people find good for themselves, for others, and for the Church and, sometimes, the state.

CHAPTER I

Universalizing correction as a moral practice

When the Margery Kempe constructed by her *Book*[1] is cast out of the Archbishop of York's presence and then his archdiocese, one of her prime offenses has been practicing fraternal correction of sin. In late 1417, she has been reproving York clerics and lay people for their sins, urging them to amend their lives. In doing so, she is what Meili Steele calls, in familiar post-structuralist terms, "a constructed subject."[2] Just as the *Book* constructs her as an exemplary holy woman in general, the clerics who have catechized her and counseled her over the years have shaped her into an active participant in their program of pastoral care, designed for two centuries to "inspire correct belief and correct behavior,"[3] especially to extirpate sin. The sins she rebukes are clerically designated and defined, and the most common of them, blasphemy, was rated the gravest among all Sins of the Tongue, a violation of the Ten Commandments, certain to bring damnation (as she reminds the culprits) unless repented of and abandoned.[4] Moreover, the rhetoric Kempe employs in rebuking sin hews, as we shall see at the other end of this book, to norms laid out in pastoral texts. One of the reasons she escapes the nets cast by her learned accusers is that she is so fully a subject of clerical power, so fully conformed to pastoral discourse on sin and its correction.

To read Margery Kempe at York through this broadly political lens, so commonly used in recent scholarship on early-fifteenth-century literature, is to read in only one dimension, to grasp only one set of relations between the clerics and the lay woman: that of power conferred by priesthood and Latin learning, both restricted by institutions to men (wholly and largely, respectively). It is to see social power only in terms of class, gender, degree of literacy, status, and law.[5] But the *Book* demands at least bifocals, especially in its exchanges between clerics and lay people. For the Margery Kempe who emerges in dialogue with the York clergy, most notably Archbishop Henry Bowet, is also (again in Steele's terms) "a constructing ethical subject,"[6] someone for whom ethical practices can be used to achieve her own sense of the good in a specific situation.

Than seid the Erchebischop to hir, "Thow schalt swerin that thu ne xalt [shall not] techyn ne [nor] chalengyn [reprove, correct] the pepil in my diocyse." "Nay, ser, I xal not sweryn," sche seyde, "for I xal spekyn of God & undirnemyn [reprove, correct] hem [them] that sweryn gret othys wher-so-evyr I go un-to the time that the Pope & Holy Chirche hath ordeinde that no man schal be so hardy to spekyn of God, for God al-mithy [almighty] forbedith not, ser, that we xal speke of him."[7]

"Nay, ser" marks Kempe as agent, and "chalengyn" and "undirnemyn" mark fraternal correction of sin as a fluid cultural resource for a woman aware of the power differential between herself and a University-educated Archbishop (indeed, a doctor of civil and canon law). For her, correction of sins, clerical and lay, is a form of divinely sanctioned speech, a way to speak of God to those who need to hear. For example, her rebuke of the Archbishop's retinue (I capitalize to underscore his institutional power) just before this exchange concludes by asserting the primacy of God's commandments over the custom of swearing "great oaths": " 'Seris, I drede me ye xul [shall] be brent in helle with-owtyn ende les than [unless] ye amende yow of yowr othys swering, for ye kepe not the comawndementys of God' " (p. 124). She rebukes sin as violation of divine law and seeks the men's amendment, goods, as we shall see below, sought for in the practice of fraternal correction. Her reply to the Archbishop exposes how he uses his position of authority in the institutional Church to attempt to silence a woman who is following an institutional practice conscientiously: Women as well as men, those subject to clerical disciplinary power as well as clerics, were obligated to correct sinners wherever they encountered them. In this, she confers upon herself a pastoral authority and power (to be defined shortly) that she uses to challenge how consistently and authentically he practices his forms of authority and power. Through fraternal correction, she reconstructs power relations in her own ethical terms.

Subject as she is to what clerics have taught her about fraternal correction, Margery Kempe nevertheless uses that in a specific situation in ways that, to appropriate Paul Ricoeur on ethical intentionality, she finds good for herself, for others, and for the institutional Church, even though those ways may be counter to what the clerics at hand find good.[8] Like Ricoeur's formulation, her speech acknowledges the close relation between ethics and politics, allowing for a passage from one to the other as she takes responsibility for others and for the life of institutions. What she accomplishes at York, and the rhetorical strategies she employs, will form the other bookend of the study, the second half of chapter 6.

As a product of the pastoral movement, the discourse on fraternal correction I will explicate in this chapter licenses criticism, especially of ecclesiastical and civil authorities, for the good of individuals and society. However, it also works to constrain the forms that criticism takes, insisting that correction be negotiated in ways that confirm existing power relations, especially the disciplinary powers of the clergy. Such a discourse demands from us a complementary ethical and political approach, just as the episode at York does. This approach must insist that "agency is embedded in complex historical languages, which can both oppress and enable,"[9] which both construct religious subjects and equip them to pursue their own sense of what is good in specific situations, even in conflicts between social groups. I believe that it is the task of the medievalist both to re-present those languages as fully as possible – to let us listen to the textual voices that speak them – and to critique how those languages implemented the power of dominant classes through their institutions. For the voices I use the first person plural whenever feasible; for the critique, the third person.

PASTORAL POWER AND SIN

The practice of fraternal correction was developed by the clergy to address the problem of sin within the Western Christian Church. It was a product of the "pastoral offensive" initiated by the Fourth Lateran Council of 1215.[10] Like preaching or auricular confession, it was an instrument of what Michel Foucault called pastoral power, a power which "implies knowledge of the conscience and the ability to direct it." Like them, too, it was designed to assure the salvation of individuals.[11] It presented as the way to salvation the individual's conformity to a law of truth, an ideal, normative way of knowing and acting derived from religious law, as it was interpreted by the clergy. In this last sentence, as in much of this chapter, I extend and critique Foucault's concept of pastoral power, sharply limited because he considers only confession (and little evidence on that) and sees all disciplinary power as oppressive.

Sin was defined by the pastoral movement as ways of deviating from that law. Consider the definitions of sin, twelve but somewhat overlapping, set forth by Magister Galienus's mid-thirteenth-century English pastoral manual, the *Speculum juniorum*. Pride of place goes to the time-honored Augustinian "Every sin is something said or done or desired against the law of God." Although "law" was commonly understood in pastoral texts as revealed moral law, the injunctions and prohibitions of the Christian scriptures,[12] the *Speculum* glosses it as eternal law, the divine plan or will ("ratio divina vel voluntas"). So, sin could be seen ontologically as violations of "the form, order, and due measure that inform creation," in Lee

Patterson's words.[13] To define sin in such moral and ontological terms is to make space in a largely illiterate society for a learned clergy that can expound revealed law and anatomize how specific sins are "inordinata," contrary to divine order. Several of the *Speculum*'s definitions locate sin in the disoriented will: a will averse to the unchanging good for all because it is directed to the sinner's own good, an inferior good involving external, not spiritual good ("voluntas aversa ab incommutabili bono communi et conversa ad proprium bonum aut ad exterius bonum aut ad inferius"). A sinful will, as another definition conceptualizes it, lacks justice, the steady disposition to render to others what it owes them, as the community determines that (Aristotle's definition of justice as a virtue of character). And sin is straying from what truth commends ("in preceptis veritatis errare") – another definition which creates the need for someone to expound law/precepts. Finally, sin is to dishonor God, to fail to acknowledge His worth and status ("deum inhonorare") – the last, like the first, an ontological definition.[14]

The pastoral movement insisted that sin, conceived of in all these ways as willed deviations from divine being, will, and law, must be eradicated by someone expert in the care of souls, the "art of arts" according to the Fourth Lateran Council. First, sin must be made known, be spoken of, in pastoral activities: characterized in preaching, labeled and defined by the priest during the confessional dialogue, identified in fraternal correction. In response, sinners were required to speak of their sins as a sign that they accepted pastoral knowledge, felt sorrow for sin, and would amend their lives. Unlike the much studied practices of preaching or confession, however, fraternal correction, as we will see, could confer pastoral power on the *subditus*, the person subject to spiritual care and discipline, as well as on the *praelatus*, the person charged with the care of souls (*cura animarum*) or disciplinary office: on the lay person as well as on the cleric, on the novice as well as on the abbess or abbot, on the penitent as well as on the confessor during confessional dialogue. It was a cultural resource shared by any Christian who acts out of charity when he or she sees something that needs correcting in someone. The sinner could stand in any social relation to his or her reprover: inferior, equal, or superior.

How did such a conferral of pastoral power develop in a reform movement usually seen as consolidating clerical authority and clerical power through its pastoral initiatives?

First of all, throughout the Middle Ages, the term "correctio" (making straight or setting right, reforming, amending, improving) applied to many overlapping spheres of life and many disciplinary agents, many of them lay: the father within the family, the judge within the civil court, the mayor within the city, as well as the priest preaching and directing confession (and, of course, God in the world at large). Pastoral texts do not shy away from these associations. The fourteenth-century Dominican John Bromyard's general entry on *correctio* in his first compendium of preaching materials, *Opus trivium* (*c.* 1330), in which he compiled canon, divine, and civil law on various topics, links the father's correction of his children to the bishop correcting his household and to superiors in general (*praelati*) correcting those in their charge.[15] All are male heads of a social unit (family, episcopal household, parish, city, abbey) responsible for knowing communal *mores* usually derived from or supposedly consonant with religious law, for inculcating them, for inquiring into violations of them, and for punishing those violations in ways they and the community deem appropriate. Paternal, civil, and other practices of correction bled into clerical practices, just as all of them, especially clerical correction, bled into fraternal correction of sin, processes I will trace somewhat below. Through pastoral texts, sermons, and moral practices, the clergy acted indirectly on the other forms of correction, not just by validating them but by prescribing what should be corrected – that is, what violated religious law. Yet this assertion of clerical power through pastoral power should not lead us to miss the simple fact that pastoral texts recognize that lay people – in these cases, those having power through the institutions of the patriarchal family, the law, and the city – could exercise a kind of pastoral power through correction.

When we turn from correction in general to papally initiated reform, other reasons emerge why a more assertive clergy might confer pastoral power on lay people, even licensing them to correct clerical sins. First of all, it is important to recognize that reformist movements targeted clerical, as well as lay, misconduct. As Maureen Miller reminds us, the earlier reform movement of the eleventh century had its origins (despite the scholarly label "Gregorian" after Pope Gregory VIII) not only in the papacy or in Cluny, but also in lay demands that the clergy be held to higher behavioral standards. Unworthy priests provoked some lay people even to question their efficacy in administering the sacraments.

Over a century after Gregorian reform, Pope Innocent III, in the sermon which opened the Fourth Lateran Council, proclaimed that unworthy priests were "the source of all evils in the Christian people," those recently focused on by R. I. Moore and others, like heresy, and those beloved of older historians, like threats to the liberty of the Church.[16] Reforming the universal Church entailed for Innocent – and, apparently, for the compliant bishops, abbots and priors, clerical representatives, and secular princes at the Council – disciplining the clergy at all levels. Every time the constitutions of Lateran IV use the word "correctio," they refer solely or especially to clerical *mores*. Provincial synods, in constitution 6, are to inflict penalties on transgressors, especially clerical ones, in order to reform their conduct ("de corrigendis excessibus et moribus reformandis, presertim in clero"). Repeat offenders (a three-strike rule) are to be removed from their benefices (constitution 30).[17] Moreover, England, as Roberto Rusconi observes, was one of only two areas that applied the sixth constitution fully, its bishops convoking a provincial council every year to ensure the theological and moral discipline of the clergy.[18] Finally, while Lateran IV's pastoral constitutions furthering preaching against sin[19] and mandating yearly confession of sin did increase clerical power over lay conduct,[20] this should not obscure the fundamental fact that priests, too, were subject to preaching and spiritual direction within confession, both designed to root out their sin. To extend correction of sinning clerics from their disciplinary superiors alone (pope, bishop, confessor) to clerical equals, clerical inferiors, and the laity, as fraternal correction did, was to greatly increase the number of reform-minded people who might admonish them and work to amend their lives.

OUT OF THE MONASTERY

Where did this universalized practice of combating sin originate? How was it made available to the pastoral movement in the thirteenth century? While I am not writing a genealogical study, I will provide a brief and general account of fraternal correction before Lateran IV in order to help explain why the pastoral movement embraced and developed it as a full-blown practice, even while it extended clerical powers.

Fraternal correction of sin within Christian communities is as old as the age of the Apostles, when Paul rebuked Peter, his superior as Prince of the Apostles (Galatians 2:11–14), an action much debated by patristic and early medieval writers (see, for example, the lively exchanges between Augustine and Jerome introduced in chapter 3). The central text for these debates was Jesus' command that all rebuke a brother's sin, with its four-stage process (Matthew 18:15–17):

Si autem peccaverit in te frater tuus, vade, et corripe eum inter te, et ipsum solum: si te audierit, lucratus eris fratrem tuum: si autem te non audierit, adhibe tecum adhuc unum, vel duos, ut in ore duorum, vel trium testium stet omne verbum. Quod si non audierit eos: dic ecclesiae. Si autem ecclesiam non audierit, sit tibi sicut ethnicus et publicanus.[21]

[But, if your brother shall offend against you, go and rebuke him, between you and him alone. If he shall hear you, you shall gain your brother. And, if he will not hear you, take with you one or two more, that in the mouth of two or three witnesses, every word may stand. And, if he will not hear them, tell the Church. And, if he will not hear the Church, let him be to you as the heathen and publican.]

Ambrose of Milan, for example, argued that this injunction provides us with both a means to encourage friends to correct one another and a procedure for correcting others with proper forethought about what we should speak and when we should speak publicly.[22] But he, like his contemporary Jerome and Pope Gregory the Great two centuries later, was far more interested in prelatical, especially episcopal, correction of sin (divine correction, too). Their fellow bishop Augustine of Hippo was another matter. He preached and wrote often on Jesus' process and on Paul rebuking Peter, developing ethical concerns that would dominate texts on fraternal correction after Lateran IV: the obligation to correct, the will of the corrector (charitable, not wrathful), the power of admonition to change lives, and the need to tailor corrective speech to circumstances, especially to avoid shaming the sinner.[23] Augustine's promotion of "fraterna objurgatio" [brotherly rebuke] reached later pastoral writers enshrined in biblical commentaries and lodged in *florilegia*, as well as in his much-copied texts themselves. Above all, it reached them in the Rule of life he forged for male religious communities, adapted, perhaps in his lifetime and possibly even by him, for nuns.[24]

In the *Regula tertia vel Praeceptum* Augustine institutes Jesus' four steps – secret brotherly admonition, then two or three witnesses to convince, then a superior's punishment, and, finally, ejection from the community – as a means of correcting fellow male religious who behave wantonly, especially in the presence of women. He argues that the religious are obligated to admonish and correct their sinning fellows: To keep silent when they see their brothers perishing is not to be "innocent" and to ignore a fellow's spiritual injury is even more cruel than to ignore a physical one.[25] The *Regula's* whole chapter on correction, based on Matthew 18:15–17, appears in the derivative Rule for women, *Regularis informatio*, where only the gender is changed.[26] While Augustine's Rule influenced other monastic Rules throughout the Middle Ages, for women as well as for men, it came to the fore in the centuries of papally initiated reform as new preaching and teaching orders adopted it. In the twelfth-century cathedrals and collegiate churches, the canons born in the Gregorian reform

a century earlier adopted the *Regula*. In England these Augustinian canons became the largest religious order of men. Hermits who had banded
together in the twelfth century to engage in preaching and teaching also
adopted the *Regula*, becoming the Augustinian friars. So did the four families of the Crutched Friars, all founded during these centuries of reform.
In 1215, Dominic chose the *Regula* as a Rule for his Order of Preachers
precisely because it "had become *par excellence* the Rule of canons, clerical religious."[27] It quickly became the Rule for Dominican nuns, as well.
Later in the thirteenth century, communities of women using forms of the
Augustinian Rule associated themselves with the Augustinian friars and
founded new convents, though none were in England.

Although the Benedictine Rule and, later, the *Regula bullata* of Francis
did not follow the Rule of St. Augustine in institutionalizing correction
modeled specifically on Matthew 18, the religious life before and during papally initiated reform promoted correction of sin in multiple ways
within monastic communities. Religious orders of all stripes made provision for correction of errant brothers and sisters by superiors, and many
orders created a daily or weekly chapter of faults (*capitulum culparum*), in
which brothers reproved each other for minor infractions of their common
Rule.[28] Monastic writers, like Abbot Ailred of Rievaulx, a twelfth-century
Cistercian, advocated informal reproof of friends within the community.
The eleventh-century Benedictine abbot and reformer Peter Damian vigorously promoted charitable correction of neighbors, citing both Paul correcting Peter and Jesus' injunction and procedure in Matthew 18. And
while the new Franciscan order stressed correction by superiors, Francis's
Regula bullata obligated brothers to reprove a brother who wanted "to walk
carnally," and the order's Statutes of Paris (1292) recognize that fraternal
correction modeled on Matthew 18 was practiced in Franciscan communities, where it could conflict with correction by superiors.[29]

Given the importance of correcting sin within religious communities, given many new orders' practice of an Augustinian Rule that bound
members to reprove errant brothers or sisters, and given two centuries
of reformist commitment to eradicating clerical, as well as lay, sin, it is
not surprising that fraternal correction emerges as a crucial, highly contested topic of academic debate in the early thirteenth century. A regent
master at Paris, Alexander of Hales, who entered the Franciscan order in
1236, treated some of the basic questions that shape discourse on fraternal correction in his *Quaestiones disputatae* and his commentary on Peter
Lombard's *Sentences*.[30] Fraternal correction emerges as a full-blown, pas-
sionately advocated practice within the program of teaching and reform

in the work of Thomas Aquinas, the Dominican pastoral theologian *par excellence*, writing in the full tide of the pastoral movement.[31] Nor is it surprising that the major Dominican (and later Franciscan) compilers of preaching, confessional, and catechetical materials drew heavily on Thomas's eight articles on fraternal correction as an act of charity in the *Summa theologiae* (before 1273), which are rooted deeply in Augustinian texts, especially the Rule. Members of other orders, along with secular clerics, followed suit. Brotherly and sisterly correction had come out of the monastery and into the wider Church. Before I examine how Thomas and his successors for over a century constructed the practice of fraternal correction, laboring to distinguish it from prelatical correction and placing it squarely in the hands of all Christians, female and male, I should turn to their main instrument, pastoral discourse.

MAJOR SOURCES

Although the Fourth Lateran Council produced no constitution directly mandating a pastoral literature, its constitutions on confession, preaching, and clerical education stimulated the writing and disseminating of *pastoralia*, catechetical material for priests to use in the religious and social formation of both clerics and lay people through preaching, private admonition, group or one-on-one catechesis, and directing confession. This is a well-known narrative. What is not so clearly recognized is the centrality of moral theologians, like Thomas Aquinas, and of canon lawyers in the reform of pastoral care and in its target: the reform of conduct. They provided the bulk of the material from which University-educated parish priests, diocesan officials, friars and monks, and scribes wove pastoral texts, though they also took material from biblical commentaries, biblical *distinctiones* (schematic groupings of biblical texts on topics), and collections of *exempla*. Scholastic theologians had been agents of reform since the twelfth century. Early scholastics, as Marcia Colish has demonstrated, worked to adapt the Church's teachings and practices to contemporary needs, not least of all more effective and informed pastoral care. Aware that the Church was a "historical phenomenon whose theological and canonical traditions were neither static nor monolithic," they combined analysis of authoritative texts with a sense of historical context.[32] Decretalists likewise addressed pastoral concerns, so much so that their canons and even their commentaries are quoted in collections of preaching materials and even sermons, as well as where we would expect them to be: in the quasi-legal *summae* for confessors.[33] It is easy to think of popes and councils as instituting reforms in belief and practice, but Colish notes acutely that Lateran IV was the only ecumenical council to do so from the twelfth to early fifteenth centuries. Crucially, reform was formulated and fostered by multiple voices in the theological and canonical traditions over the centuries.[34] It was those scholastic voices who took fraternal correction out of the monastery (and the friary) and into the wider Church.

Moral theology, canon law, and other materials were all synthesized in the alphabetical compendia for preachers, the *summae* for confessors, and the sermons that are the main sources for our knowledge of fraternal correction in England. Because of the fundamental, unavoidable canons and biblical texts on correcting sin and because of Thomas Aquinas's influential theological treatment, pastoral writing and preaching on fraternal correction possesses a great deal of continuity from the late thirteenth century to the mid fifteenth. Much of the long chapter on fraternal correction in the *Speculum spiritualium*, compiled primarily for the religious probably in the first quarter of the fifteenth century, can be found almost verbatim in Johann von Freiburg's widely disseminated *Summa confessorum* of 1297–8.[35] And Thomas's treatment of the procedures governing fraternal correction (2.2.33, 7–8) dominates both. Despite this continuity, I will limit pastoral sources in this and the next two chapters to those written and disseminated before 1375, for the reasons I gave in the introduction.

Let me introduce the major sources for this chapter and the next: first, entries (those mini-treatises on fraternal correction) in collections of pastoral materials and *summae* for confessors, then sermons. (I will describe less frequently used sources in these and other pastoral genres when I first cite them.) I exclude theological texts, like William of Ockham's *Dialogus* (except insofar as they are appropriated by pastoral writers), because this book considers only material designed to be disseminated to clergy and laity alike.[36]

Of the eight alphabetized compendia circulating before 1375 that contain entries, I draw on all more than once, but extensively on only three, the most capacious. Ranulph Higden, a Benedictine chronicler at St. Werburgh's, Chester, finished in 1340 a sizeable pastoral manual, *Speculum curatorum*, containing a chapter on fraternal correction (following a chapter on charity).[37] The Oxford-educated Dominican John Bromyard's vast *Summa praedicantium*, finished between 1348 and 1352, has an extensive entry on *correctio* (fraternal at the outset, but then mainly correction by disciplinary authorities) that is dense with canons and with biblical and patristic authorities, but enlivened by metaphors,

satiric sketches, beast fables, and *exempla*. Given this mix, it is not surprising that the *Summa* was mined extensively and in depth by writers
of sermons for at least a century.[38] From the third quarter of the century
comes the encyclopedic *Omne bonum*, described in the introduction. Of
its three entries on correction, the last, made up largely of passages from
Thomas Aquinas's *quaestio*, deals with fraternal correction.[39]

We know much more about the Continental authors of the two main
confessional *summae* I cite frequently, both surviving in more manuscripts in British collections than Bromyard's *Summa* (four, with two
more attested) and *Omne bonum* (one). The German Dominican Johann
von Freiburg's *Summa confessorum*, extant in fourteen manuscripts in
Britain, was, in Leonard Boyle's words, "the most influential work of
pastoral theology in the two hundred years before the Reformation."
(His fellow Dominican John Bromyard quotes it in his *Summa*.) As a
Dominican lector, Johann shapes a more theological entry on fraternal correction, pulling in the great moral theologians and canonists of
his order as he addresses fundamental questions: Is fraternal correction
required by precept? How should the precept be carried out? Should all
correct or only disciplinary superiors? Is a subject bound to correct his
disciplinary superior? May a sinner correct another? Should one withhold
correction if one fears the sinner would become worse if corrected? What
process should be followed in fraternal correction? While his answers to
all digest Thomas Aquinas, he pulls in canonists, twelfth-century scholastics, and patristic texts, including the Augustinian Rule.[40] The last of the
five main compendia for this study, the Italian Dominican Bartolomeo
da San Concordio's *Summa de casibus conscientie* (1338), is derived from
Johann's *Summa*, though it takes account of more recent juridical texts,
certainly on the exhaustive procedures for correction. Surviving in eight
fourteenth-century manuscripts in Britain, its alphabetical organization
made it especially handy for priests engaged in preaching, catechizing,
admonishing, and directing confessions.[41]

Of these forms of pastoral instruction, the record of only one survives,
of course: the sermon – and the texts we have differ to varying degrees
from what was actually preached. Often built out of materials on fraternal correction in pastoral texts, the sermon, as that influential writer
of pastoral handbooks William of Pagula insists, was bent to teaching,
to "informing people in the faith," to providing information.[42] Sermons
on Jesus' precept about fraternal correction, the opening verses of the
Gospel lection (Matthew 18:15–22) for the Tuesday after the third Sunday
in Lent (the *thema* "Si autem peccaverit in te frater tuus"), often do just

that: They contain large chunks of moral theology, canon law, patristic writing, and other biblical passages.[43] Unfortunately, few Lenten cycles of sermons (*sermones quadragesimales*) survive in Britain; I use five "Si autem peccaverit" sermons from before 1375, some from mixed collections, some from Lenten cycles. Of these one is in English verse: from the expanded version of the *Northern Homily Cycle*, begun as part of the catechetical ministry of the Augustinian canons in the north perhaps as early as the late thirteenth century and expanded from the mid fourteenth century on.[44] Sermons on Matthew 18:15–22 could also be preached by the bishop or designated clerical visitor to parishes or religious houses, who would begin with a sermon on correcting sin before inquiring into the conduct of the community and its members. Visitation sermons could be very influential: They served as models of what priests should preach in their parishes.[45] In addition, sermons preached on Jesus' parable of the mote and beam, part of the lection for the fourth Sunday after Trinity (Luke 6:36–42), often dealt with fraternal correction, especially constraints on its practice (*thema* "Estote misericordes"). They survive in greater number as part of the standard cycle of Sunday Gospel sermons (*sermones dominicales*).[46] Finally, I include as a major source one biblical commentary: that by William of Nottingham, Provincial of the English Franciscans from 1316 to about 1330, on the Gospel harmony *Unum ex quatuor* (three manuscripts of the fourteenth century, though seven later). Its indices and abridgments indicate that it was "a repository of preachable doctrine which was the common property of all."[47]

An unexpected advantage to this necessary division in sources will emerge. Pre-1375 pastoral writing demonstrates that, in Michael Haren's words, "the pre-Wycliffite church contained, at its middle levels certainly, a ferment of self criticism," especially from clerics laboring to reform the conduct of their fellows, as well as that of the laity. Let me take two examples now. Both tackle avaricious clerical practices fostered by the Church's vast wealth and by the clergy's administrative, juridical, and sacramental powers. Haren's probable author for the *Memoriale presbyterorum*, an ecclesiastical lawyer in episcopal service in the 1340s (William Doane under Bishop Grandisson of Exeter), emphasized clerics' abuse of their offices. You must ask rural deans and other officers with ecclesiastical jurisdiction, he instructs confessors, if they have imposed burdensome penalties in the hopes that the guilty would offer them money to escape, if they have favored a party in a lawsuit because of a present, if hatred or bribes have led them to employ ignorant assistants who would oppress parties, if they have invested a priest with a church in exchange for a cow or a vestment. Secondly, John Bromyard's entry on *correctio* in the *Summa praedicantium* details clerics' misuses of their learning to accumulate land and wealth. They certainly know the financial canons, he adds sarcastically, even if they do not know the penitential ones, as they are required to do. And they abandon correction of their patrons' sins in exchange for bribes, including annual income from property.[48] Drawn in part from pastoral texts like these, English sermon collections impress Siegfried Wenzel with "the outspokenness and force with which preachers in this period [1350 onward] criticized and condemned failures in their own class, from simony, nepotism, and absenteeism through neglect in studying scriptures and in preaching, to misplaced personal ambition, greed, and sexual sins."[49] The Lateran Councils' concern with clerical evils was not lost in pastoral materials and sermons. Nor was it lost in the pastoral practice of correcting sin. Most of the sinners whom Margery Kempe rebukes in York, either before or during her interrogation, are clerics.

We can best think of the pastoral texts setting forth the practice of fraternal correction as making up a discourse. They are all products of the more highly educated clergy engaged in the post-Lateran combat against sin. That is, they are generated by a powerful group within an institution to influence the actions of others. They are characterized by a set of concepts, by certain modes of reasoning, by a set of rules. Thus, they display the consistency and longlastingness I have just sketched out. They are impersonal in direction, considering what all Christians are required to do. Moreover, all of them are intended to supply material for oral instruction and some (sermons) are at least partial records of what was spoken. So, although these pastoral texts could be read only by a few, mostly clerics, their influence was pervasive in late medieval England.

Such a discourse is, of course, fundamentally ideological in cast. It does not take for granted that people desire to correct the sins of those they encounter or that, if they do, they will act out of charity, instead of a malicious urge to wreck another's good name. As a result, it must be fully explicit, even argumentative and persuasive, in its claims on people. As part of pastoral discourse on conduct as a whole, it articulates self-consciously a system of beliefs that aspires "to offer a unified answer to problems of social action," the sociologist Ann Swidler's recent reformulation of Raymond Williams's classic definition of ideology. ("Aspires" becomes important in the next chapter, which explores the contradictory texts and goods embedded in the discourse as it labors to articulate firm procedural norms.) As proponents of clerical moral ideology, pastoral writers and preachers (to appropriate Swidler once again) "insist that the world be altered to fit ideology's picture of the true and the good," and they work "to bridge the gaps between beliefs and actions."[50] But their very explicitness and the obvious strain of writing that aims to shape the actions of others make that writing vulnerable to challenge, as the chapters on *Piers Plowman*, John Wyclif, Wycliffite texts, and Lancastrian texts will reveal.

Now, to turn to how that writing uses ethical reasoning to constitute fraternal correction as a moral practice – after this final set of discursive definitions. Throughout this book I use the terms "morality" and "ethics" in these broad modern philosophical senses: Morality involves questions about what we ought to do and what character we should admire, whereas ethics considers what reasons might lead us to do one thing rather than another. That is, morality is first-order, universalizing normative and prescriptive language; ethics, second-order (but also universalizing) language about morality – especially, in this study, systematic theoretical accounts of all moral obligations.[51] So, pastoral discourse, in its markedly ideological cast, works to give strong reasons why all Christians ought to engage in fraternal correction as a practice through which central human goods are realized.

SHARING IN PASTORAL REFORM: FRATERNAL CORRECTION AS MORAL PRACTICE

Pastoral texts and the sermons built from them present fraternal correction as a moral obligation for Christians. They read the "evangelical law" of Jesus' words in Matthew 18:15–17 as Augustine did: as a binding precept. A fourteenth-century visitation sermon on this text quotes in full a canon traditionally assigned to Gratian to prove that fraternal correction – in the commonest of all pastoral phrases – "falls under what is commanded" ("cadit sub precepto"):

Tam sacerdotes quam reliqui fideles omnes summam debent habere curam de his, qui pereunt, quatinus eorum redargutione aut corrigantur a peccatis, aut, si incorrigibiles apparuerint, ab ecclesia separentur.[52]

[Priests, just like all the rest of the faithful, should take great care of those who are perishing, to the extent that they may be reformed from their sins by their rebukes or, if they prove incorrigible, may be cut off from the Church.]

In the *Decretum* this text, surrounded by canons on excommunication, serves to bind priests to correct sinners; it is an instrument of mid-twelfth-century clerical reform. In the sermon two centuries later, however, it is used to advocate fervency in correction by all Christians, lay people as well as clerics, so that no one will be excluded from reproof that has power to amend lives.[53] And in *Omne bonum*, the canon is used to refute the claim that only superiors in spiritual matters should correct the sins of others. Jesus' "Go and rebuke him" is, after all, an imperative state-ment, as *Omne bonum* reminds its readers, citing yet another canon and invoking Augustine's warning "you become worse than a sinner if you fail to correct him."[54] All three prescriptive sources – biblical, canonical, patristic – are woven together to undergird the most common of pastoral claims: That fraternal correction is a matter of precept, divinely ordained and therefore obligatory.

To claim that religious law, divine and ecclesiastical, enjoins all of us to correct sin entails for pastoral writers ethical reasoning about human ends. Precepts, as Alasdair MacIntyre writes about Aristotle, are designed to educate us in the virtues, to instruct us how to reach our true end.[55] Fraternal correction, the pastoral writers and preachers insist, following Thomas Aquinas, is an affirmative precept. Unlike negative precepts, which we must always observe since they forbid doing evil, affirmative ones should only be obeyed if we meet the circumstances required to act virtuously: in the right time, at the right place, in the right manner. To determine these, we need to consider the Aristotelian "ratio finis," the nature of an act's ultimate purpose. And that is, in any virtuous correc-tion, the improvement of our brother, amendment of life ("emendatio fra-tris"), which may include the penitent's reconciliation with those he or she has injured (as Matthew 18:15 suggests).[56] So, quoting Augustine's *De civitate Dei*, pastoral writers concede that we may decide not to rebuke a sinner on the spot, but wait for a more opportune time or even refrain altogether because reproof might make a person worse. The end governs the practice. And it is practical wisdom (prudence), acquired or infused by God, that directs us as we weigh circumstances against the end; pas-toral writers shun rules for dealing with specific situations, given their infinite variety and complexity.

Pastoral teleological reasoning is not restricted to the act itself. It also attends to the doer's will, the movement of charity that generates frater-nal correction. In Augustine's dictum about when fraternal correction should be omitted, charity is the judge, counseling us when to refrain. Moreover, he argues, letting fear of public opinion or of death overmas-ter our "fraterna caritas" makes omitting correction a mortal sin.[57] In all pastoral writing, it is charity, infused by God, that makes correction fra-ternal. As the disposition to seek another's happiness, to do what can be done to bring about another's welfare, charity directs us to seek to free a wrongdoer from sin as an evil that threatens to destroy him.[58] It is an act of friendship. So, John Bromyard also treats fraternal correction in his entry on *amicitia*, arguing that we are all bound by the law of charity to succor our neighbors. Thomas Brinton, bishop of Rochester, preached in 1376 that correcting our neighbors' sin (fornication, adultery, and usury form his list) manifests love for them, an argument he supports by citing canon law and Matthew 18:15.[59] A Dominican sermon on Matthew 18:15–22 even argues that any corrector sins whose speech is directed not by charity, but by a malign disposition of will, like vengeance or derision. Like Cham, who gazed on his father Noah's nakedness and then divulged it to his brothers (Genesis 9), such a corrector exposes someone else's moral shamefulness out of a perverse will.[60] Indeed, open correction of those who injure us is the charitable alternative to slandering them maliciously behind their backs, as a fourteenth-century sermon argues, citing another biblical text central to pastoral writing: "You shall not hate your brother in your heart: but reprove him openly, so that you do not incur sin through him" (Leviticus 19:17).[61] All of these texts understand the charity that generates and directs fraternal correction as what John Bossy calls a "state of enlarged sociability," of simple affection and regard for our fellows.[62]

In a common pastoral schema, fraternal correction becomes one of the works of spiritual mercy, of as much greater value than any corporal work as the soul exceeds the body in importance.[63] To taxonomize fraternal correction so is to conceive of it as a compassionate response to another's need, along with counseling the grieved or teaching the ignorant (other works of spiritual mercy). In another schema, it is one form of almsgiving: We relieve a person in need by striving to remedy his or her disordered will through reproof.[64] In both of these taxonomies, fraternal correction enacts charity, mercy being an inward effect of charity and almsgiving an outward. And through both taxonomies it was taught systematically as a Christian fundamental.[65] Neglecting correction, like neglecting other deeds of spiritual or corporal mercy, had to be divulged as sin in confession. To keep silent when seeing a brother sin, argues Nicolas de Byard, a popular mid-to-late-thirteenth-century compiler of *distinctiones* for preaching and other pastoral work, is a sin, a violation of the love God shares with us, akin to not assisting him if his ass or cow falls down in the street. Moreover, such silence marks us as partners in sin, as if we saw a homicide (sin kills) and did not cry out to expose both crime and criminal. To keep silent, he concludes, quoting a much-cited gloss that animates later reformist literature, is to consent: "consentire est tacere."[66]

Charity as the sufficient cause of fraternal correction is what (along with the means used) distinguishes it from correction by *praelates*, disciplinary authorities in the Church and state: bishops, confessors, judges in civil and ecclesiastical courts, abbesses. Bartolomeo da San Concordia's *Summa de casibus conscientie* makes the distinction in standard terms (although it is not as hard and fast as the terms suggest, as we shall see, when certain circumstances, other considerations, and the whole of Matthew 18:15–17 come into play):

> Duplex est correctio, una que est actus caritatis et est per simplicem ammoncionem, et hoc pertinet ad quemlibet caritatem habentem, sive sit subditus sive prelatus. Est et alia correpcio actus justicie, que non solum fit per monicionem sed eciam interdum per punicionem, ut alii timentes a peccato desistant, et hoc pertinet ad solos prelatos.[67]
>
> [Correction is of two kinds. One is an act of charity through simple admonition and this belongs to whoever has charity, subject or superior. The second is an act of justice which may work not only through admonition, but sometimes by punishment, so that others, becoming fearful, may cease sinning; this belongs to prelates alone.]

Justice, as the generating and directing virtue of prelatical correction, looks to what a sinner owes to others, to the right relations between people ("rectitudo unius ad alterum") that sin has outraged or broken. It considers the common good. So, the prelate may punish the sinner to deter others from committing the same sin. By contrast, charity looks only to relieve the sinner from the evil that is destroying him.[68] The means of correcting comprehended under the term *monitio* manifest that governing virtue: friendly, loving instruction; exhortation to good; rebuke of evil.[69]

In all these ways, pastoral texts and sermons insistently construct fraternal correction as a practice both moral and ethical. It is moral in that it is prescribed and in that it proscribes sin, in that we are constrained by revealed moral law to practice it, in that it is presented as universal and normative, and in that it is governed by norms that we ought to obey (when correction ought to be omitted, for example).[70] By articulating fraternal correction in terms of virtue and end, pastoral texts (except the most rudimentary catechesis) make it an inherently ethical practice, one that invites us to consider, again in Paul Ricoeur's terms, what is good for ourselves and for others within just institutions.

In understanding fraternal correction as a practice, Alasdair MacIntyre's definition of practice is useful, if I edit out some elements dictated by his dominant examples, athletic and intellectual games: "any coherent and complex form of socially established co-operative human activity through which goods internal to that form of activity are realized."[71] Fraternal correction is co-operative in multiple ways: It is continually re-established by pastoral activities like preaching; it is to be carried out by all Christians; its end is the welfare of others to whom we are bound by God and common humanity, the brother, the neighbor. William of Nottingham justifies making fraternal correction a precept by the common Christian analogy of the body, where the mutual aid of members is necessary to sustain life.[72] The goods internal to correction, crucial in MacIntyre's concept of practice, are several: first of all, the reformation of the sinning brother, preceded, as Ranulph Higden declares, by his or her acknowledging guilt and manifesting signs of penance; the doer's enacting of charity; reconciliation between corrector and sinner; and, in some pastoral texts, spiritual merit for the doer.[73] Furthermore, in line with MacIntyre's discussion, fraternal correction is fostered by virtue, especially charity, which not only helps achieve the goods involved, but also sustains us in our quest for the good life. It also entails obedience to authoritative rules – general ones, at least.[74] It is sustained by an institution and is embedded in traditions, "historically extended, socially embodied argument[s]." In discourse on fraternal correction, as in much of MacIntyre's work as an ethical and social theorist, those traditions are Aristotelian ethics and New Testament discourse on charity.[75]

PASTORAL POWER AND POWER RELATIONS

Pastoral writing contends that correction of sins, operating within the world of existing power relations and the institutions that maintain them, may reform abuses of power by those of high status. John Bromyard's general entry on *correctio* in the *Summa* argues at the outset that just as all share in the practice of correcting sin, all are subject to correction, no matter how powerful or elevated in status they may be ("quantumcunque sit potens vel magni status"). To illustrate, John tells the story of Ambrose shutting the Emperor Theodosius out of church (as if, he adds, excommunicating him) because he had commanded 7,000 Thessalonians to be slain. Ambrose demands not only that the emperor do penance for so monstrous an evil, but also that he alter his political practice. He must ordain that no prefects should implement a death sentence from him until thirty days have passed so that he could deliberate on whether or not it was just. Only after Theodosius embraces this remedy does Ambrose permit him to stand in the chancel amid clerics. Later the emperor acknowledges Ambrose's pastoral power by proclaiming in Constantinople that he found Ambrose alone a "minister of truth." Clerical correction serves here to expose the injustice of the act, to demand repentance for the sin, and to insist on a practical reform designed to make the exercise of power more likely to be just. The corrector's power stems not only from his office (the local bishop excluding the emperor and assigning him penance), but from his commitment to virtue, to amendment of life, and to truth as an ideal way of acting in accord with religious law. Ambrose's virtue here is not the fraternal one of charity but the prelatical one of justice because he is acting, as a *praelatus* must, for the common good, for what a ruler owes his people.[76]

Despite this idealized *exemplum*, John Bromyard recognizes that existing power relations can make correcting sin difficult, even for the clergy. When sinners have greater institutional power, he advocates that the reprover prudently use a pleasing exemplary narrative rather than direct admonishment. The rhetorical power of such *exempla* he illustrates with the most common biblical model for correction of sin, Nathan (2 Samuel 12):

Quando voluit regem david de adulterio et homicidio corripere, caute proposuit exemplum de divite qui habebat oves plurimas et de paupere qui non habuit nisi unam, quam dives pro peregrino sibi adveniente occidit. Ait ergo regi "Responde mihi judicium." Qui respondit "Vivit dominus quoniam filius mortis est vir qui fecit hoc." Cui propheta "Tu es ille vir." Ecce si aperte sine exemplo eum reprehendisset, forsitan rex indignans superbe et sine correctionis effectu respondisset. Quia vero pulcro exemplo et quasi ex judicio proprio concludit, gratanter et salubriter reprehensionem admisit, dicens "Peccavi domino." Hujusmodi igitur exemplo caute et quaestione precedente in talium correctione seu ammonitione est procedendum ut ipsi se judicent quasi in alieno negocio et contra arguentem non irascantur.[77]

[When he desired to correct King David for adultery and murder, warily he related an *exemplum* about a rich man who had many sheep and a poor man who had only one, which the rich man killed for a stranger who was just arriving. Therefore, he said to the king: "Reply with a judgment." The king answered: "As the Lord lives, the man who has done this is a child of death." The prophet said to him: "You are that man." If he had reprehended him openly, without the *exemplum*, perhaps the king, furious in his pride, would have answered without correction happening. Indeed, because Nathan argued by means of a fine *exemplum* and as if from the king's own judgment, the king joyfully and wholesomely admitted his own fault, saying "I have sinned against the Lord." Therefore, correction or admonition of such people ought to be carried out by a careful *exemplum* of this kind and an antecedent question so that they judge themselves, as if in an affair which does not pertain to them, and are not angry with their reprover.]

By exercising prudent rhetoric, the reprover secures his end of amending the sinner's life, and he does so without becoming the victim of the power the sinner has already used against the less powerful. (David, of course, was a model penitent for the medieval clergy, perhaps not least of all because he was a king who submitted to a prophet's authority.) Nathan's *exemplum* succeeds because, first, as a story, it creates a specific situation that invites King David, as a ruler accustomed to pass judgment, to judge this case. Then, as a fiction, it creates the distance ("as if in an affair which does not pertain to them") that enables the king's judgment to be just, to reflect communal standards about what we owe to each other, and that, even before the judgment is formulated, preempts a defensive visceral reaction. Finally, when Nathan discloses that his narrative is a similitude, the judge transfers his judgment of the rich man to himself. In John Bromyard's telling, Nathan has found the rhetorical means to exercise pastoral power over a man with great political power, to direct skillfully the conscience of someone who has violated religious law so that he speaks the truth of his sin and seeks salvation through amendment.

Both of John Bromyard's successful correctors of the powerful are, of course, men of power by virtue of their office: a bishop of late antiquity in a great imperial city and a major prophet in Israel (although the *Distinctiones exemplorum* presents Nathan as an *exemplum* of "corepcio fraterna"). Certainly, Ambrose, within a Christian order, was a *praelatus* in relation to Theodosius, charged with the care of his soul and dispensing penance. The practice of fraternal correction, however, licenses subjects (*subditi*), as well as disciplinary superiors (*praelati*), to reprove sin. Moreover, pastoral texts insist specifically that subjects are bound by the law of charity to admonish superiors, including their own, about anything that needs correcting in their conduct. Just after establishing that all ("sive subditus sive prelatus") are obligated to correct, Johann von Freiburg, Bartolomeo da San Concordia, and James le Palmer all devote a full *quaestio* to affirming that the obligation must entail inferiors correcting their disciplinary superiors. "Subjects," Bartolomeo writes, "are bound to that act of correction which stems from charity, if there is anything needing correction in disciplinary superiors" [Subditi ... tenentur autem correpcione illa que est caritatis si in eis [prelatis] est aliquid corrigibile].[78] The term *praelati* in these passages clearly designates both those who have sacramental power over others through priestly orders, responsible for the care of their souls, and those who have juridical power over others. So, pastoral discourse on fraternal correction unleashes, to put it crudely, down-up criticism within the relations of lay people to clerics, clerics to other clerics having sacramental or juridical power over them, and citizens to civil authorities. It does not spell out these possibilities, explicitly dividing lay people from clerics, but uses the generalizing language of "everyone who has charity" and of *subditus* and *praelatus*. However, it works explicitly to remove any constraint a *subditus* might have about correcting sin in his or her own *praelati* (due, perhaps, to deference or hostility). It argues, firstly, that he or she is obligated to show mercy to the superior. Sometimes, the *Regula* of St. Augustine is cited to authorize this argument: " 'Non solum,' inquit, 'vestri sed et ipsius miseremini qui inter vos quanto in loco superiore tanto in periculo majore versatur' " [Have mercy not only on yourselves but also on him, who, being in a higher position among you, is therefore in greater danger] – greater danger, a visitation sermon adds, of being excluded from a salvific act of spiritual mercy when he sins.[79] In addition, a *subditus* was required to correct his or her *praelatus*, indeed any *praelatus*, if he imperiled the faith or in any way threatened to harm a community (sedition, for example), a condition to be explored in chapter 2.

I use the two pronouns "her" and "his" advisedly. Pastoral discourse does use the word *frater* for the sinner (from Matthew 18), never (that I have seen) the cloistered women's *soror* from the Augustinian Rule adapted for women; its adjective qualifying the practice is always *fraterna*; its pronouns are also male ("quemlibet caritatem habentem"). The few standard *exempla* in *summae* (Paul and Peter, Nathan and David) involve only men. Nevertheless, more extensive lists of biblical correctors in preaching materials include women. In the *Distinctiones exemplorum*, Abigail exemplifies the wise corrector who does not reprove someone drunk (1 Samuel 25). The wealthy widow Judith, as well as Nathan, demonstrates how effective fraternal correction of superiors operates: She reproves the elders of her besieged town for telling their people that God will abandon the town to the Assyrians if He does not aid them within a certain time. By means of her reproof she persuades them to change the course of the action – surrender to which they were committed ("Benigne reprehendebat Judith cives suos et fecit ab incepto proponito removeri. Judith 8").[80] Some pastoral writers, at least, took "fraterna" as a generic term ("fellow Christian," from "frater," *DML* 4) applying to women as well as to men. (The language of fraternal correction is, on the whole, generic, as I noted with *subditus* – as open-ended and inclusive as possible.) However much some medievals may have felt "fraterna" as a gendered term, even an exclusionary one, no pastoral text down to 1440 that I have read excludes women from voicing fraternal correction.

The very arguments often made by scholastic theologians that pre-vented women from preaching may have helped solidify – indeed, mark out – a role for them as fraternal correctors of sin. As scholars have observed frequently, discussions of preaching from the late twelfth century had worked to keep lay people from addressing belief and conduct from the pulpit, limiting access totally, except in unusual circumstances, to the ordained, even the licensed.[81] In the process, these discussions distinguished women's edificatory and instructive speech from preaching by confining it to the private sphere of "familiar conversation" ("privatim ad unum vel paucos, familiarite colloquendo," in the words of Thomas Aquinas), which is the realm of fraternal correction. (Notice that Thomas's language does not confine women's teaching to the household, as is sometimes asserted.) Secondly, theologians routinely denied women the prerogative of preaching because the female sex, according to Genesis, is subjected ("subditus") to the male sex, whereas public teaching in the church belongs only to *praelati*: "Docere autem et persuadere publice in Ecclesia non pertinet ad subditos, sed ad praelatos." Behind these arguments lies Paul's prohibition against women teaching and his injunction that they keep silent in church (1 Corinthians 14:34 and 11:5).[82] Since discourse on fraternal correction emphasizes that *subditi* are particularly obligated to correct the sins of their *praelati*, conventional thinking about women as *subditi* (generally, as well as in the case of teaching) may have reinforced their obligation to correct.

Despite bestowing fraternal correction on lay people and subordinate clerics, pastoral texts, by framing their entries in terms of the binary *praelati* and *subditi*, insist that existing power relations be acknowledged. Thus, they embody and reinforce them. They also insist that power relations, especially those between superiors of all kinds and those subject to them, be negotiated in certain ways if correction is to be practiced morally and successfully. To share in the pastoral power of directing the consciences of others in light of religious law entails obedience to pastorally dictated norms and constraints, themselves rooted in that law as construed by the clergy.

Some pastoral texts acknowledge openly the threat that allowing anyone to correct sin may seem to pose to power relations. In his *Summa de poenitentia* (1295), the German Franciscan Johann von Erfürt begins to explore the question of who may correct sinners by admitting that it seems that the practice should not be open to anyone whomsoever – the standard scholastic method of entertaining objections to the position the writer will advocate. Johann cites a canon from the *Decretals* stipulating

that sons and disciples should be so faithful and so restrained as followers
of their spiritual fathers and masters ("devoti esse debent ac sobrii") that
they would never speak to them with temerity. This objection he answers
by distinguishing types of reproof: the imperious that stems from a power
to command ("imperio potestatis"), like that of a *praelatus* over *subditi*,
a father over his sons, and a teacher over his students; the impetuous or
thoughtless ("temeraria"); and the social or charitable ("socialis ac carita-
tiva"), under which *subditi* may reprehend *praelati*.[83] First of all, such a
distinction protects – indeed, it foregrounds and reinforces – a superior's
disciplinary power to command, coerce, and punish through the apparatus of Church and state. Pastoral writers underscore this power repeatedly
in the very ways they define fraternal correction as a moral practice: Love,
not justice, generates it; the subject and the superior may both admonish
others to set them straight, but only the latter punishes to achieve the same
end; the subject and the superior may both be concerned for the individual's spiritual welfare, but only the superior is obligated to look after the
good of the whole community. Pastoral writing even observes consistently
that the duty of fraternal correction weighs more heavily on those who, as
praelati, have the care of souls ("cura animarum").[84] Secondly, Johann's
distinction dictates that charity must govern a *subditus*'s manner of rebuking a *praelatus*. Charity entails recognizing the superior's status, speaking
meekly and reverently, not impudently and harshly ("non cum protervia et
duricia, sed cum mansuetudine et reverencia"). Sometimes, pastoral texts
include the *exemplum* of the monk Demophilus, who was reproved by
Dionysius because he had corrected a priest irreverently, striking him and
throwing him out of a church. Speak to a spiritual father as you would an
older man and your own father, the pastoral texts argue by analogy, citing
Galatians 2:11: "Do not rebuke an older man, but exhort him as you would
a father."[85] One text goes so far as to use this analogy to forbid *subditi* to
rebuke *praelati* in public, reserving public correction for the latter.[86] You
must, pastoral writers insist, pay attention to the estate (*status*) of the person you are correcting. Johann von Freiberg extends this proper reverence
even to nobles and other great persons.[87]

Discourse on fraternal correction reinforced existing power relations,
too, by casting superiors' correction of inferiors as charitable when punishment is not involved – or not yet involved. Indeed, it allowed *praelati*
to claim the virtue of charity as what prompts their correction of others.
The clerical visitor in a fourteenth-century visitation sermon on Matthew
18:15–22 begins preaching to those he will correct by asserting that mercy
ranks first among the virtues of *praelati* because they have compassion on

others and extend themselves to others through the uniting power of love. By acknowledging that charity also unites subjects to their superiors, he scripts their responses as well (loving, obedient). But the charity of a superior is more lofty ("precellentior") because he shows compassion on inferiors, seeking to remove their sins. Then he quotes "If your brother sins against you" to cast his pastoral visit as fraternal, not prelatical correction.[88] Such a rhetorical move would be particularly easy to make for the likely monastic audience of the sermon, a community of *fratres*, but it depends upon the overlap between prelatical and fraternal correction: Both involve admonition and a disciplinary authority may perform both.

The very structure of the Gospel reading encouraged using fraternal correction to bolster the authority and power of disciplinary authorities. As the Gospel of Matthew constructs the process of correction (to be examined in detail in chapter 2), it comes to an end with the brother who dismisses correction being cast out of the religious community. This act of exclusion is followed directly by one of the "bind and loose" statements beloved by medieval clerical authorities: "Amen, I say to you, whatsoever you shall bind upon earth shall be bound also in heaven, and whatsoever you shall loose upon earth shall be loosed also in heaven" (Matthew 18:18). So, Jacopo da Varazze, the popular preacher and author of that most influential of hagiographies, the *Legenda aurea*, argues that just as Christ established fraternal correction in this Gospel passage to combat ubiquitous sin, he also authorized correction by superiors at the same point so that it would not be despised. Therefore, he concludes, superiors ought to correct inferiors and inferiors ought to hold superiors in great reverence.[89] Reinforcing clerical power, preachers and pastoral writers even imagined Peter, Prince of the Apostles and future Pope, as the specific recipient of all these words about correction, although he is not mentioned until the end of the reading, when he asks how many times one should forgive a brother (in verse 21). A collection of biblical *exempla* appends Matthew 18:15 to its Old Testament *exempla* of "correpcio fraterna," characterizing it as the perfect rule Christ gave to Peter ("perfectam regulam dedit dominus petro"), and the *Northern Homily Cycle* begins its sermon on Matthew 18 with "Unto Saint Peter said he thus."[90]

The virtues which generate fraternal correction could be used even more broadly to reinforce basic social and political hierarchies. The many Middle English versions of the catechetical handbook *Somme le roi* expound "castiga," a general term for reproof and correction, as an act of spiritual mercy within existing power relations, ecclesiastical and civil. In the words of the popular late-fourteenth-century *Book of Vices and Virtues*, the third branch of spiritual mercy is to "chastise and withtake [rebuke] the fooles and schrewen [sinners] and here [their] folies and this bilongeth specialliche to prelates of holy chirche and to princes and to grete lordes and othere riche men. They schulle chastise here servauntes and sugetes [subjects] whan they witen [know] wel that they ben schrewen and done evele …"[91]

The very act of laying responsibility on the powerful here serves to justify their political, ecclesiastical, and social roles as necessary disciplinary agents in their spheres. They are obligated to police their households and, more broadly, all in their jurisdiction. Moreover, extending the obligation to "othere rich men," who, of course, do have servants and other dependants to look after, baptizes and confirms economic power relations as well as those based on offices of Church and state. So, correction as a moral act, not just as obligation but as compassionate concern for another's spiritual welfare (the end is to amend a life), serves to entrench hierarchies by moralizing their social control of those subject to their power.

For all that pastoral texts and sermons used discourse on fraternal correction to build up existing clerical, even secular, powers, two simple facts remain. Firstly, the clergy used fraternal correction to engage the laity in reproving and reforming sinners. As John Bromyard indicates, the institutional Church depended upon their help, due to the enormity of the task.[92] Secondly, pastorally promoted fraternal correction licensed *subditi*, including lay people, male and female, to reprove the sins of their superiors, those civil and ecclesiastical authorities who exercised disciplinary authority over them. Pastoral texts and preaching had taken fraternal correction, as a moral practice, out of the monastery and out of the religious orders and into the general life of the Church. Even as it did so, it also labored to shape correctors who could use ethical reasoning, know pastoral norms, and observe established constraints in judging whom to correct, when to correct, to whom to divulge sin, and what model of corrective speech to try out – the subjects of the next chapter.

CHAPTER 2

Negotiating contrary things

A fourteenth-century Dominican sermon extant at Magdalen College, Oxford, made up of authoritative statements about fraternal correction by several distinguished members of the order, begins expounding Jesus' precept establishing fraternal correction ("But, if your brother shall offend against you, go and rebuke him"), with the expected firm statements. We are obligated to correct anyone who has injured us. God wills that no one should perish, so He commanded that we correct evildoers, just as He commanded that we forgive the penitent, as a way of leading humans back to Him. So, if anyone has directly injured us or even sinned in our presence, we must honor Christ's imperative. Moreover, we must exercise the greatest patience and care so that they will be reformed, neither flattering nor insulting them, being neither bashful nor brazen. Then the writer of the sermon reconsiders. Is not this command contradicted by another: "But if anyone strikes you on the right cheek, turn to him the other also" (Matthew 5:39)? Therefore, it seems, we should not speak out against those who do evil to us. I respond, the writer continues, that we turn the other cheek if we exercise patience when we rebuke. So, he concludes firmly, rebuke should not be omitted.[1] This same material, with its scholastic structure of question, statement of contradiction, and response, appears almost verbatim in the Franciscan Provincial William of Nottingham's early-fourteenth-century exegesis of the passage. William is more explicit about the principle he uses to reconcile what seem to be conflicting moral imperatives: the intention of Christ. In Matthew 5:39, His intention is to lead us to practice patience ("Dicendum est quod intencio xristi [Matthew 5] est suos inducere ad pacienciam"), not to have us choke back reproof.[2]

This material, incorporated into biblical commentary and sermons, presents the basic method of discourse on fraternal correction. Its drive is to use authoritative texts to establish norms and constraints governing how non-disciplinary correction could be practiced with moral authority.

In this case, sermon and commentary advocate patience as a disposition governing the reprover's decisions and speech. Sometimes pastoral norms are much more specific. The process in reaching these norms involves displaying seemingly contrary authorities, not just different, but seemingly opposed in nature and tendency. It even teases out opposing features, the method pioneered in the early twelfth century by Abelard's *Sic et non* and used by Gratian and other canonists in the *Concordia discordantium canonum*. Such a method, as Catherine Brown argues, "makes especially clear what is the case in all exegesis, poetic or not, monastic or scholastic: finding solutions, finding meaning, is a labor of *invention*."[3] In discourse about fraternal correction, that labor of discovery almost always entails ethical reasoning: William resolves the seeming contradiction, like a good student of Aristotle, by seeking the ethical intention of the speaker, the way he directs us toward the good life. In this case, texts that seem to demand opposite responses to injuries (either "Reprove the person who injures you" or "Do not resist those who injure you") are reconciled so that the one response, fraternal correction, becomes a means of enacting the other, patience in the face of evil. Contrariety provokes thought and discourse, first of all that of Christian biblical exegesis, which affirms that "Truth" is, in Brown's words, "at once and paradoxically single and multiple," that Truth may reside "in one biblical proposition and, equally and simultaneously, in its apparent opposite."[4] Then, ethical reasoning is brought in as an exegetical tool to resolve the contradiction, not through a judgment that accepts one text and rejects another (an either/or logic) but through discovery of the common ethical end of both: in this case, resisting evil patiently.

In this chapter, I will take up successively the central questions framed by pastoral writers as they struggle not only with seemingly conflicting authorities, but also with textual ambiguity and with competing claims about what we owe to each other. Given that we live in a world full of sin, whose sin are we bound to correct? Is it ever justifiable, let alone efficacious, for a known sinner to correct a fellow sinner? When are we justified, even required, to divulge someone's sin to the public in the process of reproof, running the risk of being seen as a treacherous slanderer? And, when we are, who needs to know? Are harsh words ever acceptable in reproof generated and governed by charity? Driving these fundamental questions, pushing the pastoral writers to research, weigh, and determine, is what Geoffrey Harpham characterizes as the perplexity ethics involves: "*Both* options available for choosing embody principles that can be considered worthy."[5] So, pastoral writers negotiate the claims of not intruding into others' lives but of feeling obligated to extend charity to all, of acting from charity to reprove the sins of others but of confronting one's own sins, of protecting others' reputations but of being concerned for the threats evil poses to the community as a whole, and of speaking in a mild, obviously charitable manner but of moving sinners to contrition.

The ethical reasoning that weighs these competing claims and imagines how they play out under certain circumstances does not always issue in the kind of reconciliation achieved with the seemingly contrary authoritative texts above. While logical distinctions resolve some of them and normative principles promise to resolve others in the course of correction itself, sometimes one claim and the good it involves must be sacrificed to a higher one. One, not the other, must be honored in certain circumstances. In such cases, the weight of the contrary claim will still be felt when acting on the other. But even where pastoral writers achieve reconciliation, they still embed in their texts the ethical reasoning that supports each claim and the position that comes from responding to that claim alone, just as they embed the apparent contradictions generated by authoritative texts. This embedding is due, in part, to the scholastic format of argument – question, argument for one side, argument for the other side, synthesizing response – which shaped the academic genres of disputed questions (*quaestiones disputatae*) on fraternal correction and their subtype, quodlibetal questions, and then shaped that genre of moral theology, the *summa*, on which pastoral texts draw so heavily.[6] Given its argumentative methods and multiple authorities, pastoral discourse makes contrarieties and, through them, the perplexity of ethical thought available to its readers and auditors in the very process of working its way to answer questions and to arrive at norms. Even though it is ideological in this drive toward norms, in its explicitness, and in its insistent argument, it thus has ample textual and dialectical play – an apparent, but far from real contradiction in a discourse that explores apparent contradictions.

UNIVERSALIST CHARITY AND AVOIDING INTRUSIVENESS

Whose sins are we bound to correct, given that charity obliges us to seek to deliver our brother from doing evil and that the world is full of sinners who are all our neighbors? The ambiguous wording of the text that founds fraternal correction opens up this question, calling for more precision: "Si autem peccaverit in te frater tuus." What does "in te" mean? Only "contra te" [against you] in the sense of personal injury, as Ambrose of Milan and Jerome thought in their exegesis of Matthew 18:15?[7] Or any sin of which we have direct knowledge, as Augustine thought ("in te" as "in front of you")? "What does it mean that he has sinned against you?" Augustine asks, answering "You know that he has sinned" ("Quid est, in te peccavit? Tu scis quia peccavit").[8] If the latter, are we obligated to seek to discover sin so that we can set evildoers straight? Driving these questions in thirteenth- and fourteenth-century pastoral texts are the competing claims of open-ended Christian charity, with its universalizing imperatives ("Love your neighbor as yourself"), and of aversion to prying into the lives of others – not to mention aversion to having our own lives scrutinized by others, an aversion authorized, too, by Christian scripture.

The potentially conflicting readings of the "evangelical law" are usually resolved by embracing them all with a flexible construction of "in te," with what Catherine Brown labels the "both/and" method of exegesis. So, Jacopo da Varazze begins demonstrating his claim that the text shows how we ought to practice fraternal correction by glossing in this way:

"Si peccaverit in te frater tuus" et cetera. Id est, te solo sciente: vel "in te," id est, contra te injurias vel contumelias irrogando vel "in te," id est, contra te, id est, malo exemplo te corrumpendo.[9]

["If your brother shall offend against you" and so on. That is, with you alone knowing: either "in te," that is, by injuring or insulting you or "in te," that is, against you, namely by corrupting you with a bad example.]

In Jacopo's neat, emphatic phrasing, Augustine's reading that we should correct when we alone know of the sin is reconciled with Ambrose's and Jerome's insistence that only personal injury should prompt correction: Only we know of a sin when we have been maltreated. "In front of you" always means "against you" because evildoing involves influencing others as well as insulting or assaulting someone. Not all sermons, commentaries, or pastoral texts word their glosses as deftly, but most embrace these three non-exclusive justifications for reproving others: direct personal injury, evil example, and exclusive knowledge.[10]

The unexpected personal encounter with sin also becomes the answer to the specific pastoral question of whether or not it is fitting to seek out those whom we should correct ("utrum oporteat quercre quos corripiamus") and the more general one of how we should fulfill the precept ("Qualiter hoc preceptum impleri debeat"). As the latter question suggests, a precept creates an obligation. In the analogy which Ranulph Higden, Johann von Freiburg, and James le Palmer use to explore the question, a monetary debt requires us to seek out the creditor, when the debt comes due, in order to repay him. Shouldn't we do the same for sinners, whom we are bound to correct out of fraternal charity? Pastoral writers contain the open-endedness of precept and of charity with a firm distinction between the good deeds ("beneficia") that we owe to a specific person because of an exchange with him or her and those we owe to all people. In the latter case, that of fraternal correction, it is not fitting for us to seek out individuals to whom we may discharge our general obligation; we should simply act on it when people come our way by chance.[11] Otherwise, we would become pryers into the lives of others ("exploratores vite aliene"), something forbidden by the Wisdom tradition of scripture: "Lie not in wait, nor seek after wickedness in the house of the just" (Proverbs 24:15a).[12]

Drawing both on the multiple interpretations of Christian exegesis and on ethical distinctions, pastoral texts resolve the issue of whom Christians are obligated to correct in a way that combats sin in the community and practices charity without probing into the lives of others. Such a resolution does more than honor the seemingly contrary claims of both Gospel precept and cautionary proverb by invoking the common pastoral category of the affirmative precept, one which we ought to practice only when the circumstances are proper. It also restrains the activity of the corrector. Reproof of sin is only justifiable when we unexpectedly encounter sin. Crucially, it also tends to limit reproof to individual sinners, not social groups. No pastoral texts or sermons consider, in treating fraternal correction, the question of when any Christian may – let alone, ought to – voice criticism of corporate or institutional evils, though some warily allow (in adjunct material) correction of a sinning multitude by a disciplinary authority.[13] A non-prelatical rebuke of a social group is never directly forbidden by any pastoral text I have encountered, but the practice of fraternal correction is usually phrased in the singular, following the authorizing text of Matthew. 18:15: "correction of the evildoer," "amendment of your brother" ["correctio delinquentis," "emendatio fratris tui"]. The standard biblical examples of fraternal correction also work to limit it to individuals: Paul rebuking Peter for breaking off his practice of eating with the Gentile Christians of Antioch (to be considered in the next chapter) or Jesus rebuking Judas before the betrayal. Some less common ones involve rebuke of more than one person, but not a whole social group: for example, Abraham rebuking Lot's shepherds (Genesis 12), and Lot the people of Sodom who demand to have sex with his guests (Genesis 19).[14] Post-biblical reprovers also tend to speak only to individuals, like the monk of the vernacular *Northern Homily Cycle* (shortly to come to the fore) who rebukes a young workman in the street for eating early on a fast day.

THE DANGERS OF HYPOCRISY AND
THE IMPERATIVES OF CHARITY

While textual ambiguity sparks thought on whom to correct, the second major question raised by pastoral writers on fraternal correction springs from a collision between the evangelical "law" of fraternal correction and another set of evangelical precepts: "Nolite judicare et non judicabimini" [Judge not and you shall not be judged] and, further in the Gospel reading for the fourth Sunday after Trinity or Trinity itself, "Quid autem vides festucam in oculo fratris tui, trabem autem, quae in oculo tuo est non consideras? ... Hypocrita, ejice primum trabem de oculo tuo" [And why do you see the mote in your brother's eye, but the beam that is in your own eye you do not consider? ... Hypocrite, cast first the beam out of your own eye] (Luke 6:37, 41–2). (The version in Matthew, an occasional text for preaching, is virtually verbatim in the Vulgate [Matthew 7:1, 3].) In the sermon on the *thema* for this reading, "Estote misericordes" [Be merciful], from the *Northern Homily Cycle* (*c.* 1300 for this sermon), the preacher anticipates that his auditors will recognize how these precepts seem to contravene the precept establishing fraternal correction (Matthew 18:15–17). So he builds their voices into his sermon, making their logic a false conclusion to his paraphrase of Luke 6:36–42 and an *exemplum:*

> Bot here may some men say to me,
> If foles suld noght schastist be [fools should not be chastised],
> Bot of [Except by] tham that gude er sene,
> And no man knawes himseluen clene,
> Than thinkes me he es noght wise
> That snibbis [reproves, corrects] a fole for his folise.
> And tharfore will I hald me still,
> And lat the foles wirk thaire will.[15]

To this prudential withdrawal from fraternal correction, the preacher opposes authoritative texts: Matthew 18:15–17 in paraphase, and a saying he attributes to Bernard, "If thou se a man mistake, / And non-wise amendes make, / In sines ay thou ert his fere" [are his companion]."[16] The preacher's imagined auditors might be forgiven for asking the very question pastoral texts insistently pose: "Utrum peccator possit alium corrigere" [Could a sinner correct someone?] or, more legalistically, "Utrum criminosus possit corrigere criminosum" [Could a guilty person correct a guilty person?].[17] But their answer is faulty in the Gospel/pastoral economy of charity, where even Christians' nagging awareness of sin and worries about their own and others' hypocrisy are trumped by the single imperative "chastise him in charite." Committing a sin, *Omne bonum* declares bluntly, is no excuse for not obeying a precept, especially one directing us to perform a work of spiritual mercy.[18] How can that strongest of claims be met while facing squarely how sins discredit correctors of sin, draw God's condemnation on them, and vitiate the end of moving others to amend their lives?

Sermons, the scriptural exegesis which fed them, and the pastoral texts which often shaped them all find in the scriptural metaphor of the mote and beam ("a grete tre" in the *Northern Homily Cycle*) significant obstacles for the sinner who attempts to correct another. Generally, the mote in the eye was construed as a light sin, the beam a heavy or grave sin. Nicolas de Lyre gives a useful illustration: The beam is adultery compared to the mote of simple fornication. Those who have committed a more serious sin than those they rebuke are driven by rashness in judgment ["judicii temeritatem"]. Blinded by their own sins, they judge quickly and so can misjudge others, not discerning their will or the circumstances.[19] In the words of the Middle English version of Robert of Gretham's sermon on this *thema*, a person should not judge quickly because "he ne seth noght [does not see] his wille ne hou that he is tempted, for ther nis non [there isn't anyone at all] so wise in him selven that may se another mannes wille."[20] Such rash correctors, guilty of serious sins themselves, are obviously unworthy ["indignus"] of correcting others. They are bound to fail, writes John Bromyard, because they will be mocked by others: "That person full of worms is reproving another full of worms." Moreover, to correct another unworthily – even when we are bound to correct – is itself a sin.[21]

An even more serious obstacle than such a corrector's unworthiness, real or perceived, is the scandal correctors give if they are known sinners, the threat they pose to others' moral welfare. It looks as if they are rebuking others not from charity but from idle show or vain display ("non corrigat ex caritate, sed magis ad ostentationem"). To develop why a corrector might speak hypocritically, pastoral writers and preachers draw on Pseudo-Chrysostom, whose early medieval set of sermons on the early chapters of Matthew were copied and cited widely in the thirteenth through fifteenth centuries, not least of all by reformist writers from Wyclif on. He expands in this way Jesus' question "Or, how do you say to your brother: Let me cast the mote out of your eye; and, behold, a beam is in your own eye?":

"Quomodo?" … puta ex caritate, ut salves proximum tuum. Non, quia teipsum ante salvares. Vis ergo non alios sanare sed per bonam doctrinam malos actos celare et sane laudem ab omnibus querere.[22]

["How?" ... Perhaps from charity so that you may save your neighbor? Not at all, because you should save yourself first. You do not desire to restore others to health, but to hide your evil deeds under sound doctrine and, certainly, to seek praise from all.]

The abuse of correction is rooted in the will. To return to the multiple pastoral conceptions of sin, it not only violates divine law, but it springs from misdirected love: love of our own appearance of rightness/righteousness and of others' approbation, not love of our neighbor. To set someone else straight, to weigh and rebuke another's sin ostentatiously is to direct attention away from our own sins, to simulate righteousness. More deeply, it also springs from a pride that makes light of our own sins, while sternly judging another's: Proud correctors compare themselves favorably with their neighbors.[23] Looked at in terms of intention, this abuse of correction is also sin in itself: The beam in the eye, William of Nottingham argues, may signify the evil intention to extol ourselves by accusing others.[24] Such hypocritical misuse of correction discredits both corrector and the act of correction itself.

Resolving the competing claims of Matthew 18's precept, of the open-ended charity which sustains it, and of the dangers sin poses to the corrector, the community, and the practice itself would seem to demand just a simple act: Confess and do penance for the disabling sin. Pluck out that beam, in the Gospel metaphor. In both of his compendia for preachers, John Bromyard advocates confession as a way of fulfilling the canon which admonishes all "primo seipsum corrigat qui alios corrigere nititur" [he who struggles to correct others should correct himself first]. And in his *Opus trivium* confession before admonishing another for sin is a way of enacting the proverb cited repeatedly in discourse on fraternal correction and correction in general: "Justus prior est accusator sui" [The just person is first accuser of himself (Proverbs 18:17)]. Just as a servant may not bring an accusation in a court of law, so the servant of sin or the devil may not reprove someone else for sin. First he must become a free man. First he must cleanse himself. After all, you wash your hand before extending it to others and you clean a mirror before it can show others spots (of sin).[25]

Confession of specific sins, however, would seem not to address wholly the deeper problem: a misdirected will that can convert any virtuous practice into a vicious one. The sermon on "Estote misericordes" in the *Northern Homily Cycle*, like other pastoral texts and exegesis, construes the "grete tre" that blinds the corrector not only as specific sins but as dispositions of will: malice and envy. Its *exemplum* turns on a monk's discovery of how "miswiling," even in a habitually virtuous person, may prompt abuse of fraternal correction. In the street, the monk had come upon a young man eating early on a fast day (a Friday). At first sight, he judges the man's character and reproves him:

> The monk when that he saw this sight,
> An evill man he demid him
> And said, "Why ettes thou or tyme?" [Why are you eating before it's time?]
> This ilke [same] monk was ful haly,
> And a gudman was he forthi [therefore],
> And in his hert him thoght it skorne
> To ete so arly on the morn.

When the monk returns to his cell, his fellow monk, who, unlike the corrector, has a gift of discernment, immediately perceives that he has fallen from God's grace, that he has angered Him somehow. Then the corrector recognizes that his will was misdirected when he reproved the young man:

> "In my hert had I hething [contempt or hostility] grete,
> For he was so arly at mete.
> And wele may be I did foly,
> For of his hunger noght feled I.
> For suth [truth] it es that hunger grete
> Makes a man gredy to mete.

Instead of fraternal correction springing from a compassionate response to another's spiritual need, the monk's speech is malicious. His very holiness, his very set-apartness from others, his very commitment to observing the rules of fasting, prompt him to read the act as evil, blinding him to the natural necessity ("hunger grete") behind it. In terms of the Gospel metaphor, the beam in the eye (his self-righteous malice) has made him blind, has skewed his perception. Prolonged penance then becomes the only way to redirect his will and so to restore true perception of himself and others. Both monks pray for a fortnight before they get a sense that God has charitably forgiven him and "That the penance was fulfild / For his miswiling that he wilde." This example shows you, the preacher concludes, that you must discern the cause of actions and "mak thyself ful clene / That non-kins [no kind of] filth in the be sene, / And then may thou ful worthily / Snib [reprove, correct] another of his foly."[26]

Hasn't the preacher's conclusion brought us full circle? How can anyone conscious of his own sins correct another if being fully "clene" of sin must come first? In fact, it is at this point that the voices of the "sum men" enter the sermon and swear off fraternal correction, only to be checked by the preacher quoting Bernard and the Gospel precept. Such a response as theirs misses, in the eyes of the preacher, the radical nature of both the Gospel precept and the reading from Luke, which begins with the absolute imperative "Bese mercifull to ilk a [each] man." Charity is a virtue of the will and mercy an inward result of charity. "Will" and "hert" are the constant refrains of the sermon: The blind man of the reading who falls in the ditch "walkes all will" [goes about wholly as he pleases]; the sinner with the "balk" finds it "in hert" to reprove his brother with the mote; the preacher exhorts him "To remu clene out of thy hert / All malice and envy so hate [hot]"; the young man breaks the fast from need, not will; finally, the monk's "miswiling" leads him to reprove.[27] This sermon might be seen as more voluntaristic than most pastoral discourse on fraternal correction because it was composed for the evangelizing missions of the Austin canons, deeply influenced by Augustinian theology. However, texts heavily influenced by Thomas Aquinas, as we have seen, insist that fraternal correction springs from charity, and Thomas places charity in the will, in the intellective appetite that apprehends supernatural goods and directs us to supernatural ends (our neighbor's rescue from evildoing, from violating divine law).[28] Therefore, it is because confession and penance redirect the will to desire to love God and then others that confession, in this sermon and in pastoral discourse on fraternal correction in general, is the means for correctors to correct themselves so that they may correct others rightly. Charity then ensures the proper perception and intention that enable us to remove the sin in our brother's eye, the action that concludes the Gospel metaphor (and the Gospel reading): "then you shall see clearly to take the mote out of your brother's eye" (Luke 6:42). The order of charity, writes Nicolas de Lyre on Matthew 7, begins in the self ("ordo charitatis incipit a seipso"); only after a person is restored to friendship with God through penitence can correction proceed from charity, not from audacity and hypocrisy. Charity is like a fountain that springs up from the self of the corrector, writes John Bromyard; then it flows down to others. As the preacher of the *Northern Homily Cycle* rehearses the imperative of Matthew 18 to refute his imagined interlocutors, "chastise him in charite."[29]

In the very process of correction this charitable will should direct sinners to humbly acknowledge their own sins, at least to themselves and often to the sinners they are reproving. Even reflection on our own sins, the pastoral writers claim, following Augustine, is enough to prompt us to rebuke with mercy. And mercy arises, in late medieval moral theology, from a perception of shared weakness.

Cogitemus, cum aliquem reprehendere nos necessitas cogerit, utrum tale sit vitium quod nunquam habuimus. Et tunc cogitemus nos homines esse et habere potuisse. Vel tale quod habuimus et jam non habemus, et tunc tangat memoriam communis fragilitas ut illam correptionem non odium sed misericordia precedat. Si autem inveneremus nos in eodem vitio esse non objurgemus, sed congemiscamus et ad equaliter penitendum invitemus.[30]

[When necessity forces us to reprove someone, we should consider whether we have ever had such a vice, and then let us realize that we are men and could have had it. Or that we did have it, but do not now, and then a sense of common fragility should touch our memory so that mercy, not hate, may come before our reproof. However, if we find ourselves in the same vice, we should not reproach the person we are correcting, but should sigh together with him and invite him to repent along with us.]

Sermons on "Estote misericordes" sometimes develop Augustine's three stages of reflection into five conditions necessary for correcting in the way God ordains.[31] While all of the conditions (paraphrased in the note) loom large in pastoral treatises and sermons, the first is always primary: We should never attempt reproof if we are committing the same sin we observe in another. Only mutual contrition is possible.

These sermons on "Estote misericordes" have engaged us so long because they not only develop how sin could subvert correctors, the practice of correction, and even sound teaching, but because they offer a way of surmounting obstacles. To acknowledge your sin is to avoid drawing fresh condemnation on yourself ("Judge not that ye be not judged" and "Hypocrite"). It is also to become capable of reproving others with mercy, with that heartfelt compassion for another's needs which should direct all the seven spiritual works of mercy, as it directs the seven corporal works, because it springs from a sense of shared vulnerability.

Thought on this question of whether or not a sinner may correct is driven by more than concern for the efficacy of correction and for the spiritual welfare of corrector and sinner alike. Bartolomeo da San Concordio places this *quaestio* not in his entry on fraternal correction, as he does the other six he adapts from Thomas Aquinas, but in his entry on disciplinary correction. Reworking Thomas's claim that sin does not wholly destroy a corrector's judgment, he argues that sinful *prelati* are still competent to reprove the evil doings of those in their charge ("peccatum autem non tollit quin remaneat in peccatore aliquid de recto judicio, et secundum hoc potest sibi competere delicta subditorum arguere").[32] (Thomas's thinking about the effects of sin is more confident about the powers of the intellect than the more voluntaristic sermon from the *Northern Homily Cycle*.) Bartolomeo's use of pastoral discourse on fraternal correction to resolve a question about disciplinary correction, despite moral theology's distinctions between the disciplinary and fraternal, indicates how profoundly clerics were concerned with the laity's questions about the efficacy, even the validity, of disciplinary actions performed by immoral priests. The popular late-thirteenth-century French pastoral compiler and preacher Nicolas de Byard devotes much of his third entry on "correctio" to exhorting clerics to correct themselves before they attempt to correct others. What is at stake, he insists, is nothing less than their authority ("corrigere qui vult alios primo aliter ammitit auctoritatem alios corrigendi ut medicus infirmus alios curandi"). Like the physician, the cleric must heal himself first or face the mocking response from those he attempts to correct: "Physician, heal thyself."[33] The homily in the Middle English *Mirror* goes further: It declares that if a priest who habitually commits deadly sin reproves a subject in confession, he commits a deadly sin – and does so if he attempts to celebrate any of the sacraments.[34] How these and other clerical failures endanger the practice of disciplinary correction will emerge more fully in the following chapters on *Piers Plowman* and Wycliffite texts. It is enough here to suggest that passionate concern for the efficacy of disciplinary, as well as fraternal, correction drives extended thought on the question of whether sinners may correct.

GOOD REPUTE AND THE COMMON GOOD

The Gospel precept authoring fraternal correction would seem to obviate altogether the third question (in two parts) posed by pastoral writers: When should the reprover make another's sin public? And, when he or she should, who needs to know of it? Matthew 18:15–17 sets forth a firm, step-by-step procedure to govern when and how reproof should extend beyond the injured speaker and the sinner. The *Northern Homily Cycle* gives us a mid- to late-fourteenth-century vernacular version, slightly expanded in ways that work to spell out when the Gospel specifies privacy, when disclosure to a few, and when fuller disclosure.

> If thy brother, what-so he be,
> In this erth trispas to the,
> Thou sal [should] him blame bitwene yow twa,
> That of yowre wordes wit no ma [no man knows],
> Ne of yowre cownsail lat wit nanne
> Bot thou and he by yow allane;
> And if thy brother with gude chere
> Thy blameing and thy wordes will here,

And so amend him of his sins,
Thy brother than ful wele thou wins.
And if he sett noght by thy saw [counsel]
Bot fra [away from] thy counsail fast will draw,
Than unto the sall thou ta [take]
Of thy best frendes ane or twa,
For in the mowthes of twa or thre
May ilk a [each] word wele witnest be.
And than if he will noght tak hede
To yowre counsail, than es it nede
That thou tell unto haly kirk
The sins that thou sese [see] him wirk.
And than if he will noght be boun
To haly kirk and to resoun,
And do what-so may him availe,
Als [as] haly kirk will gif counsaile,
Onence the thou hald him slike [Consider him among you as]
Als a puplicane [publican] or ane etnike [alien]
That in this werld will never wirk
By the counsail of haly kirk,
Bot lifes out of Goddes law
And will no heleful [wholesome] counsaill knaw.[35]

Whether or not sin should be disclosed depends upon the sinner's response to the salvific counsel he or she is offered as a violator of divine law. So does how far it should be disclosed. The reprover only goes public if the sinner rejects being set straight.

Even such a sharply defined procedure could perplex. Adam of Eynsham's life of Hugh of Lincoln, the *Magna vita Sancti Hugonis*, written shortly after the bishop's death in 1200, records how a group of experts in canon and civil law, discussing a range of topics, became divided over how to bring in witnesses and how a brother's sin should be spoken to the Church ["de forma dicendi ecclesie peccatum fratris"]. Bishop Hugh resolved these issues himself with an account of how he, as a young deacon newly in charge of a parish, dealt with a notorious habitual adulterer, whose flagrant, repeated sins were subverting religious practice and authority. After ascertaining the truth of his reputation for evil ("famam mali"), the new deacon summoned him to a private interview. When the man not only denied his guilt but insulted and abused Hugh, he, mindful of the evangelical precept ("precepti vero hujus evangelici memor"), reproved the man again in the presence of two or three witnesses who already knew of his sin. Only when he refused to amend did the bishop rebuke him very publicly: before the whole congregation on a feast day.

As the bishop drove home the heinousness of his sin and threatened him with excommunication, the terrified adulterer confessed his sin before all and accepted penance. Adam retells this story (he tells us) because it manifests the solicitude, zeal, discretion, and wisdom young Hugh possessed in the care of souls, enabling him to decide how to fulfill ("adimplere") the Gospel precept in a specific case.[36]

Adam's story, of course, involves a clerical corrector admonishing and imposing punishment on behalf of the parish community he heads. Correction carried out by a disciplinary inferior (*subditus*) or equal (in disciplinary systems) raises more acutely the competing claims that surface repeatedly in the anecdote: protecting the sinner's reputation and looking out for the common good. Each claim is complexly bound up with the end of fraternal correction as a moral practice: amendment of life. And to ignore either claim could lead to devastating consequences: slander that imperils the sinner and the integrity of the process of correction alike and failure to expose major threats that, if unchecked, would harm the lives of others, even the community itself. So compelling are these claims, so destructive the potential consequences, and so various the circumstances in which they must be weighed and adjudicated that most pastoral writers devote more space to the intertwined questions of when and to whom to divulge sin than to any other question. No question prompts so heavily juridical a discourse.

A text that might seem to contradict the Gospel procedure, taken together with it, authorizes the basic moral principle governing procedure: "Peccantes coram omnibus argue ut et caeteri timorem habeant" [Reprove those who sin before all so that the rest may also have fear] (1 Timothy 5:20). Citing this, Ranulph Higden, Bartolomeo da San Concordio, Johann von Freiburg, and James le Palmer begin considering the question by arguing that public sins ought to be publicly rebuked, while hidden sins ought to be rebuked in private, following Matthew 18:15's "between you and him alone."[37] When we alone experience wrongdoing, when it is a private affair, charitable concern for our brother's welfare generally dictates that we work in ways that preserve his or her reputation as much as possible ("corrigens fratrem debet quantum potest conservare ejus famam"). Good repute is commonly reckoned among the greater human goods, writes the influential early-fourteenth-century exegete Nicolas de Lyre, as he argues that charity dictates that we keep secret the sins we reprove, akin to how a doctor tries to restore health without cutting open the body.[38] Johann von Freiburg and James le Palmer develop *fama*'s worth by arguing that it is valuable ("utilis") in temporal affairs, surely a general reference to the overlapping legal and commercial uses of *bona fama*, explored recently by Barbara Hanawalt, Thomas Kuehn, and F. R. P. Akehurst. Its loss brings on temporal losses of many kinds. And fear of such a loss may draw the sinner back from sin. Moreover, they claim, a sinner is much less likely to reform – indeed, he or she is likely to cast aside all moral constraints – if publicly shamed. Others may profit, too, when a sinner's good name is preserved because divulging sins may provoke others to sin similarly – a domino effect.[39] Sins made public may also tar others, including whole communities of which they are members (the phrasing suggests religious communities).[40]

Given the multiple values of good reputation and the dangers of infamy, to desire to rebuke someone publicly for a hidden sin makes us treacherous people, not correctors – at the very least slanderers unjustly wounding our brother's reputation. So argues Augustine in a passage from his sermon on Matthew 18:15, which then presents St. Joseph as the model of the fair-minded corrector who respects the reputation of someone he suspects of sinning against him. This passage, incorporated into the *Decretum*, is pulled wholesale into Simon of Boraston's entry on "correptio" in the widely disseminated *Distinctiones* (1327–36):

Nam si solus nosci quia peccavit in te et eum vis coram omnibus arguere, non es corrector sed proditor. Attende quemadmodum vir justus Joseph, tanto flagicio quod de uxore fuerat suspicatus, quanta benignitate pepercit, antequam sciret unde illa conceperat: quia gravidam senserat et se ad ipsam non accessisse noverat. Restabat igitur certa adulterii suspicio, et tamen quia uxor solus sciebat quid de illo ait evangelium? "Joseph autem cum esset vir justus et nollet eam divulgare." Mariti dolor non vindictam quesivit; voluit prodesse peccanti, non punire peccantem. "Joseph voluit occulte dimittere eam."[41]

[If you alone know that he has sinned against you and you wish to reprehend him before all, you are not a corrector, but a traitor. Pay attention to how that just man Joseph spared his wife with such exceeding kindness, despite how great a crime he had suspected her of before he knew by whom she had conceived. He grasped that she was pregnant and knew that he had not approached her. Therefore, a certain suspicion of adultery remained, and still because he alone knew it, what does the Gospel say of him? "However, because Joseph was a just man and did not wish to expose her publicly ..." The grief of the husband did not seek vengeance; he wished to assist the sinner, not to punish her. "Joseph decided to set her aside secretly." (Matthew 1:19)]

Here a popular fourteenth-century English pastoral text disseminates a fundamental pastoral and legal constraint on reproof: To reprove others publicly is to use reproof as a tool of vengeance rather than of correction. It is to seek covertly to expose sinners out of malice, to destroy their social selves, not to amend their lives out of charity. So that fraternal correctors avoid even the appearance of malicious slander, pastoral writers affirm emphatically, as a guiding principle, that correctors should resort to charitable admonition in private before making sins public.[42]

Nevertheless, sometimes the claims of justice demand that we set aside the claims of our brother's temporal and spiritual welfare as they are tied up with reputation. First of all, the corrector must distinguish when the evil done to him or her also affects others. If someone who injures us does so with others present, we must rebuke him in front of them because he has also disturbed them. They must be protected from scandal, from threats to their morality, just as he must be dissuaded from evil. They must be dissuaded from imitating him. In a much-quoted saying of Isidore's, "Manifesta peccata non sunt occulta purgacione purganda, palam enim arguendi sunt, qui palam nocent, ut dum aperta objurgacione sanantur, illi, qui eos imitando delinquunt, corrigantur" [Manifest sins ought not to be cleared away by secret cleansing, for anyone who inflicts harm openly ought to be rebuked openly so that, while they are healed by open rebuke, those may be corrected too who do evil by imitating them].[43] The spiritual welfare of all – the common good – must be considered. If a sin is known by others or even likely to become known, argue Ranulph Higden and Johann von Freiburg, bring in a *praelatus* rather than correct the sinner on your own so that the punishment he inflicts may remove scandal or at least may work against scandal when the sin becomes public. Secondly, pastoral writers reason that the common good simply outweighs the good of reputation when hidden sins – like conspiring with the state's enemies, stealing habitually, or spreading heresy – endanger the community. Then the person who discovers the sin ought to move at once to secure a judicial summons (*denuntiatio*). Even in such a case, however, the writers try to reconcile the claims of both charity and justice, allowing for private admonition first if the corrector has firm grounds for believing it will head off the evil threatening the community.[44]

The Gospel procedure, pastoral writers also argue, requires us sometimes to denounce our brother, when private admonition fails, in order to deliver him from a sin, even at the cost of his good name. The value of salvation outweighs that of reputation. Even then, however, we ought to disclose sin to as few people as possible – and only to ones chosen with an eye to containing public knowledge as far as possible. Pastoral discourse develops elaborate procedural rules for achieving this, rules which need concern us little here. So, Bartolomeo da San Concordio, Johann von Freiburg, and James le Palmer insist that, despite the open-ended

Gospel command to take one or two witnesses, we should first divulge an unrepentant sinner's "private offense" only to a *praelatus* (the Gospel's one witness) because his paternal admonitions, commands, and threats of ecclesiastical censure may be more effective in securing amendment and because he will contain knowledge of the affair.[45] If both fraternal and prelatical admonition fail, the wrongdoing must be disclosed to one or two other witnesses, who should seek to gain a confession and then admonish the sinner charitably. Only after the witnesses do all they can, resourcefully adapting their methods to the sinner's response, does the wrongdoing become public (Matthew 18:16's "tell the Church") as the unrepentant sinner is excommunicated. If that, too, fails in securing amendment of life, all should join in excluding him or her from the religious community, just as, John Bromyard remarks, the Israelites did by all – not just the priests – stoning blasphemers and adulterers.[46] William of Nottingham develops how the Church ought to regard publicly revealed impenitents in his gloss of Matthew 18:17's terms for them: "ethnicus" is what a gentile is to a Greek; "publicanus," someone who seeks the rewards of the world through fraud, theft, or assaults or who exacts taxes.[47] So, the extent to which the sinner's reputation is tarnished depends on his or her response to correction, with the corrector(s) always setting first the claims of reforming the sinner. So crucial is the latter that if the initial corrector judges that bringing in witnesses would not work, but might make the sinner worse, he or she should abandon altogether correcting the sinner.[48]

Although no pastoral writer I have studied acknowledges this, these carefully reasoned considerations of when to divulge sin publicly call into question, in several ways, the hard-and-fast distinction most writers draw between prelatical and fraternal correction. To weigh and act from either fear of scandal or danger to the community is to be moved, at least in part, not by the charitable concern for the sinner that marks fraternal correction, but by the concern for the common good that marks prelatical correction. This is notably so even when disciplinary inferiors publicly correct their *praelati* because of some imminent danger they pose to the faith, as in Paul's rebuke of Peter. The end intended and the good to be realized – at least the primary end and good – are not the end and good of fraternal action: amendment of the brother's or sister's life. Secondly, even to consider when to go public raises sharply a critical question on which pastoral texts differ, without acknowledging that difference, a question rooted in the evangelical law/precept of Matthew 18:15–17 itself: When does correction extended past private admonition cease being fraternal and become prelatical? The heavily juridical *summae* and other texts close to moral

theology and canon law usually stop their entries on fraternal correction
with the corrector denouncing the sin to a *praelatus* (*denunciatio*), a specific act that could initiate a legal process leading to penance or excommunication, even a trial.[49] However, homilies in the ancient form, just
like biblical commentaries, are bound to explicate the whole of Matthew
18:15–22. Some of them explicitly include within fraternal correction the
final stages of telling the Church/*praelatus*, including excommunication.
The widely disseminated Lenten cycle of sermons by Jacopo de Varazze
divides the process into three types of correction, all of which are fraternal: correction by love of the humble and mild (admonition in private);
correction by reason of the crafty (by bringing in witnesses); correction
by fear of the proud and presumptuous (by a *praelatus* acting as judge
coercing through punishment).[50] All actions may be considered fraternal
correction because all are aimed at the sinners' spiritual welfare and work
to amend their lives. Both of these ambiguities – mixed ends or intentions and whether punishment by the *praelatus* is fraternal or not – erode
the distinction between a fraternal correction that anyone may perform
involving charitable admonition to amend sinners' lives and a prelatical
correction involving punishment that only an authority may perform for
the common good. That distinction, as we have seen, serves both to justify
opening the practice of correction to *subditi* and to shore up a prelatical
sphere of power and authority. It also protects *praelati* from being subject
to coercive punishment by disciplinary inferiors, as a visitation sermon in
British Library MS Royal 7.A.VIII states bluntly.[51] These ambiguities open
up ways for reformist writers like Langland and John Wyclif to transform
radically the practice of fraternal correction, extending it to lawful public
protest against communal evils (chapter 3) and to a disciplinary process in
which lay people punish sinful clerics (chapter 4).

COURTLINESS AND HARSHNESS

Pastoral writers' labors to distinguish proper correction from deviant
speech do not stop with marking correction off from its illegitimate
cousin slander as they weigh the sometimes conflicting goods of preserving the sinner's good repute and of acting for the communal welfare and,
under some circumstances, the sinner's salvation. Their labors extend to
the mode of corrective speech itself, especially the ambiguous mode of
chiding (*objurgatio* or *contentio*). Private, charitable correction, comments
William of Nottingham, ought to be utterly benign and courtly ("curial-
issime"), sparked by love. It ought to avoid threat, insult, and any other

kind of verbal violence. Yet earlier in his commentary on Matthew 18 William insists that only vehement speech can move someone to grieve for the injuries he is inflicting on others.[52] Does the need to move sinners to contrition and so to redeem them outweigh the claims of gentleness, justifying harsh speech?

In speech, as in many other aspects of practicing fraternal correction, pastoral texts advocate a leniency or mildness rooted in charity and in the correctors' sense of their own moral fragility. So reasons the entry on "correccio" in a mid-fourteenth-century treatise on the virtues, capping its argument with the common analogy of physicians and a popular saying ascribed to Seneca:

Sicut medicus nimia potacione occidit egrotum, sic ille qui corripit nimis dura correpcione. Seneca: "Vicia animi sicut vicia corporis leviter tractanda sunt."

[Just as a physician slays a sick person with too much of a potion, so does the person who corrects with excessively harsh rebuke. Seneca: "Vices of the soul, like those of the body, ought to be treated gently."]

Just before using the same metaphor and *sententia*, a collection of *distinctiones* argues for mild or light correction, especially when sins are light ("pro levi culpa"). You don't fight against flies and fleas with a sword, it adds.[53] As the stress on "nimia"/"nimis" indicates, however, what pastoral writers endorse is a measure of moderation (*modum* or *moderamen*) that strikes a balance between mercy and harshness in emotion, tone, and words. For they are equally wary of excessive leniency. The most common *exemplum* of misjudged correction is Eli's overly mild (and thus ineffectual) rebuke of his sons, who kept abusing their priestly office to the point that they were slain in battle, that Eli died, and that the Ark of the Covenant was captured by the Philistines. We should all be compassionate and loving to other sinners, realizing we could be Peter, the earthly vicar of Christ hearing the cock crow his betrayal of Christ, writes John Bromyard. But if that keeps us from fervor, we are like scarecrows or nets spread to scare off birds, which become ineffective over time as the birds become accustomed to them.[54]

In speech, the balance to be struck involves avoiding both caressing and flattering (*blandus*) speech and threats, insults, or, especially, violent chiding (*increpatio*). In fraternal correction, as in disciplinary, the pleasing images that the flatterer constructs to sell for his advantage obviate that amendment of life which is the end of reproof. That false praise, proclaims the second sermon on "Corripe eum" in British Library MS Royal 7.A.VIII, deceives sinners, seducing and softening them so that they cannot tolerate the hard truth about themselves.[55] On the other hand, the standard marginal gloss on Luke 6:42 warns that the acrimonious words of chiding often signal that hate or anger generates and governs correction, not the desire to amend a sinner's life. Chiding ought to be used rarely. It should never be excessively harsh or coarse, moving beyond the bounds of social expectations and so threatening to break the social bonds between corrector and sinner, like "thou dronkelwe harlot" or "thou holour" [lecher], Chaucer's Parson's illustrations of chiding and uncharitable reproof.[56]

How does a corrector judge what words are fair, balanced, measured, and so more likely to be efficacious? In an early-fourteenth-century collection of *exempla*, when a monk of Clairvaux corrects a friend by scolding him beyond "the measure of just correction," he loses a longstanding, God-given grace: a sweet taste which had accompanied his reception of the Eucharist. Instead, it tastes like the most bitter absinthe or wormwood.[57] Does such a measure exclude harsh language, like vituperation or chiding? Johann von Freiburg distinguishes amicable admonition from the noisy chiding (*increpatio*) that may characterize disciplinary correction. (Clerical correctors, Bartolomeo da San Concordio writes, may even use insults, just as they use threats of material loss, in the process of discipline.) As fraternal correctors, Johann argues, we must determine the proper measure of our words case by case on the basis of four considerations: the relative gravity of the sin ("quantitas culpe"), the opportuneness of the moment, the status of the person being corrected (here we find his advice on speaking reverently to superiors – not just *praelati*, but also secular magnates), and the zeal that drives us (which should be love, not envy or rancor). In all these things, we should keep the spiritual profit of our brother in mind.[58] Thus, the corrector must apply in specific situations the moral and ethical principles pastoral discourse provides in order to steer between the deviant extremes of flattery and contentious chiding, extremes we will encounter in *Piers Plowman*, then in later visionary literature and *The Book of Margery Kempe*.

MORAL AUTHORITY

For speakers to discern properly what words to use in correction signifies that they possess pastoral power. They show the ability to direct conscience by knowing it – their own and the sinner's – and by judging how conduct deviates from religious law. Moreover, their success in negotiating the other ethical questions pastoral discourse explores – When should they become involved in correction? Should they, as sinners, engage in correction? When and to whom should wrongdoing be divulged? – shows this knowledge of both self and other in terms derived from religious law. Yet this law regarding sin in general and its correction in particular is transmitted, interpreted, and analyzed in pastoral discourse. To master how pastoral writers resolve these questions and adjudicate the seemingly contrary powerful claims that drive them is to become a sharer in the pastoral power of correction with the *praelati*, the priests who write pastoral texts and catechize and preach. To internalize this textual thought and know how to speak in accordance with it is to have the texts' and the clergy's pastoral power and moral authority, if not their disciplinary authority.

Moral authority is constructed in several ways that pastoral discourse makes available to those who conform to it. This discourse roots the practice of fraternal correction in what Josiah Ober calls an "originary grant": the evangelical precept of Matthew 18:15–17.[59] It then shapes norms ("Do not divulge sin unless the common good is threatened") according to the opinions and, presumably, the practice of authoritative individuals and groups over time: Jerome as biblical scholar, Augustine as bishop engaged in pastoral care, Gregory the Great as Pope, the twelfth-century canonists working from papal and conciliar decrees and patristic texts, Thomas Aquinas disputing about a precept of charity within an Aristotelian ethical tradition at the University of Paris. The pastoral use of canons in constructing norms, of course, enmeshes moral authority and legal authority in an interesting way. The canons have moral authority in part because they are rooted in the writings of past authorities like Augustine, and they contribute to making that authority known and observed in the present. But, as positive ecclesiastical law, they also have a power to bind fraternal correctors. Beyond making available this originary grant and its authoritative development over time, pastoral discourse offers moral authority to correctors through establishing a basic reciprocity: The right to reprove others for sin and to urge them to amend their lives comes from a willingness to reprove oneself for sin and to repent. And this construction of basic fairness in the practice points to the way in which pastoral discourse works in general to confer moral authority. It presents the learned clergy's agreement on the conditions for the practice of fraternal correction: proper subjects, proper procedure, proper speech, proper judgment of circumstances, proper means, and above all proper directing of moral affections (the virtues, not the vices). For if pastoral discourse generates norms for carrying out the practice – which also serve as constraints, of course, on how correctors operate – it grounds all of them in charity. The charitable will and the charitable end of amending an evildoer's life confer unassailable moral authority.

For all that pastoral discourse, in its insistent, ideological way, resolves seemingly contrary texts, honors seemingly competing moral claims through ethical reasoning, answers the questions it raises, and does all fairly consistently from text to text and time to time to the last quarter of the fourteenth century, it also makes contraries available to its readers and auditors. The seemingly contrary texts ("Turn the other cheek" versus "Go and reprove") and the competing claims ("Preserve the sinner's reputation" and "Protect society from subversive acts") are quite fully presented in the *distinctiones, summae*, and sermons. So are the basic tools of exegetical and ethical reasoning used to adjudicate them. Semantic multiplicity, distinctions between what we owe to individuals and to the community, hierarchies of goods, the ethical importance of circumstances, the radical open-endedness of charity, the importance of reciprocity – all become the property of those informed by pastoral discourse. So, in the very process of negotiating apparently contrary things authoritatively, in establishing norms/constraints for those correctors outside the established disciplinary structures, who might be pulled by competing claims and troubled by seemingly contrary texts, pastoral discourse gives them the means to reflect ethically on the practice of correction, even, given the close association between the disciplinary and the fraternal, correction by their own *praelati*. Also, of course, it gives them the means to contest superiors' adjudication of issues and questions. So, as we shall see more fully in the next four chapters, this pastoral discourse becomes a cultural resource for writers engaged in social, ecclesiastical, and political reform, not only the reform of individuals. It shapes the moral agents they create in narratives or conceive of in treatises; it should also shape, they argue, the lives and speech of their reform-minded readers, giving them pastoral power and moral authority.

CHAPTER 3

Managing the rhetoric of reproof: the B-version of Piers Plowman

Reformist discourses crowd *Piers Plowman*, moving in and out of the seven dreams and twenty narrative *passūs* of its B-version. Satiric, pastoral, inter-clerical and anticlerical, Franciscan, apocalyptic – each discourse is voiced recurrently, by different figures and by the wandering dreamer/narrator himself, an open persona in a world of contending discourses and contentious interlocutors and of the often contrary texts shaping both.[1] Each becomes part of a search that, in David Aers's words, "resists attempts to generate a 'spirituality' abstracted from the embodied practices of the virtues and vices."[2] As *Piers* explores – and activates – the potential of each discourse to reform the individual, social and economic relations, the Church, and sometimes the state, each one's contrarieties and limitations, as well as its promise, begin to appear. Some discourses endure to the end of the poem; others are rejected; some recur in several dreams, their potential coming to matter at specific points in the narrator's journeys. Among the last is discourse on fraternal correction as a moral practice, shaped by moral theologians and canonists intent on reforming the conduct of individuals, lay people and clerics alike, then transmitted by pastoral text and sermon. *Piers Plowman*'s open field of multiple discourses provides fertile ground for the interplay of seemingly conflicting, even contrary, goods, texts, and voices that we find in pastoral discourse – and for its many ways of negotiating them. However, in place of the systematic structures of pastoral genres with scholastic roots – the sermon, the *distinctio*, the commentary, the *summa* – *Piers* as a dream vision presents loosely associated fictive situations in which allegorical figures, with different fixes on fraternal correction, collide with the dreamer, whose own eagerness to reprove others raises ethical questions and sparks passionate responses. The partiality of each speaker and the dreamer's angry, contentious, and sometimes miscalculated reaction to the evils he observes work together to lead readers of the poem, in David Lawton's words, "to experience, rather than observe, moral conflict and spiritual quest."[3]

57

Reproof of sin is first vexed in the poem by the wily initiator of so many of the poem's recurrent topics, Lady Meed (Lady Reward, Lady Profit Motive), who uses pastoral discourse on sin itself to discredit, with some justice, her chief reprover as a slanderer and chider in the poem's first dream. In the third dream, the narrator's initial search for living a good life, Clergie (Pastoral Teaching) insists upon the obligation to practice correction, fraternal and disciplinary, provided that reprovers first correct their own sins. Then, when the dreamer comes to realize his confessor's greedy exploitation of pastoral offices, Lewte (Lawfulness) both constrains his anger and licenses him to correct publicly his friar-confessor and his whole convent. Crowding upon them, an unidentified speaker insists that charity obviates harsh rebuke, and Reason reproves the dreamer's overly hasty reproof, mistaken in its target.[4] Taken together, the clustered speakers of the third dream explore most of the questions that occupied moral theologians, canon lawyers, and pastoral writers: Are we obligated by precept to correct sinners? Should charity be the directive virtue? Is harsh speech ever justified? Should sinners correct? Should disciplinary inferiors ever reprove their superiors? These explorations work together to shape a corrective speech that can best resist being discredited by figures like Meed. Together, too, they serve as narrative examples in relation to pastoral norms and ethical reasoning, with "all the possibilities of servility, deflection, deformation and insubordination that role implies," as Geoffrey Harpham says of the relations between imaginative literature and ethics.[5] And *Piers* does not scant any of these possibilities: It deflects private fraternal correction of sinning individuals into public reproof of communal evils, especially those committed by disciplinary authorities.

The dreamer's own uncertain, even fluctuating status – educational, occupational, and social – aids this process of testing. Clearly a recipient of some types of Latin education clerics would normally receive, he is also a married man, with a daughter, in later dreams. Textual details most often identify him as a clerk in minor orders, though some details at some points can be taken to suggest that he is lay. In England such clerks could retain the tonsure, clerical clothes, and clerical legal privileges if they married, but they could no longer hold any ecclesiastical office and were placed among the laity during services, separate from the celibate clergy. Always lesser in ecclesiastical and social status than priests in the poem, such as his friar-confessor, the dreamer is particularly open to the possibilities of fraternal correction, with its conferral of pastoral power and moral authority. And his ambiguous status, with its tensions between "clergie" (learning; Latin literacy; the clergy) and "lewedness" (ignorance; the laity), enables him to use clerical discourse in order to raise new questions and, sometimes, reject conventional clerical answers, as Fiona Somerset has argued.[6] Thus, the poet uses his dreamer's status, much as he does the weaving of Latin quotation into his vernacular text, as a means to do vernacular moral theology in Nicholas Watson's twin senses. In the first sense, the poet translates the largely Latin textual tradition on fraternal correction, making its moral and ethical complexities accessible to those readers not well versed in Latin. This was far from a new enterprise, of course. Vernacular sermons, like that on "Estote misericordes" in the *Northern Homily Cycle*, entertained and worked to resolve conflicting texts, precepts, and goods, even by using, as *Piers* does, conflicting voices. And the more complex sermons recorded or digested in Latin may very well have been preached in English, at least on certain occasions.[7] In addition, pastoral catechesis, though often quite rudimentary (devoted to the fundamentals, like the Seven Sins or the Works of Spiritual Mercy), could become as sophisticated as Latin *quaestiones disputatae* when the recipient was as eager, tenacious, and disputative as Margery Kempe.[8] Nevertheless, the very association of English with the rudimentary opened the way for the poet to critique clerical culture and its moral theology, especially in terms of experiential knowledge (*sapientia*, as opposed to *scientia*) – Watson's second sense of vernacular theology.[9] More rapidly evolving and less regulated than ecclesiastical Latin, English could also be more open to semantic multiplicity and slipperiness, to renaming correction ("lakken" [find fault with], for instance) in ways that could make it morally dubious and expose its kinship to petty fault-finding or even chiding.

What kind of readers were drawn to such an open and contentious text invested in reform of society, the Church, and the individual? What kind of public voice does the poet create that engaged them?

All three versions of *Piers Plowman* achieved nationwide circulation: the A-version, probably composed in the 1360s; the more extensive B-version, almost certainly written before the Uprising of 1381; and the C-version, a partial revision of B in the 1380s.[10] The known or strongly suspected readers of the poem in the late fourteenth and early fifteenth centuries (including scribes and owners), were secular clerics, regular clerics, and literate lay people, like estate managers and civil servants. The poem often appears in manuscripts and in wills among Latin and vernacular pastoral texts or other types of didactic literature.[11] These readers, lay people and clerics alike, were concerned deeply with pastoral care and with "the broader moral, social and legal issues it raised."[12] Their day-to-day work involved counsel, education, discipline. This was a readership interested in attaining "right relations" within Christian communities and in penetrating to "historical precedents and foundations of both temporal and spiritual imperatives"[13] – to the sources of moral authority.

Ecclesiastical and economic conflicts throughout the latter half of the fourteenth century, as well as training and work, fueled these readers' interest in *Piers Plowman* and would especially have engaged them in its treatment of correction. From the middle of the century, as the first chapter indicates, clerics had been accused often – and often by fellow clerics – of avarice for accepting bribes as ecclesiastical officers and confessors. From about 1373, John Wyclif, then his followers at Oxford and elsewhere, mounted a campaign against clerical ownership of property (clerical dominion), clerics' appropriation of tithes, and clerical wealth and hypocrisy in general.Within the clergy, there were conflicts throughout the century between secular clerics (and monks) and the mendicants, accused of seducing lay people into their pastoral care, in part by relaxing penitential discipline and encouraging financial penances. These controversies over clerical wealth and pastoral activities helped to create a readership for a poem focused on ecclesiastical, social, economic, and personal reform.

These controversies also generated *Piers* itself and what Anne Middleton calls its "public voice," the voice created for the public, the readership, Langland imagined. No matter what the education or status of the poet who seems to sign his name as William Langland,[14] *Piers* is rooted in – and often built out of – post-Lateran-IV catechesis in its many written and oral forms.[15] Like clerical catechesis, its rhetoric is directed to the twin ends of moral reform in the present and salvation in the afterlife. It has designs on its audience. Its general voice, like the voices of its dreamer and many of his interlocutors, is public, retaining "the social activism, the militant readiness to rebuke high and low on issues of public policy or spiritual welfare, that we associate with late medieval teaching and preaching."[16] As a hortatory text in the public voice, *Piers Plowman* works to license its imagined readers as correctors of sin, disciplinary and especially fraternal, and so as agents of personal, ecclesiastical, and social reform in an age of crisis. And it does so on the basis of biblical precept, theological debate over God's response to moral action, and the debilitating effects of individual and corporate evildoing. Indirectly the poem's recursive treatment of fraternal correction also licenses the poem's often pastoral rhetoric of reform, in part by indicating how correction of an individual exposes the communal dimensions of sin. But first I will take up the first dream's staging of the failure of other forms of correction – penitence and public, non-fraternal accusation – where the dreamer is a silent observer, not a speaker of reproof himself.

In the first vision's jostling anatomies of economic, legal, political, and religious corruption, where money seduces and wealth has almost irresistible power, Lady Meed soon becomes the object of reproof. The range of meanings, some contradictory, that her name involves – reward, profit motive, gift, bribe, fair wage, and salvation – suggests that she promotes semantic confusion among those who encounter her, try to evaluate her effects on society, and attempt – or should attempt – to reform her. The narrator's first interlocutor, Lady Holy Church, characterizes Meed as an opposite of the truth she expounds in *passus* 1 and promotes: fidelity in social relations of all kinds, lawfulness, integrity, accurate speech, correct belief.[17] Generally a deviant and untrustworthy speaker (her father is Falsehood), Meed works to discredit Lewte, a central figure for lawfulness and for loyalty to the community and to others, who will become, in the third vision, the main figure to advocate fraternal correction of sin (2.20–7). She has told lies and found fault with him ["ylakked"], "lak" being one of the poem's recurrent terms for correction of sin, along with "blame," "reprove," "rebuke," "chastise," and "correct" itself. In *passus* 3 Meed seeks to invalidate public reproof of her vices in ways that threaten the practice of fraternal correction: Creating semantic confusion, she relabels reproof as the deviant speech that pastoral discourse on fraternal correction demands that reprovers avoid.[18] And she does so in ways that mingle truth and falsity. In her slippery way, the poem's first reprover of others is its most successful figure in discrediting reproof when it threatens to disclose the darker sides of her polymorphous identity.

Meed's aversion to correction of sin appears first in her acceptance of a friar's offer to absolve her for a pack horse-load of wheat, no matter how many men she has slept with (3.35–42).[19] They then drive a larger bargain. Meed will decorate his friary lavishly as long as he does not find fault with women that love lechery: "While ye love lordes that lecherye haunten / And lakketh noght ladies that loven wel the same" (3.53–4).[20] What Meed gains is not merely confession without shame,[21] easy absolution, and a light penance (that wheat), but an escape from disciplinary rebuke. In pastoral discourse the most serious impediment to rigorous, effective prelatical correction is bribes, the Latin *munera* being one sense of the Middle English "meed."[22] The friar's bribe-taking allows Meed to emerge unreproved and unamended from that most potent clerical occasion for correction of sin: auricular confession.

Key to Meed's escape is her slippery naming of disciplinary correction: "And lakketh noght." This colloquial verb casts correction here as mere fault-finding: overly critical, uncharitable, and even trivial in its focus on what people lack, on their deficiencies ("lakken," *MED* 2). And it is clear elsewhere in *Piers Plowman* that such a pejorative view of reproof is often justified: Envy confesses to sinning in speech by "lakking" the goods of his rival (5.130–4); lords and debauched religious "lak" their servants (10.316); those who seek to discredit Jesus after he raises Lazarus claim that his teaching is lies "and lakken it alle" (15.602). The polysemous noun behind the verb makes this pejorative use possible, as we have already seen in Meed's "lakking" of Lewte. While "lak" may mean deficiency or want, or even physical disfigurement, things for which one is not always responsible, it also may mean misdeed or sin, a morally blameworthy action ("lak," *MED* 1a, 2a). And pastoral discourse on the Sins of the Tongue specifically forbids rebuking others for physical deformities (see Reason's speech, p. 81). As a vernacular text, *Piers* can explore how English speakers may detach reproof from its construction in pastoral discourse and render it morally suspect simply by renaming it. According to Meed, confessors find fault; they do not correct in the Latinate sense of setting right or straight.

Meed's talent for renaming reproof of sin later enables her not merely to deflect prelatical correction, but to discredit public reproof in the form of accusations, or charges. When the first vision's king proposes to reform her by marrying her off to Conscience, the latter resists the proposal by playing his proper role as accuser: He publicly exposes her looseness in speech and sexual conduct, her subversion of relationships based on loyalty and even law or contract, her corrupting of the Church through temporal wealth, and her destruction of the king's father (3.120–69 altogether):

> crist it me forbede!
> Er I wedde swich [such] a wif wo me bitide!
> She is frele of hire feith, fikel of hire speche;
> She maketh men misdo many score times.
> In trust of hire tresor she teneth [troubles] wel manye.
> Wives and widewes wantounnesse techeth,
> Lereth hem [Teaches them] lecherye that loveth hire giftes.
> Youre fader she felled thorugh false biheste [promise],
> Apoisoned popes, apeired [impaired] holy chirche.

Is noght a bettre baude, by him that me made,
Bitwene hevene and helle, and erthe though men soughte.
She is tikel of hire tail [easily aroused sexually], talewis [glib] of tonge,
As commune as the Cartwey to knave and to alle,
To Monkes, to Minstrales, to Meseles [lepers] in hegges. (3.120–33)[23]

In response, Meed accuses him of violating the conventional constraints on reproof: "thou hast famed me foule bifore the king here" (3.186). Conscience could be seen to have violated proper procedure by bypassing private admonition, to have assaulted her reputation in ways proscribed by pastoral discourse on fraternal correction. Pastoral texts did, as chapter 2 explains, permit the first form of reproof to be public if there was an imminent threat to the common good. Although Conscience tries to make that case, he is still vulnerable to the appearance of slander because he speaks publicly. He is also vulnerable to the charge of slandering her through false accusations, a charge she makes throughout her rebuttal. The reader, of course, knows the truth of many of his accusations from Meed's behavior in *passus* 2: She is sexually promiscuous and leads others to be the same; she is untrustworthy in speech; and she has impaired the Church, not to mention the royal system of justice. However, the king, her audience, does not know much of this. And *Piers* makes its readers aware elsewhere that falsehoods often accompany reproof.[24] In a neat sleight of hand, Meed recasts Conscience's speech as both slander and chiding by ostentatiously claiming to eschew them in her own speech: "And thow knowest, Conscience, I kam noght to chide, / Ne [Nor] to deprave [disparage] thy persone with a proud herte" (3.178–9).

In pastoral discourse on the Sins of the Tongue, chiding may be virtuous if it attacks falsity – as the reader, again, but not the king, knows Conscience is doing – and if it does so with that judicious amount of acrimony prescribed by writing on fraternal correction. But chiding may be vicious if it attacks the truth, transgresses rhetorical bounds in its excessive harshness, or if it springs from pride in one's own opinions and also from anger – as Meed claims of Conscience's speech: "Why thow wrathest thee now wonder me thinketh [it's a wonder to me]" (3.183). Above all, it is sinful if it accuses others of sin with the intention not of amending them, but of winning a personal dispute, even by maintaining falsehoods.[25] Moreover, Meed goes on to claim with some justice, Conscience has committed the very evils he has accused her of: He has been fickle, sometimes clinging to her and sometimes rejecting her; he has misadvised the king's father, resulting in the loss of territory in France (3.180–227).[26] In Meed's construction, Conscience is the proud and hypocritical reprover described by pastoral discourse, the one who sternly judges the sins of others while ignoring or making light of his own. More specifically, he violates the charitable corrector's obligation to commiserate privately with the sinner if he even might sin, let alone has committed the same sins.

As rhetorically slippery as she is semantically slippery, Meed has succeeded temporarily in discrediting Conscience's reproof of her sins. The king acknowledges her victory: "by crist, as me thinketh [it strikes me], / Mede is worthy, me thinketh, the maistrye [upper hand] to have" (3.229–30).[27] She has cast doubt on Conscience's will and intention as a speaker: His reproof springs from sin, wrath, and pride, and it commits sin by its harshness and its injury to her reputation. In a double sleight of hand (or tongue!), Meed has slandered and chided Conscience, indulging deftly in the very types of deviant speech she so noisily denounces. And Conscience is vulnerable to such an attack for more reasons even than the public nature of his reproof, his insults, and the partial validity of her counteraccusations. He is not a cleric, but a knight, and his reproof operates outside the clerical preserve of disciplinary reproof. Yet his end is not that of the fraternal corrector either. He avowedly reproves her, in part, in order to escape marriage to her, not wholly to amend her life or further her salvation.

In Meed, the poet foregrounds the response to reproof, present in much pastoral discourse in only subordinate ways. Like galled horses, John Bromyard says, the reproved kick back when their sores are touched. Their weapon is harsh words, especially chiding and slander designed to take away the good name of the reprover.[28] Even for the reader, who knows the truth of Conscience's accusations and his concern with reforming the kingdom, her accusations have some force. Are Conscience's will and intention – not to mention his choice of words – fully directed by one of the virtues which should govern correction: justice or charity? If so, how can he make that apparent to others? And, even if they are, are such crude public accusations and such harsh language justified?

In this fictive episode, the complexities of character (not least of all, of allegorical ones like Conscience and Meed), of semantics, of contrary claims, and of the uncertain relationship between speech and the inner self all make the reprover himself morally suspect in the eyes of other characters and, to some extent, of readers. Meed's attempts to discredit Conscience, like her evasion of disciplinary correction, raise questions about whether reproof backfires in a world outside of pastoral discourse, a world where pastoral discourse on normative speech itself – that on the Sins of the Tongue as well as that on fraternal correction – even becomes a tool, in the hands of deceptive speakers, for subverting the reprover himself. How can the social, economic, and ecclesiastical evils associated with Meed – bribery of jurors, prostitution, violation of feudal obligations, simony – be confronted at all in ways that might convincingly expose and amend them without the reprover being cast aside as a deviant speaker and a hypocrite? Even more fundamentally, is the purely or fully charitable reproof imagined by pastoral discourse ever possible in specific situations? As Meed's exchange with Conscience establishes, *Piers Plowman* is fundamentally concerned both with the ethos of the corrector – that is, with the character corrective speech projects (habits of emotion and of thought, will, intention) – and with the character others attribute to the speaker.

CLERGIE AND THE CORRECTOR'S INTEGRITY

Piers Plowman returns to the rhetoric and ethics of reproof in the poem's third dream, where the wandering dreamer/narrator struggles with many of the reformist concerns and the difficulties of reform raised in the contending discourses of the first dream. And it does so four times, with four different speakers, over two *passūs*, 10 and 11. As the dreamer defines himself more insistently as a Christian actively pursuing salvation and as a writer concerned with the value of his work, he seeks the good life for himself and others in just institutions: In narrative terms, he asks those he encounters to explain what Dowel, Dobet, and Dobest are. Now named Will (first at 8.129), he becomes more and more identified in the course of the dream not only with the rational will or *voluntas* (the power of the soul responsible for moral choice and moral action – for desiring, for intending, for choosing, and, to some extent, for knowing) but also with *affectus*, will as a power of desire or appetite, closely linked to the passions.[29] Because of this great range of activity and because of the fierce thirteenth- and fourteenth-century theological debates over the nature of the will that *Piers* registers, the dreamer remains an open persona, registering all that he encounters, though he is more verbally and intellectually active (read "willful," "critical," and "cantankerous") than in the first dream. This interplay of the open and the disputatious makes Will an immensely fertile figure for exploring the education of the will through contentious encounters with interlocutors promoting certain discourses and social practices, all embedded in institutions.[30] In the formation of the will – the central psychological, social, and theological drama of this dream[31] – fraternal correction of sin emerges as an urgent, recurrent topic.

It provides a major vehicle for Will, as he seeks a good life in all social relations, to counteract the vice he encounters, if he can foil potential discrediting by the vice-ridden, overcome disruptive passions in himself, and come to read scripture in socially and personally productive ways.

In his desire to grasp the three related degrees of doing well, Will is directed to Clergie, a figure, as Nicolette Zeeman has established firmly, for Christian teaching, especially of a practical, pastoral cast,[32] but also a figure identified at times with the clergy as a *status*, a social group defined by its work, its rhetoric, and its forms of social power. Not surprisingly, Clergie defines Dowel as belief in Christian fundamentals as transmitted by authoritative texts (10.238–57). Dobet then becomes obedience to scriptural and ecclesiastical injunctions (258–63), which will guarantee integrity, making action conform to what is professed. "Thanne," he adds, "is dobest to be boold to blame the gilty, / Sithenes [after, since] thow seest thyself as in soule clene" (264–5).

Even Clergie's teacherly cast of character, his investment in pastoral work, and his loyalty to authoritative texts (he is married to Scripture) does not prepare us fully for his simple dogma: that correcting the sins of wrongdoers is the highest degree of moral action. To amend the lives of "alle maner men," he declares, is the best way to heal them ("to salve with othere") (274–6), an analogy pervading discourse on fraternal correction. And he considers correcting sin unproblematic, provided that the correctors remove the obstacle of their own sin – that proviso forming the sole, insistently sounded theme of his fulsome speech about Dobest (264–96). Clergie is concerned with only two aspects of pastoral discourse on the question "Should a sinner correct someone?": the effect of sin on the corrector's perception and the efficacy of correction. True to his nature as Christian teacher and to his class, he develops these concerns with pastoral rhetoric, a mélange like that we find in the entries on correction in John Bromyard's *Summa praedicantium* or Simon of Boraston's *Distinctiones*: biblical texts, learned and proverbial sayings, brief *exempla*, metaphors, reasoning, imperatives:

> God in the gospel grimly repreveth
> Alle that lakketh any lif and lakkes han hemselve [have themselves]:
> *Quid consideras festucam in oculo fratris tui, trabem in oculo tuo & c?*
> [Why do you see the mote in your brother's eye, the beam in your own
>   eye, etc.?]
> Why mevestow thy mood for [do you get exercised over] a mote in thy
>   brotheres eyghe,
> Sithen [when] a beem is in thin owene ablindeth thyselve –

Ejice primo trabem de oculo tuo & c –
[Cast first the beam out of your own eye, etc.]
Which letteth thee to loke [hinders you seeing], lasse outher [or] moore?
I rede [advise] ech a blind bosard do boote to [buzzard to remedy]
　　himselve. (267–72)

The Gospel's – and pastoral discourse's – central metaphor for hypocrisy in the corrector, the beam in the eye, is simply translated by Clergie, not explicated as specific sins. What matters to Clergie is its effects: Sin prevents or obscures moral perception in correctors. As in pastoral writing and sermons on Luke 6 and Matthew 7, sinners who reprimand others have no sense of the relative gravity of their own sins and of the sins of those they reprimand. Consequently, they become angry at others' sins, perhaps at sinners themselves, correcting them out of a vicious will. And, already doubly blameworthy (for the greater sin and the vicious will), the corrector only succeeds in sinning more by violating the biblical injunction against hypocrisy. In the end, such hypocritical, self-deceiving reproof only awakens contempt in others, raising questions about the speaker's intention and failing in its end of amending others' wrongdoing. Clergie's metaphor for the sinful and ineffective corrector, the "blind bosard," is an inferior sort of hawk to begin with (a buzzard), then made wholly useless for hunting because of its blindness.

Clergie presents the remedy for this obstacle to correction, despite its complexity, as unproblematically as the moral obligation to correct: You must simply see yourself "as in soule clene." "Clene" recalls John Bromyard's washed hand and polished mirror of chapter 2. You are able, respectively, to join in the co-operative act of correcting your neighbors and to show them their sins. It suggests that the simple cleansing of penance is all that is necessary to eradicate sin. Then, you can simply avoid sin: "*Si culpare velis culpabilis esse cavebis*" [If you wish to blame, then shun being blameworthy] (266a). In Clergie's account, charity is as absent as a virtue that directs us to confess and is strengthened by confession, as it is as a virtue that moves us to extend ourselves to others in reproof and then governs how we carry it out. For Clergie, removing the obstacle of sin, like engaging in fraternal correction, is simply a matter of obeying biblical precept.

After advocating correction in general, Clergie's discourse veers wholly to correction by clerics as teachers (272–96), as we would expect of a figure defined by pastoral care and connected to those in holy orders. In this, he follows general entries on *correctio* by pastoral writers like John Bromyard or Nicolas de Byard, who acknowledge the general obligations of all

Christians to correct, but then largely concern themselves with *praelates*, especially with their disciplinary responsibilities and failings.[33] In fact, Clergie's pronoun shifts from the singular "thou," addressing individual Christians, to the plural "you," addressing clerics as a group ("persons and parissh preestes, that preche sholde and teche" in some *Piers* manuscripts [273] and "For Abbotes and for Priours and for alle manere prelates" in others).[34] As in pastoral discourse on clerical correction, Matthew's and Luke's hypocrite becomes the evil disciplinary superior hypocritically and inefficaciously trying to correct the lay person, while the blind man leading the blind, the metaphor that precedes the mote and beam in Luke 6, becomes the ignorant priest misdirecting the lay (279–81).[35] The commonest of all pastoral *exempla* of overly mild correction, Eli and his wayward priestly sons, is focused, in Clergie's account, on the consequences of the sons' sin of greed for the Israelites as a people: loss of the Ark of the Covenant and the death of their high priest (282–8).[36] Everywhere Clergie opens up the distinction between the cleric – with his Latin learning, his pastoral office of preaching and teaching, and his obligation to correct sins in himself and others as imposed by both his learning and his office – and the "lewed" [the lay, the uneducated, those unable to read Latin, *MED* 1a], who fault clerics for their hypocrisy in rebuking others. That is, Clergie shifts the reader's attention to how this obstacle affects correction within existing power relations. He is concerned with the authority and the efficacy of scriptural imperatives in general when lay people perceive clerics, especially those who have disciplinary authority over them, violating the precept to cleanse their own sins before they correct others. As a result of their hypocrisy, the lives of many lay people remain unamended.

When Clergie urges those charged with the care of souls to heed the example of Eli and his sons by correcting themselves first, he argues from professional advantage:

> Forthi [Therefore], ye Correctours, claweth [clutch] heron and correcteth
>   first yowselve,
> And thanne mowe [may] ye manly seye, as David made the Sauter
>   [Psalter],
> *Existimasti inique quod ero tui similis; arguam te & statuam contra faciem*
>   *tuam.*
> [You thought unjustly that I would be such a one as yourself, but I will
>   reprove you and lay charges before your face]
> Thanne shul burel [supposedly learned] clerkes ben abasshed to blame
>   yow or to greve,
> And carpen noght as they carpe now, and calle yow doumbe houndes:

Canes non valentes latrare,
[Dogs unable to bark]
And drede to wrathe [anger] yow in any word youre werkmanship to lette
   [hinder],
And be prester [prompter] at youre preyere than for a pound of nobles,
And al for youre holynesse; have ye this in herte. (10.289–96)

Lay people with pretensions to learning ("burel clerkes"), Clergie claims, will not reprove his fellow clerics if they correct their own sins and will not call them dumb hounds, the standard pastoral figure for clerics who shirk correcting others' sins out of greed.[37] Moreover, he draws on Psalm 49, which was joined to the metaphor of the mote and beam in Gratian's *Decretum* and then cited by John Bromyard in order to bind the pastoral clergy to correct their own sins before those of their *subditi*.[38] Clergie's great incentive for his fellow *praelati* to remove the obstacle of their sins, then, is immunity from fraternal correction by those *subditi* who know pastoral teaching well enough to recognize that correction is their responsibility as Christians and to invoke its metaphors in reproving ignorant, sinful, and ineffective priests. Integrity and holiness should matter to clerics because they silence lay critics and make them obedient, leaving the clergy free to carry out its pastoral work of correction without lay hindrance. Not to sin, or at least to confess sin, is to make manifest both the power to direct souls according to divine law and the reciprocity in handling sin that confers moral authority on correctors. It is also part of the ethos, the expected character, of the clerical caste. In Clergie's argument, the efficacy of correction, and of religious teaching in general, depends upon his caste maintaining its moral authority and pastoral power, while his exaltation of correction in general ("is dobest to be boold to blame the gilty") serves, by the end of his speech, mainly to bolster correction by clerics. Not so for Lewte, the next speaker to advocate correction, who, amidst the crux of Will's encounters with biblical texts (and Scripture herself), promotes vigorously correction of clerical sin by disciplinary inferiors.

ABIDING BY LAW: THE "LEWED" PERSON'S AUTHORITY TO CORRECT COMMUNAL SIN PUBLICLY

Piers Plowman returns to correction as a way of reforming lives in the imaginative re-beginning in *passus* 11, which gives Will himself a figure who begs to be corrected, which challenges him to act on biblical injunctions to voice correction publicly, and which suggests ways to negotiate

carefully apparently conflicting texts and goods as he obeys that imperative. In the process, Langland deftly makes his readers aware of the communal dimensions – indeed, roots – of individual sin, extending the
reach of fraternal correction to communities and institutions, with their
entrenched power relations, their claims on individuals, their protective
discursive strategies, and their social practices. Against these *Piers* sets
not just biblical authority but the multiple goods that may be realized by
practicing fraternal correction of sins at once individual and corporate.

Ironically, Clergie's very promotion of correction contributes to the
intellectual and emotional impasse Will reaches at the end of *passus* 10.
After Clergie's long discourse on correction in several modes and with several social groups (160–327), Will attacks him and Scripture. Clergie has
insisted in general that to do well to any degree is to obey God's written
law, and he has confidently affirmed that the corrector can be free of sin.
However, Will is sure from his visionary experience that no human can
meet the demands of revealed law. So, he believes, neither the moral life
nor the pastoral learning that claims to direct that life can achieve either
salvation or reformation of the self and society. Moreover, Will reaches
despair over the implications of the predestination preached by some clerics. If grace alone can save humans who cannot fully obey God's law, he
asks, of what value is moral action and the pastoral learning/teaching that
sustains it?[39] When Will's clever and passionate disputation with Clergie
and Scripture, full of many turnings, leads the latter to rebuke him with
the famous saying *"Multi multa sciunt et seipsos nesciunt"* [Many know
many things, but they do not know themselves] (11.5),[40] Langland directs
the reader's attention to Will's own character, to the habits of emotion,
thought, and intention that engender such disputatious speech. As Will's
anger and sorrow at Scripture's reproof plunge him into a dream within
a dream, the search for Dowel is temporarily suspended, enabling Will
to grapple with what perplexes and haunts him at a more intuitive level,
more at the roots of the self.

It is mercenary abuse of pastoral care by the friars that drives Will to
corrective speech within this inner dream. When his despair leads him
first to abandon the moral life and the life of learning for a "land of longing," his hedonistic way of life is abetted by his friar-confessor, who, time
and again, grants him easy absolution in exchange for donations, without
admonishing him or demanding contrition and restitution – that is, without correcting sin (shades of Meed's friar). The friars also hold out promises of postmortem masses and prayers for Will if he buys a burial plot
from them (11.6–60). When Will reaches old age, the friars abnegate their

compact with him because he is too poor to make payments and because his conscience has moved him to seek burial at the parish church where he was christened (10.62–8). He rebukes his confessor for his convent's neglect of baptizing and preparing candidates for confirmation because they find directing confessions and burying the dead more lucrative:

> Ac [And] yet I cride on my Confessour that so konning heeld him
>   [considered himself so clever]:
> "By my feith! frere," quod I, "ye faren lik thise woweris
> That wedde none widwes but for to welden [control] hir goodes.
> Right so, by the roode! roughte ye nevere [you couldn't care less]
> Where my body were buried by so ye hadde my silver.
> Ich have muche merveille of yow, and so hath many another,
> Why youre Covent coveiteth to confesse and to burye
> Rather than to baptize barnes [children] that ben
>   Catecumelinges." (11.70–7)[41]

Will's impassioned rebuke leads him to imagine a public to which he can appeal: "Loke, ye lettred men, wheither I lie or noght" (83). This invitation to judge the truth of his admonition conjures up Lewte, who has been referred to throughout the first half of the poem, but has never spoken. From the Prologue, Lewte is linked to the obligations to provide law, to administer it fairly, and to keep it oneself. Therefore, Lewte becomes central in the king's program (once he rejects Meed's power) to have Conscience and Reason reform political, legal, and social life: "I wole have leaute in lawe" (4.180). Lewte is also linked to love by Lady Holy Church, whose favorite or lover he is (2.19–21), by Meed's adherents, by Piers himself as a reformer of society and individuals, and by Will's interlocutors in the search for Dowel, Dobet, and Dobest.[42] In these ways, Lewte – the term is uncommon – emerges as a virtue of political, social, and religious action: a disposition to promote the value of law, to observe law, and to desire to do both because of a commitment to loyal, loving, and fair relations with others. So, the reader is well prepared for Lewte to emerge as the poem's great champion of fraternal correction as an obligatory charitable practice founded in evangelical law and for his speech to be insistently ethical.

With a laugh and a hard look, Lewte is quick to distance himself from the lowering indignation that prompts Will's reproof of his confessor and the friar's whole convent.[43] As in the Meed episode, the reader recognizes the truth of Will's reproof, but, led by the reaction of other characters, is troubled by the reprover's will and intention: here not just Will's anger, but his long life of sin – indeed, his past complicity with the very friars he

aims to correct now.[44] Lewte responds to the troubling ethos of the corrector not by insisting, as Clergie has already done, on a "clean life," but
by taking a different tack: He urges Will to go public because scripture
demands that.

> "Wherfore lourestow?" qoud Iewtee, and loked on me harde.
> "If I dorste [dared]," quod I, "amonges men this metels [dream] avowe
>   [tell, declare]!"
> "Yis, by Peter and by Poul!" quod he and took hem bothe to witnesse:
> *"Non oderis fratres secrete in corde tuo set publice argue illos."*
> [You shall not hate the brothers secretly in your heart, but rebuke them
>   publicly] (85–8)

Lewte's response goes to the heart of Will's situation. His biblical imperative, Leviticus 19:17, presents public reproof as an alternative to silent
anger, in its settled form of hatred, always inimical to fraternal correction in pastoral writing. Within the liturgical year, Leviticus 19:10–19
took a prominent place as a lection: It was read in place of the epistle
on the Thursday between Passion Sunday and Palm Sunday, and so was
occasionally preached on.[45] Pastoral writing and sermons use this Mosaic
precept, like the evangelical one of Matthew. 18:15, to authorize the practice of charitable reproof, often in the full form that, John Alford argues,
is always invoked by *Piers*'s incomplete biblical quotations: "non oderis
fratrem tuum in corde tuo sed publice argue eum ne habeas super illum
peccatum" [You shall not hate your brother in your heart: but reprove
him openly, lest you incur sin through him]. As we saw in chapter 1, this
Mosaic law was invoked in preaching on another text to urge listeners
to counter the malicious urge to slander those who have injured them
by enjoining open reproof "according to the manner of charity."[46] Simply
to invoke this imperative is both to confront Will with the demands of
charity and to offer him a central good involved in fraternal correction as
a moral practice: enacting charity, here a way of dissipating anger at the
friars that could settle into hatred.

    Lewte neatly alters his biblical text in three ways to point it even more
closely to Will's situation. He adds "secrete," making Will face this state of
will: the pent-up anger revealed by his lowering, the anger of the aggrieved
who will not disclose the grievance to others (the now contrasting phrase
"publice argue"). Then in a crucial sleight of the pen-holding hand, the
brother of Leviticus ("fratrum") becomes the brothers ("fratres") of the
convent as a group and, by extension, the fraternal order or all fraternal
orders, an extension pointed up by omitting the personal pronoun "tuum,"
the third alteration.[47] These last two simple, but cunning, changes make

the social group subject to fraternal correction, insisting that sin is not just an act of an individual friar ("your brother") but of a community ("the brothers") in the very way it carries out its central work of pastoral care. This deft pluralizing of a biblical imperative fits neatly the episode Langland has crafted. What Will's confessor practices – absolution in exchange for money, without contrition, penance, or correction of sin – is what his whole convent practices and what (perhaps some of the time) the fraternal orders practice, just as the greed that directs this abuse of pastoral care is common to his convent and, to some extent, the fraternal orders. It also fits *Piers* as a whole, which confronts its readers with this friarly sin from Meed's friar-confessor to the apocalyptic last *passus*, where sinners admitted by corrupt friars through lax confession penetrate the Church's barn of Unity. Lewte's rhetorical strategy explains his seemingly odd omission of the evangelical precept enjoining fraternal correction. Matthew 18:15–17 focuses on reforming the individual, as pastoral writing on fraternal correction had insisted. Moreover, its four-part structure prohibits public correction until admonition in front of witnesses (as well as private admonition) has failed, in order to protect the sinner's reputation.[48] By contrast, the less often used originary precept of Leviticus enjoins public fraternal correction from the outset. Just like Clergie addressing only the mote and beam and related biblical texts about sinful correctors, Lewte is not uttering a full *quaestio* on fraternal correction, binding him to treat a conventional range of texts and use them to adjudicate the usual conflicting goods and demands. Instead, Lewte is addressing a specific situation in which the communal, even institutional, nature of sin is readily apparent and, as a result, public correction is needed. (If the early readers of *Piers* were aware of the large role of the fraternal orders in universalizing and teaching fraternal correction, the mocking plural "fratres" would have ironic resonance, satirizing those who championed fraternal correction as, now, its all-too-obvious targets.)

What matters about Will's friar-confessor in terms of correction, in addition to the corrupt practices of his community, is his status as Will's disciplinary superior. Lewte addresses the power differential between them by invoking Peter and Paul as witnesses to the Mosaic precept. Paul's rebuke of Peter in Antioch was the central biblical *exemplum* adduced in pastoral discourse to justify subjects' correction of their *praelati*. The incident was simple enough. When Peter broke his practice of eating with the Gentiles of Antioch because Judaizers from Jerusalem were visiting the city, Paul "withstood him to the face because he was to be blamed." He reproved Peter before all who had been seduced by him into this breaking of religious community (Galatians 2:11–14). The sheer fact that the Prince of the Apostles was reproved publicly by a later and lesser Apostle provoked fierce differences between patristic commentators, first Jerome, who argued that Peter had not erred and that Paul's speech was not truly a rebuke, and Augustine, who argued the opposite. In Augustine's reading, Peter had sinned because his act led the Gentiles to believe that they could not be redeemed unless they lived according to Jewish ceremonial law. To Paul this violated the "evangelical truth" of grace. To correct Peter before all was to witness faithfully to this truth.[49] Jerome's and Augustine's heated exchange of letters was pulled into medieval glosses and commentaries on Galatians, then into pastoral writing on fraternal correction.[50] For James le Palmer and Johann von Freiburg (following Thomas Aquinas), Paul's reproof demonstrates that subjects must rebuke their own *praelati*, even publicly, when the faith is endangered, especially by actions that disturb others, threatening to seduce them by bad example (on scandal, see chapter 2):

ubi immineret periculum fidei etiam publice essent prelati a subditis arguendi. Unde et paulus, qui erat subditis petro, propter imminens periculum scandali circa fidem petrum publice arguit.[51]

[When danger to the faith nears, superiors must be rebuked by their subjects, even publicly. On this account Paul, who was subject to Peter, publicly rebuked him on account of imminent danger of scandal in a matter of faith.]

So, Lewte's opening reference to Peter and Paul also speaks directly to Will's immediate situation: A man who is certainly not a priest (at most a clerk in minor orders) longs to, but hesitates to, divulge publicly conduct of his own confessor that creates scandal.[52] Taken together, Lewte's references to Peter and Paul and to Leviticus serve forcefully to place the initiative – indeed, the responsibility – for correction of communal evil in the hands of the individual Christian, even if he is a subject.

In a world of pastoral discourse, with its apparently contrary texts and goods, however, even Lewte's deft handling of texts is not sufficient, as Will quickly points out. Facing the threat of public correction, the friars, he claims, will cite a countertext of seemingly greater weight, one from the Gospels: "'They wole aleggen also', quod I, 'and by the gospel preven [prove]:/ *Nolite judicare quemquam* [Do not judge anyone]'" (89–90). The Latin half-line drives home the blunt, seemingly indisputable text. But it also alerts readers to friarly sophistry. "Quemquam" is added, and the second half of the verse is omitted: "that you may not be judged" ["ut non judicemini"] (Matthew 7:1) or "and you shall not be judged" ["et non judicabimini"] (Luke 6:37). This countermove is shaped, of course, by scholastic debate, even by the *quaestio*, just as in some pastoral discourse on the contrary texts and goods involved in fraternal correction. This is a imagined debate of the learned: the friars with their training in pastoral texts and Lewte with his knowledge of religious law. "Nolite judicare" became a key text in exploring the question of whether sinners should correct because in both Gospels it prefaces the metaphor of the mote and beam; pastoral discourse here furnishes the friars with their resistant countertext. However, rather than forbidding moral judgment of others, as the friars allege, it is usually taken, in commentary and sermon, to forbid rashness (*temeritas*) in judgment. One form of rash judgment is reproving others' light sins when our own are greater or the same: the vice of the hypocritical corrector that preoccupies Clergie. Another is wrongful judgment: We judge someone guilty of a sin, not on the grounds of witnessing it or of discovering manifest signs, but of construing from tenuous signs ("levibus signis").[53] Both forms violate fraternal charity. So, this evangelical precept is widely glossed as forbidding abuse of reproof, not reproof itself. Pseudo-Chrysostom's widely disseminated sermon on Matthew 7 even begins its exposition of "Nolite judicare" by forestalling the false interpretation Will's friars will proclaim:

dominus hoc mandato non prohibet xristianos ex benevolencia corripere alios xristianos dignos correpcione, sed ne per jactanciam justicie sue xristianos despiciant peccatores, derogantes frequenter de multis et ex solis frequenter suspicionibus odientes ceteros et condempnantes, et sub ipsa pietate proprium odium exequentes.[54]

[By this commandment the lord does not prohibit Christians from rebuking, out of good will, other Christians worthy of rebuke, but commands Christians not to despise sinners by boasting of their own justice, frequently belittling them for many things and on the grounds of suspicions alone frequently hating and condemning others and, under the guise of piety itself, acting out their own hate.]

The friars' countertext serves, as such texts do in scholastic debate, to challenge Lewte to formulate fuller, more explicit, more thoroughly grounded arguments for public correction of communal sin by disciplinary inferiors, to develop the implications of his tersely presented initial authorities. This he does, first of all, by the pragmatic argument that, if religious law is to fulfill its purpose of shaping our conduct and of directing us to our ends, we must correct false teaching and practice: "'And wherof [to what purpose] serveth lawe', quod lewtee, 'if no lif undertoke [if no one reproves] it / Falsnesse ne [and] faiterie [fraudulence]?'" (91–2). Lewte's reasoning is often heard in reformist texts of the late fourteenth

century, like the vernacular *Book to a Mother* (1370s), in which lovers of the
world cry out against those who rebuke them with the very same countertext: "Wolle not ye jugge."[35] In this context, Will's confessor and his con-
ventual brothers have, after all, left those in their pastoral care in deadly
sin – and not only by easy absolutions. Like Lady Meed's friar, they have
not used confession for correcting sin, instructing their confessional subjects and reproving their vices so that the latter conform their lives to religious law. Thus, they practice deception and they receive money under
false pretenses ("faiterie"). The salvation of others depends upon public
exposure of such communal threats to the faith; only then can religious
law be fulfilled through pastoral direction of confession and through sinners' repentance. Of course, Lewte is drawn by his very nature to advocating fraternal correction of communal sin on these grounds. He promotes
the authority of religious law, not just what is realized in penitence but also
the biblical imperatives to correct, as he emphasizes by then recalling Paul's
witness to the Mosaic precept to correct sin publicly (92–3).[36] He advocates
actions that preserve the community. And he insists on fidelity to what is
true: Christian scripture and Will's experience with his friar-confessor and
his convent. As a result, the good inherent in fraternal correction, the end
that Lewte holds out to Will, is not so much the conventional pastoral one
of amending the life of the individual as a new one: reforming a corrupt
practice by a powerful group within the Church as an institution.

   The need to correct established more explicitly, Lewte can directly refute
the friar's "Do not judge anyone" with a new authoritative text: "And in
the Sauter also seith david the prophete, / *Existimasti inique quod ero tui
similes &c*" (94–5). Clergie had summoned up the same Psalm text – "You
thought unjustly that I should be such a one as yourself: but I will reprove
you, and lay charges before your face" (Psalms 49:21) – in the full form
pulled into the poem by the etcetera. For him it voices the ethos, the
rhetorical character of the cleric who corrects himself before correcting
lay people in his charge. He may speak these words confidently to establish that innocency of life qualifies him to rebuke sinners. In contrast,
Lewte uses it to suggest that the friars read others in terms of themselves,
thinking that correctors violate Jesus' prohibition because they themselves judge and speak viciously. Moreover, the second half of the text
reinforces what legitimates correctors, especially given the interpretation
by one of the most widely disseminated of moral writings, the *Libellus de
conflictu vitiorum atque virtutum*. In the *Libellus*'s debate between Slander
("detractio") and the Freedom Given to Just Correction ("libertas justae
correptionis"), Correction uses the Psalm text to justify open reproof out

of fraternal charity. What scripture prohibits, Correction claims, is slander behind your neighbor's back, engendered by hate.[57] Correctors may appear similar to slanderers because they expose the sins of others, but their willingness to engage in open reproof, when allowable or even necessary, as Lewte insists, marks their wills as moved by solicitude for others' spiritual welfare, not by the hatred that engenders slander.

Having disposed of the friars' seemingly contrary text, Lewte turns directly to them as resisters of correction by their subjects and to Will himself, who hesitates to divulge publicly his reproofs of those who have disciplinary power over him. As in pastoral writing on the questions "Are we bound to correct our superiors?" and "Does the precept extend to all?," Lewte's dense weaving of texts and reasoning leads to a firm conclusion: "It is *licitum* [lawful] for lewed men [laymen, the uneducated] to legge the sothe [allege the truth], / If hem liketh and lest [if it pleases them]; ech a law it graunteth" (96–7). Whereas Clergie opened up the power differential between the learned and the unlearned, between the cleric and the lay person (especially the somewhat learned lay as critics of the cleric), Lewte, with his fierce commitment to scriptural precept and its social benefits, insists that the gap may be crossed. Will is the case in point. Although his status in the poem may be uncertain at times and even fluctuate, he is at most a married cleric in minor orders and so "lewed" in relation to his confessor: less lettered (supposedly), of lesser status.[58] When we come from pastoral writing negotiating if and how subjects may rebuke *praelati*, what is striking about Lewte's conclusion is the absence of provisos hedging in the subordinate, the "lewed." He does not note carefully, as pastoral writers do, that disciplinary superiors of *praelati* (heads of monastic or fraternal houses, say, or bishops) have first dibs in correcting them and that their subjects should intervene only when those superiors fail to act.[59] Nor does he insist that subjects speak reverently. His concern is to refute the naysaying cleric (like the friars with their injunction against judgment) and to license the subject: to overcome the weight of entrenched disciplinary authority, the habit of subjection. His very use of the Latin term *licitum* underscores all of this. Legal permission has been given.[60] It now rests with the will of "lewed men" like Will to desire and to choose to speak out ("If hem liketh and lest").

Lewte voices one stipulation from pastoral texts, the central one in Paul's rebuke as interpreted by Augustine and commentators following him. Only manifest sins may be rebuked publicly:

> Thing that al the world woot [knows], wherfore sholdestow spare
> To reden [give counsel about] it in Retorik to arate [blame] dedly sinne?

Ac be thow neveremoore the firste the defaute to blame;
Though thow se yvel seye it noght first; be sory it nere [it's not] amended.
Thing that is prive, publice thow [make known] it nevere;
Neither for love loove [praise] it noght ne [nor] lakke it for envye:
Parum lauda; vitupera parcius.
[Be spare in your praise; be more spare in your blame] (101–6)

Why would Lewte devote nearly half of his speech to developing the pastoral prohibition about revealing secret sin? (He has just forbidden confessors from engaging in open reproof, even of true sins [98–100]; they must keep secret what they have learned in confession.) He does not even qualify it, as many pastoral writers do, by allowing us to divulge only cloaked threats to the community, like heresy or sedition (see chapter 2). First of all, obeying this prohibition is central to fulfilling the imperative the friars love: "Nolite judicare." As Jacopo da Varazze's sermon on "Estote misericordes" argues when it comes to "Nolite judicare," we are to judge manifest sins, like blasphemous utterances, not hidden ones, which would entail passing judgment on what we do not know: the hearts of others.[61] More fundamentally, it is in the nature of Lewte – his concern for loyal, loving, and fair relations between people, his fidelity to religious law that binds and demands us to witness to it – to desire what we are obligated to do: follow the apostolic example and the Mosaic precept for the benefit of the community. To divulge secret sin is to open us to Meed's criticism of Conscience's will and intention: that reproof springs from deadly sin and that it commits deadly sin by destroying reputations, people's social selves. To follow this stipulation is to deliver impeccable reproof, reproof that cannot be discredited.[62] And even while developing this proviso, Lewte keeps his argument directed to the point launched by the apostolic example: that scripture authorizes – indeed, enjoins – all Christians, specifically subjects like Paul, to practice public reproof of manifest sin. Will should will to broadcast his dream about his confessor's and the convent's/order's corruption of pastoral care.

In hewing to Lewte's voicing of traditional pastoral constraints and reasoning, I do not want to scant the radical use to which Langland is putting this material. Like Clergie, Lewte uses dense, argumentative speech to convince an audience that authoritative texts demand that wrongdoing be reproved and that obstacles to effective correction be surmounted. However, after championing correction in general, Clergie speaks to his own kind, urging them to amend their lives so that they can be effective disciplinary authorities. Lewte, through Will, speaks to an audience of those subject to the pastoral care of others, exhorting them to voice publicly reproofs of those with disciplinary power: not only individual sinners but the communities, even institutions, that foster sin by their very practices and structures. Only such public reproof can free observers of sinners from their anger, allowing them to act charitably, to deliver irreproachable reproofs, and to take responsibility for the Church's welfare.[63]

MISMADE REPROOF: FALLIBLE WILL

After Lewte's impassioned advocacy and, before that, Clergie's high valu-ation of correction, fraternal correction slips into a subordinate, though recurrent, *topos* in the third dream. No other speaker marshals the full armature of biblical precept, scholastic logic, proverbs, figures, and embryonic *exempla* to move Will and the readers' wills to practice frater-nal correction. Instead, in the context of a new understanding of charity – divine, then human – two later speakers in *passus* 11 caution Will, prone as he is to anger, rash judgments, contentiousness, and harsh speech, against miscasting the rhetoric of reproof and choosing an improper tar-get. Langland continues to stage a discursive drama in which allegorical figures as partial as Clergie and Lewte – an unnamed advocate of charity and Reason – later adopt reasons and goods sometimes different from those of Clergie and Lewte. There lies Langland's originality as a ver-nacular writer rethinking pastoral discourse on fraternal correction: Each of the four speakers on fraternal correction brings to the fore a different strand of that discourse, and Langland uses their monological positions, as he uses a Will prone to mismake correction, to appropriate pastoral discourse for his own reformist purposes with his reform-minded read-ers. In this sequence, the two speakers work to rein in the harsh chiding, the mere fault-finding, the hostile accusation, and the hypocrisy or com-plicity in sin that Lady Meed accuses Conscience of in the first dream, all of which would invalidate the public corrective speech Lewte has just championed.

The first of the two remaining speakers is unidentified.[64] An electronic pop-up in Will's inner dream, he or she appears after Will's new impas-sioned exchange with Scripture (11.106–39), which, in James Simpson's persuasive reading, moves him from worries about predestination to con-fidence in God's merciful response to humble contrition for sin.[65] This re-engagement with Scripture after Will's long truancy, I would argue, is precipitated in part by Lewte's insistence that biblical precept provides the way to deal with social evils that enrage Will; Scripture begins with

"He [Lewte] seith sooth." And the profound theological shift Will makes in this exchange provides the very basis for amendment of life, the end of the corrective speech Lewte has championed. This exchange, then, is broken off by the Roman Emperor Trajan, who, directed by love even as a non-Christian, so promoted observance of the law and was so loyal to his community (his subjects) that he was redeemed after death. In this sequence beginning with Lewte, moral action sparked by charity now becomes the way of life God not only enjoins, as Lewte had argued, but rewards. So, when the unidentified speaker explores the demands of love and "lewte" in specifically Christian terms, he or she takes up correction of sin while enjoining readers to be generous with their goods and their learning:

> *Alter alterius onera portate.*
> [Bear one another's burdens.]
> And be we noght unkinde of oure catel [ungenerous with our financial
>   resources], ne of oure konning [learning] neither,
> For woot [knows] no man how neigh it is to ben ynome fro [taken away
>   from] bothe.
> Forthi lakke no lif oother [Therefore find fault with no one else] though
>   he moore latin knowe,
> Ne undernyme noght foule [Don't correct bitterly], for is noon withoute
>   defaute. (11.212–15)

In this context, the emphatic prohibition "Ne undernym noght foule" voices the traditional pastoral position that charity and its offshoot mercy forbid unduly harsh and contentious reproof, in part because they prompt us to face our own sins before we reprove others.[66] The speaker first uses the vernacular "lak" to indicate that mere fault-finding needs to be curbed, then the more neutral or at least plastic "undernyme" for reproof where the manner needs to be controlled by charity ("undernimen" as "to reprove," *MED* 8a and b; less often it has the negative sense of "to find fault with" or even "to make accusation," 8c and d).[67] The speaker imagines the target of reproof as, particularly, the learned clergy, whose very moral and disciplinary authority and, often, whose hypocrisy tempt inferiors to correct them contentiously, as we have heard from Clergie and have seen with Will and his friar-confessor. Fraternal correction of clerics emerges here as a work of human mercy, now founded in divine mercy, and a concomitant consciousness of the corrector's fallibility. So, charity as an absolute good must direct the will, shaping the words and the tone reprovers use toward their neighbors. Indeed, pastoral discourse often resorts to the speaker's biblical imperative, "Bear one another's burdens," in order to claim that fraternal correction involves bearing with sinners by remaining benevolently disposed to them (even though they are annoying) and then seeking to change their lives for the better.[68]

Although Will has been instructed in charitable correction twice in the *passus* and has embraced divine mercy, his desires, intentions, and appetitive habits can still misdirect his judgment and skew his speech. The last speaker on reproof in the *passus*, Reason, is driven to voice constraints on corrective speech by Will's own willful rebuke of Reason. When Will envisions how Reason, the principles of divine law manifest in nature, orders the lives of animals and even of plants, he faults Reason for not directing the moral lives of humankind: "I have wonder in my wit, that [you who] witty art holden, / Why thow ne sewest [don't follow] man and his make [mate] that no misfeet hem folwe [so they don't sin]" (11.373–4). Reason critiques this fault-finding on two grounds. In terms familiar to us, he counsels Will to amend his own life before he finds fault with ("lakken") others (11.376–91). Will has violated Clergie's rule against hypocrisy. With this mismade reproof, Langland makes us aware of the habitual nature of hypocrisy, of the need to recall regularly pastoral norms and constraints on correcting sin so that the will is properly directed. New to *Piers* is Reason's second constraint: that we should not reprove others for the way God has made them (as Will has just done in reproving him): "For be a man fair or foul it falleth noght to lakke / The shap ne the shaft [looks] that god shoop [fashioned] himself, / For al that he wrought was wel ydo [done], as holy writ witnesseth" (11.396–8). Reason here voices a traditional pastoral distinction: The object of reproof must be a sin (*peccatum*), something we will that violates divine law, not a flaw we are born to or are otherwise subject to (*pena* or, in the vernacular, "default" or "peine"). To reproach someone for "peine" like leprosy or a crippled limb (to say "croked harlot") is, according to Chaucer's Parson, to reprove God as creator.[69] What Will needs, according to Reason, is verbal self-control, a reflective reining in of a tongue habituated to be hasty and quarrelsome: "'Forthi I rede [advise],' quod reson, 'thow rule thy tonge bettre'" (11.387).[70] Reason does not work to silence reproof; after all, Reason is himself rebuking Will ("Reson arated me" [11.376]). With his fix on how divine law is manifest in the natural world, Reason simply insists upon two commonsense principles: Reprovers should look first to their own sins and should reprove only what is manifestly sin. In this, he advocates the habits of ethical self-reflexivity and careful scrutiny of others demanded in pastoral discourse on fraternal correction. And in this Reason displays the practical wisdom that, according to pastoral texts, should direct specific acts of correction, applying principles to a situation. These principles, habits, and virtues, like the earlier speaker's charity, can control fallible Will's fault-finding, harsh language, and hypocrisy, making reproof irreproachable and more likely to achieve Lewte's end of reforming corporate ecclesiastical practices – and Clergie's end of amending individual lives.

LICENSING REFORMIST FICTION

Piers Plowman's recurring concern with the fallible will, as with the will's formation, makes readers continually aware – in this dream, at least – that the reform of others rests on the reform of the individual agent's will.[71] But why does Langland never craft an exemplary act of correction by Will, either in his rebuke of his confessor or of an allegorical interlocutor? Why are his rebukes radically flawed? Dowel, writes Vance Smith, "cannot take precise form *within the poem*, for its only true form is as action." Like any "meaningful work" in the fourteenth century, *Piers Plowman* "must also imagine the form in which its injunctions can be achieved practically."[72] One such form is fraternal correction practiced by readers whose wills have been directed by Clergie and Lewte's biblical precepts, moved by their rhetoric, informed by their reasoning, stirred by the unnamed speaker's charity, and directed by the prudential reflectiveness of Reason. Those readers' wills to reform others have been guided, as Will's has, in the third dream, to steer between the extremes of willful or even sinful reproof and of inaction in the face of one's own sin or the resistance of a disciplinary superior. That is, Will's very fallibility is the occasion for the formation of readers' wills, both by exemplifying miscast correction and by prompting instruction from a Lewte or a Reason. Now, those readers are equipped to utter fraternal correction as pastoral texts imagine it, a form of reproof that neither Will's confessor nor Lady Meed can discredit.

Moreover, reformist readers are equipped to practice correction ably not despite, but in part because of, *Piers*'s notorious lack of closure, on fraternal correction as on most other *topoi* in which it is invested.[73] To have partial speakers pick up different strands of pastoral discourse and not to attempt an authoritative synthesis, just as to create Will as a fallible corrector, is to make readers primary ethical agents. Readers must negotiate the seemingly contrary ethical demands of Lewte, bent on lawfulness, and of the advocate of charity; they must decide if Lewte's "It is *licitum* for lewed men to legge the sothe" supersedes Clergie's professional contempt for "burel clerkes." In the process they become the kind of engaged, reflective, and self-reflexive agents pastoral discourse, written and oral, labored to shape.

Piers Plowman works at more in the third dream than moving its readers to correct communal evil when they encounter sinning individuals and more than providing them with the rhetorical resources and ethical reasoning needed. It also delivers that correction itself. While Clergie's discourse about Dobest informs Will and the reader about the necessity for integrity, it also reproves habitual lack of integrity in correctors of every social position, but especially the clergy. They are charged with the pastoral care of souls; they are educated in the scriptures. Yet they have violated biblical injunctions in the very act of correcting while they still know themselves to be sinners. And by doing so, they have inhibited lay sinners from the very amendment of life which is their life's work as priests. That is, to build Clergie's reproof of hypocritical correctors into the poem is to reprove all such hypocrites much as *The Book of Margery Kempe* reproves all blasphemers through Margery's rebukes of Archbishop Bowet's household at York. Likewise, when Langland builds into the poem Will's angry but potent reproofs of his confessor and the man's convent, Will's longing to broadcast them, and Lewte's firm advocacy of properly governed public reproof, Langland writes correction of embedded corporate evil and of the institutional practices that foster it – here communal ownership of property in the mendicant orders and their intrusions into the lucrative kinds of pastoral work. In this way, the fallible reprover becomes Langland's fictive device not only for examining what constraints are necessary but also for drawing into the poem highly polemical correction of sin.[74] Will may hesitate to divulge his dream experience publicly (" 'If I dorste,' quod I, 'amonges men this metels avowe' "), but Langland, like Lewte, harnesses discourse on fraternal correction to do just that: Through the fictional episode he employs "Retorik to arate dedly sinne." If discourse on fraternal correction licenses reformist speech, it also licenses reformist writing. Just as Langland takes pastoral injunctions and negotiations of seemingly conflicting goods and extends them to the sinning social group, he extends fraternal correction's domain from speech to writing.

Critics over the last thirty years have read Will's exchange with the friar and then with Lewte – and sometimes the whole Lewte–Indeterminate Speaker–Reason sequence – primarily in terms of Langland's worries about, and defense of, his own writing. Often this form of reading has taken on a biographical and autobiographical cast. Will's voice is "the personal voice of the poet" struggling between the urge to speak/write and the awareness of his own imperfections, his lack of moral authority.[75] I have turned last to this dimension of the episode because that preoccupation has deflected attention from Lewte's advocacy of fraternal correction as a social practice that makes disciplinary authorities in the Church subject to moral criticism, especially for abuses of their disciplinary duties. And it has dissociated Lewte from Clergie, his twin in rebuking communal evils in pastoral care. As a result – and as a result of their lack of awareness of the pastorally constructed practice of fraternal correction – readers have missed Langland's originality and boldness as a vernacular writer who recasts that practice in ways that, far from regurgitating it, do theological ethics in radical ways. Whoever he was, Willliam Langland did not have the power and status of the moral theologians and canonists who developed the pastoral ethics of correction, let alone the position in the Church to alter how fraternal correction was being preached and taught in the parishes of his England. Nevertheless, in the third dream of his *Piers Plowman* he advocates and enacts a public fraternal correction that takes aim at corporate evil by those in authority in the Church and elsewhere in society. In the process, he slyly critiques pastoral writing for failing to do so, for largely restricting the practice to individuals' sins, and he works to shape ethical, alert readers who discern that failure.

CHAPTER 4

John Wyclif: disciplining the English clergy and the Pope

When *Piers Plowman* was revised in the mid to late 1380s, the reviser (mostly likely Langland himself) sheared off all material encouraging subjects to reprove disciplinary superiors in the Church and all material extending fraternal correction from individuals to social groups.[1] Gone in the C-version is Clergie's hefty reproof of hypocritical clerical correctors, plus his forceful assertion that the highest form of moral life for all Christians is to reprove sinners boldly.[2] Gone is Lewte's apostolic precedent of Peter rebuking Paul, his firm claim that it is licit for "lewed men" to correct superiors, and the sly "*fratres*" that makes the convent of Will's confessor, even all friars, a biblically authorized target of correction. Even Will's original accusation against the friars is cut to less than a third, with any reference to the friars as a community removed. Only Will's confessor is rebuked (a traditional pastoral rebuke of a single person who has sinned directly against the reprover), and he sins only by abandoning Will in his penury. All that remains of the heart of the third vision's sequence on correction of sin is Lewte's general insistence that correction is necessary if religious law is to be observed, plus his cautions about making private sin public. Even those are refocused on the needs for corrective speech to be accurate and for the speaker to be loyal to institutions.[3] Lewte may still offer Will, as a public writer, general encouragement and practical advice, as Kathryn Kerby-Fulton argues, but the reviser has gutted the B-version's firm licensing of subjects criticizing their superiors in the Church and state.[4] What drove the reviser to withdraw from exploring explicitly how extending and recasting the traditional practice of fraternal correction could give his readers, notably his lay readers, and his poem authoritative voices to protest against the social, economic, political, and, especially, ecclesiastical corruption of his England?

The rebels of 1381 had drawn from *Piers Plowman*, in Stephen Justice's remarkable reading of their brief and now elliptical letters, a language of "rural articulacy" with "a conceptual utility" and "a public force."

And one of their leaders, the priest John Ball, reshaped passages from the poem's third dream.[5] The C-reviser's response was to excise or recast into general reformist sentiments material used by the rebels for their purposes and material that might be seen to relate to the events of 1381.[6] This general strategy could account for his revisions involving fraternal correction, both for what he removes – subjects correcting their disciplinary superiors and all Christians correcting corrupt social groups, practices, and institutions – and for what he leaves: a general argument that faithful people must practice reproof to preserve religious and moral norms. Lewte's reformist urgency remains, but now "it is out of the reach of censorship (whether of scribes or the authorities) and volatile readers" (Kathryn Kerby-Fulton on the C-version in general).[7]

Even more important than the Uprising in prompting the reviser's retreat from the potentially more explosive ways of practicing fraternal correction, I believe, is John Wyclif's radical transformation of fraternal correction into an instrument for promoting specific reforms of the institutional Church: removing pastoral care from the avaricious, disendowing corrupt clergy, refusing to receive the sacraments from sinful clerics – all punitive actions to be taken by the laity. The Oxford theologian began preaching and writing about fraternal correction in 1377, and his recasting of the practice attracted papal censure almost immediately. But it was not until a year after the Uprising that the English Church and state began to suppress Wyclif's teaching. Archbishop William Courtenay summoned to London a select committee of bishops and doctors (a few bachelors, too) of theology and law, the Blackfriars Council, who condemned twenty-four theses extracted from Wyclif's writings. (Wyclif, however, was not named in the Council's documents.) The first half of the seventeenth of these had been central to Wyclif's teaching on fraternal correction for six years: "That temporal lords can at their own judgment withdraw temporal goods from ecclesiastics habitually delinquent or that the commonalty [*populares*] may at their own judgment correct delinquent lords."[8] Moves to silence Wyclif and his followers (discussed below) followed directly. The revisions of *Piers* were, from the outset, acutely responsive to ecclesiastical conflict.[9] As Justice himself thinks, Langland (for he believes Langland was the reviser) realized "that his voice had entered the public world along with another, one that sounded uncannily like his and that he had good reason to distance himself from."[10] Why Langland might distance himself so far from Wyclif's writing on fraternal correction will become clear at this chapter's end.

In 1377 and early 1378 John Wyclif (early 1330s–1384) was at the center of political and ecclesiastical controversy in London. Early in 1377,

Wyclif was preaching in London against the wealth of the clergy. On February 19, he was arraigned by the bishops of the Canterbury province at St. Paul's, although the trial broke up in violence when his ally John of Gaunt threatened to drag Wyclif's chief opponent Courtenay, then bishop of London, out of the Lady Chapel by his hair and Londoners rushed in from the nave to rescue their popular bishop. Although we do not know the specific charges against Wyclif, the chronicler Thomas of Walsingham, always a disparager of Wyclif, claims that he had been preaching about London that no one should make grants to the Church in perpetuity because lay lords should take away such endowments if clerics were habitual sinners.[11]

On May 22, Pope Gregory XI singled out as erroneous nineteen conclusions or propositions out of fifty "blameworthy" ones sent to him by Wyclif's clerical opponents at Oxford.[12] In a series of bulls, Gregory proclaimed that they were "contrary to the faith" and that they "threaten to overthrow and weaken the state of the whole Church."[13] He demanded that Wyclif be arrested if it were true that he taught the propositions; he cited Wyclif to appear in Rome within three months; he warned the University of Oxford to guard against erroneous teachings; and he urged Courtenay and Archbishop Simon of Sudbury to have doctors convince the royal family that Wyclif's propositions "infer an utter destruction of all polity and government."[14] Last among the nineteen, Pope Gregory placed Wyclif's teaching about how to practice fraternal correction of clerics. It was one of two propositions, Wyclif claimed to have heard, that the papal curia considered especially heretical.[15] I give first its form as enclosed with the bulls, then the fuller form that Wyclif, according to Thomas Walsingham, used in defending it:

Ecclesiasticus, immo et Romanus Pontifex, potest legitime a subditis et laicis corripi, et etiam accusari.[16]
[Any ecclesiastic, indeed even the Roman pontiff, can lawfully be reproved, and even arraigned, by those subject to him and by laics.]

Ecclesiasticus, etiam Romanus Pontifex, potest in casu a subjectis corripi, et ad utilitatem Ecclesiae, tam a clericis quam a laicis, accusari.[17]
[Any ecclesiastic, even the Roman pontiff, can be reproved with cause by those subject to him and be arraigned, for the benefit of the Church, as much by clerics as by laics.]

The parallel structure of both ("a subditis et laicis" and "tam ... quam") stresses that lay people and clerics are equally responsible for correcting their ecclesiastical superiors, an explicit statement of lay action I have not found in pastoral discourse before Wyclif.

Wyclif circulated widely two closely related defenses of his propositions: one before the council summoned by Archbishop Sudbury (before
March 27, 1378), in which Wyclif was requested to clarify the meaning of
the nineteen propositions (the *Protestacio* or *Declarationes*), and the other
composed for some public forum or, perhaps, for members of Parliament
in late 1377 (the *Libellus*).[18] Both at first present irreproachable standard
pastoral teaching on fraternal correction, rooted in Jesus' injunction and
in the moral theology of Thomas Aquinas:

omnis talis ecclesiasticus est frater noster peccabilis, et per consequens ex lege
correptionis fraternae, Mat. xviii, 15, si peccaverit in quemcunque, assistente de
possibili opportunitate, debet eum corripere.[19]

[every ecclesiastic is our brother capable of sin, and, as a result, given the law
of fraternal correction (Matthew. 18:15), if he shall have sinned against anyone
whomsoever, that person is bound to reprove him, when circumstances are
opportune.]

Fraternal correction is obligatory, delivered to the individual, admonitory,
dependent on proper circumstances. But then the radical implications of
the proposition's second verb, "accusari," and of the reference to the welfare of the Church come clear, as Wyclif states of the Pope and, by extension, any cleric:

et cum totum Collegium suum potest esse deses in correptione pro necessaria
prosperitate Ecclesiae, patet quod residuum corpus Ecclesiae, quod possible
est secundum plurimum stare in laicis, potest medicinaliter eum corripere,
accusare, et ad frugem melioris vitae reducere.[20]

[and when his whole company [specifically, perhaps, in the Pope's case,
the college of cardinals] is inactive in the reproof necessary for the Church to
flourish, it is clear that the rest of the body of the Church, which, possibly, will
be made up mainly of lay people, can healthfully reprove, arraign, and lead
him back to the fruits of a better life.]

In his defenses, Wyclif violates the frequent hard-and-fast pastoral
distinction between the fraternal and the prelatical, designed not only
to confer the pastoral power of admonition on *subditi*, but also to preserve disciplinary actions – judging and punishing – for *praelati* and so to
make them immune from coercive punishment by disciplinary inferiors,
lay or clerical. Wyclif has transformed fraternal correction into a disciplinary process, involving not only admonition, but also punishment, and
performed not only for the soul of the cleric, but also for the common
good of the Church. The *Libellus* underscores this "end" by omitting any
reference to the sinner's life and by redirecting reproof solely "ad finem ut
ex ejus correctione periculum ecclesiae caveatur" [to the end that peril to

the Church may be avoided by his correction]. In this reasoning Wyclif writes within the tradition of the reforming moral theologians and canonists who universalized and constructed norms for fraternal correction, analyzing authoritative texts in light of contemporary needs. Among those norms was the need to correct sinners publicly, including disciplinary superiors, when their actions, like Peter's at Antioch, imperil the faith ("ubi immineret periculum fidei"). Wyclif even gives the two traditional pastoral examples of such peril: persistence in heresy and in turning others to sin ("si affuerit obstinata defensio pravitatis haereticae, vel alterius peccati vergentis ad spirituale damnum ecclesiae").[21] For Wyclif, clerics' misuse of the Church's endowments and tithes is heresy.[22]

Where Wyclif moves beyond any previous pastoral writer I have studied is in envisioning a legal process, usually first in ecclesiastical courts and then in secular ones, initiated by the laity as a political group in the Church. In the *Libellus* he even claims that many popes who acted contrary to canon law ("papae irregulares") were deposed by emperors, adding them to the traditional pastoral *exemplum* of the subject reproving his disciplinary superior: Paul reproving Peter, the first pope.[23] This nineteenth proposition is closely tied to the seventeenth: that kings may take away the temporal goods of clerics who habitually abuse them, an action which Wyclif presents, using traditional pastoral categories for fraternal correction, as spiritual almsgiving, a work of mercy.[24] In the hands of Wyclif the reforming moral theologian, fraternal correction has become a tool to remove sinful clerics from office and so deprive them of their control over the Church's temporal goods. To fraternal correction he has welded prelatical correction, a move somewhat prepared for by those sermons that present as fraternal correction the whole four-stage process of Matthew 18:15–17, including initiating legal processes and imposing punishments, right up to excommunication. The radical step, of course, is to place the third and fourth stages in the hands of the laity when the clergy fail to carry them out.

The proposition on correction, like all those condemned by Pope Gregory, was lifted by Wyclif's opponents at Oxford from his massive 1376–7 treatise *De civili dominio*, part of the theological *summa* in ten treatises that occupied him into the 1380s. Although its mode is academic argument, in the *summa* Wyclif extensively analyzes and provides solutions for the religious, ecclesiological and political problems of his time, especially problems of an institutional nature. Before the *summa* Wyclif had written about fraternal correction in traditional pastoral terms and genres (and he would later, as well, especially in sermons). For example, a slightly earlier part of the *summa*, *De mandatis divinis*, makes the traditional distinctions between insults and charitable correction, but warns, again in a traditional vein, that it is a sin to shun obligatory fraternal correction from a fear of insulting a sinner. And in his *Postilla* on the whole Bible, he reproduces standard commentary on the mote and beam and on Paul correcting Peter.[25] What drove Wyclif to alter profoundly traditional pastoral teaching? Ironically, it was, in part at least, his eagerness to promote pastoral reform in two traditional areas: educating the laity in moral theology and the scriptures and rooting out corruption in the institutional Church, especially in the administration of pastoral care. He had a deep affinity for the writings of the thirteenth-century promoter of pastoral reform, Bishop Robert Grosseteste of Lincoln (also an Oxford master), and he was educated at an Oxford engaged in debating Archbishop Richard FitzRalph's polemics against the friars' mercenary exploitation of pastoral care. His contemporaries at Balliol College from 1355 on were kinsmen or protégés of the great pastoral prelate John Thoresby, Archbishop of York, who may have been Wyclif's early patron and certainly was a patron of his kinsmen.[26]

De civili dominio clearly establishes fraternal correction as the practice priests must use first, instead of excommunication from the outset, in seeking to reclaim tithes which avaricious parishioners have withheld. Thomas Aquinas and canon law authorize the claim that all Christians who have the opportunity to correct are bound by Christ's precept to do so and to hew to the four-step process of Matthew 18:15–17, which Wyclif sets forth in detail with the usual ethical reasoning. (For example, first we reprove our brother privately and mildly so that he will not become irritated, lose shame, and become obstinate.) Always, Wyclif argues, the process must be rooted in its governing principle of fraternal charity ("fundatur racione caritatis fraterne"). Within the domain of charitable action, Wyclif presents the process in terms of three traditional stages ("correpcio amoris" involving admonition, "correpcio timoris" involving witnesses, "correpcio rigoris" involving punishment by the Church), much as Thomas Aquinas or some homilists do (though not always with these labels). While Thomas and the writers of confessional *summae* stop short of considering the coercive punishment of the third stage as fraternal correction *per se* (the corrector, in effect, turns the process over to a *praelatus* once witnesses fail), Wyclif, like Jacopo da Varazze, firmly includes within fraternal correction not only coercive punishment, but also a fourth stage of excommunication. Thus, Wyclif melds seamlessly the fraternal and the prelatical or disciplinary, a continuity suggested by his term *gradus* (step or degree) for each of the four. Moreover, while he introduces the process in a chapter on tithes, he presents it firmly as a general exhortation and a practice all Christians must follow all the way through, if necessary, whenever they encounter a sinning fellow Christian.[27] Book II then makes the radical turn: It places this carefully articulated process in the hands of secular lords correcting clerics who are manifest sinners.

In Book I Wyclif had argued his crucial theory of dominion: that lordship of any kind – power and ownership of property, the right to govern, the authority to administer the sacraments – depends on being in a state of grace. All things belong in common to the just, those whom God's grace allows to act virtuously. Those who have sinned mortally without repentance are mere usurpers; they cannot justly administer what they hold.[28] So, habitual sinners who are ecclesiastics forfeit dominion and the temporal goods that accompany it, and they may be deprived of these by lay lords, acting for God and for the Church as His stewards:

> quod quacunque communitate vel persona ecclesiastica habitualiter abuente diviciis, reges, principes, et domini temporales possunt legitime et valde meritorie ipsas auferre, eciam quantumcunque tradicionibus humanis eis fuerint confirmate.[29]
>
> [When any ecclesiastical community or person whatsoever habitually abuses its wealth, kings, princes, and temporal lords can lawfully and even meritoriously take it away, however much it may be established by human custom.]

By "wealth" Wyclif had in mind not only ecclesiastical endowments, but tithes, paid, in his view, to enable the clergy to meet the fundamental needs of the poor. If greed or sloth keep a cleric from fulfilling this parochial duty, the laity should withhold their tithes, giving them directly to the poor. In addition to this general theory of dominion, Wyclif's advocacy of lay disendowment as a means of reforming the English Church rests on an ecclesiology that sees the English realm as coterminous with the English Church. As William Farr has amply argued in *John Wyclif as a Legal Reformer*, Wyclif rejected the "Hildebrandine" Church that, in order to protect the Church's liberty, subsumed the political community into the Church under a papal theocracy. "Turning the papal argument on its head, his desire was to integrate the Church into the actual political construction of the realm." Therefore, reformation of the Church must involve the whole political community, all of its estates.[30]

Given Wyclif's melding of fraternal and disciplinary correction, the Gospel of Matthew's four-part procedure provides the authoritative mechanism for disendowment and withholding tithes. Indeed, Wyclif flatly states that temporal lords, including kings, are obligated to practice fraternal correction according to the order taught there ("secundum ordinem ibi doctum … processum ewangelicum").[31] This is quite in keeping with Wyclif's *summa* as a whole, where the "law of Christ" ("lex Christi") is at once, in Williel Thomson's words, "the source and standard for all earthly laws, secular and canonical alike."[32] Of course, it is quite out of keeping with the major traditional pastoral uses of the procedure: to mark out the limited circumstances when correction should be made public, to protect the reputation of the sinner as far as possible. Wyclif envisions two admonitory stages in the process, then two punitive ones. First, secular lords should enjoin the higher clergy to carry out visitations of any clerical group and perhaps also any individual cleric subject to them ("clerum subjectum" ["clerus," *DML* 2 and 3]), lest they abuse temporal possessions.[33] If the group remains in sin, then the clerical superiors should take as witnesses unbribable clerical or lay lords, who will warn the community about forfeiting temporal goods. If they are obstinate, then the whole Church of the kingdom, lay people and clerics, should be informed so that it takes away from them all goods not strictly necessary for fulfilling their ministry. (It may even reduce the number of clerics so that it is proportionate to the needs of the kingdom.) Finally, if the clerics refuse to surrender temporal lordship, all communion with them should be forbidden, following Matthew's fourth step.[34] While the agents Wyclif describes in this process are sometimes both lay lords and clerics, the clergy are to be engaged only in exhortation (in the first two steps), while the laity handle the coercion involved in steps three and four. For the clergy's God-given dominion is spiritual only, the power to preach and teach. And civil dominion for the lay, especially the king and other lords, entails providing for the right operation of the Church and for the pastoral ministry of its clerics.[35] Throughout the process Wyclif writes of both individuals and communities being admonished and deprived of temporal goods. Since he has welded prelatical to fraternal correction, he can freely extend to groups, even the entire English clergy, the practice of correction designed in pastoral discourse to deal with individuals.

What Wyclif envisions his melded fraternal/disciplinary correction accomplishing is nothing less than returning the entire English clergy, willy nilly, to apostolic poverty – a radical extension of the goods involved in fraternal correction. Ownership and power over temporal goods, he insists, by a clergy that should follow Jesus the possessionless, itinerant religious preacher[36] inevitably draws the clergy into vice, chiefly the habit of avarice. Group by group, these possessioners would be stripped of their possessions by the four-step process of fraternal correction. The obdurate would be shut out of the Church altogether by the fourth step. The remaining clerics would exercise their spiritual dominion untainted by the wealth and exercise of temporal power inevitably tied up with dominion over temporal goods. They would own nothing, simply living from the material goods donated by lay lords. Wyclif believed, as Michael Wilks has demonstrated, that this disendowment would come about in two steps. First the king would remove the civil power, temporal rights, and civil wealth of prelates (bishops, heads of religious houses) in particular. Then the king would deprive the whole clergy of the power of jurisdiction, returning endowments to lay lords.[37] This sequence indicates why Wyclif can imagine prelates taking part in the whole process. Those prelates who accept being stripped of all civic property admonish their clerical subjects, then assent to the laity disendowing the English Church as a whole, then join with the laity in thrusting the unreformed clerics out of the newly reformed Church.

If clerics are so corrupted by temporal goods and powers, how could lay people, even if they were exercising (unlike clerics) a legitimate dominion over temporal goods, carry out disendowment without being motivated by greed for clerical property or by envy of clerics' temporal status, rights, and powers?

Wyclif justifies investing the laity with the power of disciplinary correction of the clergy, first of all, by giving clerical superiors first dibs on their clerical subordinates, but then insisting that they usually fail to act effectively. Instead of giving reproofs that might transform lives, they, caught up in the temptations of dominion, only assess financial penances for sin. Thus they nourish the sins of those in their care and commit mortal sin themselves – a reformist theme of the 1370s, as we have seen with Meed's and Will's friar-confessors in *Piers Plowman*. Then the secular arm must step in, acting from its responsibility over temporal goods and aiding the clergy in its duties, as the clergy aids the laity spiritually.[38] Such a procedure, Wyclif insists, hews to the proper order for fraternal correction of sin. Moreover, it is consistent with his concept of theocratic kingship, for sin becomes a civil crime to be tried in the king's courts according to his law.[39] Secondly, Wyclif alters the traditional power relations between clergy and laity by arguing that a person's spiritual state, not his office alone, gives him the authority to correct. This argument he anchors repeatedly in the canon law of the twelfth-century Decretists, a major source of authority in the second and third books of *De civili dominio*. (By contrast, he refuses to cite the Decretalists after 1200, corrupted by the texts of imperialist popes from Innocent III on.[40]) A decretal says, he concedes, that no one should reprehend or accuse his own teacher – a decretal traditionally used in pastoral materials to exact reverence from correctors. But it adds that not all prelates are to be considered prelates: The life, not the name, makes a bishop. Wyclif then cites Jerome: Conduct, not appointment, determines the position of superior.[41] So, it is clear, Wyclif concludes, that any pope, bishop, priest, or clerk in mortal sin loses his dignity, even though his ritual actions, done by the power of God, may still be valid. Then, if a person subject to that cleric is in a state of grace, he is superior ("senior") in grace and dignity; therefore, he may correct his disciplinary superior, as canon law acknowledges that Paul corrected Peter.[42] Finally, Wyclif gathers together all of his thinking on lay fraternal correction of the clergy into the conclusion condemned by Pope Gregory: "Ex istis patet quod superiores, eciam Romanus pontifex, possunt legitime a subditis eciam laicis accusari et corripi."[43] To claim that this conclusion, along with the seventeenth, is most damnable, Wyclif states elsewhere as he anticipates the papal bull, is to maintain that the laity ought to be subservient to the clergy when it comes to the whole clerical order's copious temporal goods.[44]

How can a lay person determine if he is in a state of grace entitling him to correct clerics? Because Wyclif cleverly treats disciplinary correction as fraternal correction when a *subditus* is taking action against a disciplinary authority, traditional ethical reasoning can give him his answer: if he acts from charity.[45] It is our love of God, to whom we are bound by the law of homage, and the love of our neighbor, whose salvation we ought to seek, that should move us to overcome our sense of clerical rank and indifferently correct those above and below us. Once again Paul's reproof of his superior Peter becomes Wyclif's major *exemplum*. When authorities and laws seem to oppose correction or accusation by disciplinary inferiors, he argues, we should understand that they are simply proscribing imprudent or rash correction, the reasoning pastoral writing before Wyclif gave.[46] Thus, Wyclif turns even the usual tools for reconciling seemingly contrary texts – distinctions, the charitable will and intention of the doer – to his use in promoting lay disciplinary correction of clerics.

Traditional ethical reasoning also supplies Wyclif with an answer to the question of how to determine if a cleric is in a state of mortal sin. Deadly sin must be made manifest by conduct: prodigal consumption or unjust seizure of temporal goods, violence, direct injury, clerical concubinage. So Wyclif writes in a sermon on fraternal correction in general. A corrector cannot act on deadly sins that, he thinks, lie hidden in the heart, without risking defaming the sinner, a traditional pastoral prohibition.[47] On the other hand, any cleric who holds civil lordships necessarily is committing mortal sin because he is forsaking his duty, as a holder of ecclesiastical office, to live an exemplary life, as the poor Christ did.[48] So, his sin is manifest.

While Wyclif insists that the duty of correction falls most heavily on civil and ecclesiastical lords (and not only in *De civili dominio*, where we would expect it, but also in a slightly later sermon on fraternal correction and in *De veritate sacre scripture* of 1377–8), he also extends the duty of disciplinary correction to all subordinates. They are bound, as members of the English Church, to correct any notorious sinners placed over them, including parents and their own lords, civil and ecclesiastical. Instead of continuing to minister to them for the sake of worldly reward and out of fear, they should decline to serve them any longer: to take the sacraments from priests, to defend their superiors' temporal goods, and to engage in spiritual communion with them. If a lay person even attends the mass of a priest who is keeping a concubine, he or she violates Matthew 18's law of fraternal correction and should be excommunicated. Parishioners should withhold all offerings from such obdurate sinners, making them the shunned aliens of Matthew 18:17. Only if they later repent may they receive any goods of the Church – and then only as alms given in dire necessity.[49]

Such a struggle for reform, brother against brother, Wyclif acknowledges in the sermon, is bound to cause great disturbance in the Church and break its peace. But, he counters, there is no peace in a Church infected by notorious sin. Wyclif envisions Christ bringing not peace, but a sword, and separating a man from his friend and a mother from her daughter. In such a divided Church, to persist in correcting others out of love for God and our neighbors, he claims, may involve martyrdom, the result of loving others' souls more than our own bodies. To maintain silence when we see our neighbors sin – Wyclif invokes an old pastoral argument rooted in Augustine and canon law – is to consent to the sin and so to work on the devil's side.[50] Wyclif compares such tacit approvers of sin to knights who violate their homage (baptism) and fail to earn their very great stipend (temporal and spiritual goods) by refusing to fight against their lord's (Christ's) enemies. In this apocalypticism, new to writing on fraternal correction, correcting sin becomes a struggle to the death against evil powers.

Neither the exhaustive treatment of fraternal correction as disciplinary action in 1377–8 nor the silence imposed on Wyclif by the new king, Richard II, and his Council for Wyclif's *Responsio* of 1377, kept Wyclif from returning to fraternal correction in the next volume of his *summa*, *De potestate pape* of 1379. (Wyclif's *Responsio* had reaffirmed most of the condemned nineteen propositions.) By then Wyclif's nemesis Pope Gregory XI was dead, and the election of the Italian Urban VI in April

1378 had led to schism. By then, too, Wyclif's hopes for Urban reforming the Church had been dashed by his vilification of his rival Clement. So, Wyclif turned his transformed fraternal correction against popes, whom he had treated in *De civili dominio* and in his defenses of the condemned propositions just as the supreme example of a clerical class that could be reproved and arraigned.

What popes share with other ranks of clerics, from Wyclif's perspective, is, of course, endowments – in their own case, the pivotal Donation of Constantine. In Wyclif's declinist four stages of the Church, the Donation ushered in the second Church, corrupted by temporal goods, power, and rule. Wyclif acknowledges Peter's primacy and its succession, but he defines as pope the bishop who most lives in Christlike and Petrine poverty and holiness, engaged in pastoral care. Among Peter's virtues as leader of the apostolic Church, he argues, was humility, supremely manifested in submitting graciously to Paul's rebuke, as pastoral writers on fraternal correction had claimed.[51] For a Roman pontiff to accept reproof, instead of denying that an inferior should correct his disciplinary superior and plotting against his reprover, is a sign of spiritual leadership, of being an authentic successor to Peter.[52] The life, not the title, makes the pope, as he had argued of bishops in general in *De civili dominio*. Since the Roman pontiff, Wyclif reasons, is more open than others to temptation because of his wealth and temporal power, he must take more care to be open to correction by others. And all Christians, especially great secular lords, must not hesitate to correct him if he deviates from his role as pastor and father. They must reprove his open sin just as Paul did when Peter favored one group, failing to nourish the whole Church.[53] And if that sin is notorious and habitual, the Church, following the procedure of Matthew 18, should deprive the pope of his role as father and pastor – the point, of course, where Wyclif's practice of fraternal correction departs from traditional teaching. He has become a pseudo-pope – even, given his power, an Antichrist – and must be deposed. In these arguments, Wyclif relies on the general reason for publicly correcting superiors in pastoral discourse, theology, and canon law before 1375: peril to the faith, including peril through heresy and scandal. Then, as Ian Christopher Levy has shown, he expands heresy to include any interpretation of scripture that contradicts what theologians determine to be the Holy Spirit's meaning, including any pope's mortal sin that scandalizes the Church he should teach and serve. Wyclif broadened simony, which canon law considered grounds for correction, to any desire for worldly profit in ecclesiastical office.[54] If clerics neglect to correct a heretical or simoniacal pope, the laity, especially lay lords, is bound to do so (as with other clerics) for the common good.

Wyclif's blurring of the boundaries between prelatical and fraternal correction also allows him to defang prelatical correction. Wyclif takes up papal correction in chapter 7, devoted to pastoral care. Taking his cue from papal and clerical apologists, who insisted that all of Matthew 18 was addressed especially to Peter, he contends that Christ's precepts there must dictate how Christ's vicar corrects others. First of all, in line with pastoral texts on fraternal correction, charity must begin with the corrector himself, who must keep himself blameless. When he corrects, he must be sure to apply prudently Christ's procedure, never excommunicating until after the first three parts of the process have been completed and the sinner is clearly not capable of being corrected. And he must consult the Christian people as a whole during the process; he is only their servant.[55] In these ways, Wyclif curtails sharply the Roman pontiff's disciplinary powers: If he is a true vicar of Christ, he is subject to the same moral and procedural constraints as an inferior when it comes to when and how he corrects. And his feared power of excommunication is reduced to simply speaking for a Church that has, as a community, already decided someone is an outcast.

Once again, this time with regard to the highest office, Wyclif uses fraternal correction as a tool to redistribute power in institutional life. Christians living in charity may not only admonish a sinning Roman pontiff, but refuse to acknowledge his authority. He is not a true successor to the humble and charitable Apostle. And he cannot exercise disciplinary authority independent of his fellow Christians. He is truly a servant of servants, holder of only a spiritual authority – and that only if he is holy. In this, as in his advocacy of lay disciplinary correction of clerics in general, it is easy to see how Wyclif's reformist teaching attracted support from the lay, especially those of high status – and even from some clerics. Part of the attraction of Wyclif's and his disciples' ideas, writes Andrew Brown, "lay in their similarity to much wider patterns of piety."[56] The pastoral movement had sought to make lay people more involved in combating sin in the Western Church and had subjected disciplinary authorities to lay charitable reproof, in hope of amending the lives of sinful clerics. And pastoral writing and preaching had given lay people the means to demonstrate their pastoral power and moral authority as correctors.

When Wycif's Eucharistic teaching from 1380 to his death deeply alienated the friars who had joined him in condemning clerical endowments, he came to see them as Rome's agents, intruding papal power into all aspects of religious life.[57] Moreover, friars at Oxford accused Wyclif of fomenting the Uprising of 1381, and friars also dominated the theologians (sixteen of seventeen) at the Blackfriars Council of May 1382.[58] The three condemned propositions related to dominion and disendowment explicitly include lay lords among the sinful lords who need correction by the people (*populares*), bringing to the fore a strand in Wyclif's writing on fraternal correction that he had soft-pedaled. All of these moves by friars further discredited Wyclif among the powerful who had supported him in the late 1370s.[59] Small wonder that Wyclif turned fraternal correction against the friars in the early 1380s in works that were increasingly polemical.

While Wyclif's reformist writing had often been disputative, the product of university disputation directed to individual opponents, his late polemics became more aggressive in condemning entire ecclesiastical tribes, especially those who substitute their own new laws for the law of Christ. This, of course, provides the entry for fraternal correction: The friars abandon the precepts of Matthew 18:15–17 for internal regulations designed to protect the social status of their orders, which they love more than Christ. Friars refuse, first of all, to admonish their many sinful brothers, notorious both within the community and in society as a whole. Following suit, they refuse to cast habitual sinners out of the community, fearing that exposing sins will prompt outsiders to take away their temporal goods and the good repute so necessary for economic and legal standing. Brothers who do attempt to reprove sins within the order are commanded by the chapter or prior to keep silent; if they speak of such sins to the whole Church, they are even cast into prison. In all these ways, friars abandon the charity, the concern for their brothers' spiritual welfare, that Christ commands, instead "teaching the doctrines and commandments of men."[60] Thus, Wyclif argues that the friars violate the fundamental goods and ends of fraternal correction as a moral practice, as well as substituting their regulations for the Gospel's. However, keen searcher for polemical weapons that he is, Wyclif never faults friars for abandoning fraternal correction as a distinctively friarly practice, indicating that, despite the major role the Augustinian Rule and the Dominicans played in developing the practice and despite the ambiguous term "fraternal," it was regarded firmly as universal, not distinctive to the fraternal orders.

What marks Wyclif's writing on fraternal correction from *De civili dominio* to these polemics also marks his last major treatise, the *Opus evangelicum* of 1383–4: applying the scriptural "form of correction" to solve ecclesiastical problems, especially clerical sins. An exhaustive commentary on the Sermon on the Mount, the treatise returns to Wyclif's insistent theme: that the precepts of the Gospel are "adequate law in themselves."⁶¹ In his writings over eight years, Matthew 18 constructs a process that grace-filled, charitable clergy and laity must use in admonishing and then disendowing clerics, that a holy successor of St. Peter must use in correcting those subject to him, and that a mendicant community must use in disciplining sinful members. In *Opus evangelicum*, Matthew 7 (the mote and the beam) instructs us in the proper "forma correpcionis." Correction springs from charity, and charity begins with the self, Wyclif explains in traditional pastoral terms. Before speaking, reprovers must examine whether they have committed the same sin or a greater one, amending their own lives first. If not, they commit the sin that makes the modern clergy ineffectual in pastoral work: hypocrisy.⁶² Large chunks of Pseudo-Chrysostom's and Augustine's sermons on Matthew 7 cram these chapters, buttressing Wyclif's exposition, just as they stand behind Langland's Clergie when he castigates hypocritical clerics engaged in correction. What renders his exposition distinctive is the insistence on proper procedure, on following steps dictated by the Gospel to ensure that charity directs correction. While pastoral writers for over a century had used Matthew 7 (or Luke 6) and Matthew 18 to negotiate the competing ethical claims that arise in correction, Wyclif finds in evangelical process the means for lay people to reform sinful clerics or cast them out of the Church and to guide reformed clerics in exercising a correction that becomes only admonitory.

As Wyclif the theologian, preacher, and reformer reinvents fraternal correction as a practice, social roles in the Church have been turned upside down. Clerics from the pope on down lose their punitive disciplinary authority over sinners as lay people assume it. Indeed, all that remains for clerics is the practice of admonishing sinners that the higher clergy, ironically, had conferred on the laity early in the pastoral movement. Wyclif may weld prelatical correction to fraternal correction, but he places this potent new weapon of both justice and charity only in the hands of the grace-filled laity. In the process, he also readjusts the ends and goods involved in fraternal correction. Reformation of sinning clerical groups assumes more importance than amendment of the individual life, largely because clerics are so invested in the temporal goods and powers their positions confer on them. That reformation, in turn, involves an entirely new end: returning clerics to apostolic poverty.

Now, to return to the C-version of *Piers Plowman*, its revisions – chiefly excisions – of the B-version passages extending fraternal correction to groups and institutions done several years after Wyclif's death and several more after the Uprising of 1381 and the condemnation of some of

Wyclif's teachings at the Blackfriars Council. Wyclif had made explosive Lewte's reference to Paul correcting Peter by claiming that popes who desire worldly profit and contradict theologians' interpretations of scripture should be corrected and, if recalcitrant, deposed. Moreover, to maintain that lay people should depose a sinful or heretical pope if the clergy fails to do so, just as they should dispossess the English clergy or refuse to pay tithes to it, is to make explosive, too, Lewte's language about "lewed" men correcting disciplinary superiors – or even the unnamed speaker's reference to correcting those who know more Latin. By the late 1380s, readers might take such passages to refer to lay people disciplining clerics. So, too, might they construe in the Wycliffian vein any language about clerical groups, especially Lewte's "*fratres*," since Wyclif accused the friars of abandoning fraternal correction, and his followers, as the next chapter sets forth, demanded that the extrabiblical orders be disbanded. After Wyclif, even Clergie's disgust at lazy and sinful clerics could seem subversive, supplying material for Wycliffite polemic.

What effect do these excisions have on the B-version's advocacy of fraternal correction as a reformist practice? First, there is no longer any sequence on fraternal correction at the heart of the poem (now C 12 and 13). Clergie's entire discourse on the high value of correction is gone, wholly cut from the poem, save for his somewhat related prophecy of a king who will discipline the English religious, which now appears, revised, in Reason's sermon to the folk of the field (5.146–79). And Lewte's rump speech (about half of what it is in B) becomes merely a carefully hedged defense of reproving the known sins of individuals (like Will's friar-confessor). As Andrew Cole's *Literature and Heresy in the Age of Chaucer* has recently shown, the C-version of *Piers Plowman* does not shrink from controversy on "lollardy" as an ideal of virtuous poverty and Christian discipleship; indeed, it develops it as a way of life.[63] Nevertheless, Langland does stifle his voice by gutting Lewte's, and even Clergie's, exchanges with Will. Even while he maintains some of the poem's sternest jeremiads against sinning groups, like the corrupt religious and those who foster minstrels' obscenities, he expunges anything that explicitly champions "lewed" men's correction of disciplinary authorities or groups. Wyclif had rendered politically and theologically suspect the expanded lay practice of fraternal correction for reformist ends beyond the amendment of individuals.

CHAPTER 5

Wycliffites under oppression: fraternal correction as polemical weapon

The radical but pragmatic reformist uses to which John Wyclif turned fraternal correction – disendowment of the English clergy, lay administration of tithes, withdrawal of obedience to errant popes – were embraced in the writings of his followers, perhaps even before his death in 1384. Embracing the practice, however, did not entail leaving it unaltered. As Anne Hudson has argued for several decades, the Wycliffites were highly conscious of their identity as a social group.[1] I use the term "Wycliffite" because no document brands Wyclif's disciples as "lollards" until the late 1380s and because I am persuaded by Andrew Cole's argument on the relation of lollardy and Wycliffism: that Wycliffism involved adhering to classifiable, condemned beliefs, while lollardy involved commitment to a radical imitation of Christ as beggar, a commitment that could engage the orthodox, the Wycliffites, and those betwixt and between.[2] In this sense, Wycliffites were heretics. They held pertinaciously and explicitly beliefs condemned by the Pope and, later, English councils,[3] fraternal correction as a lay disciplinary practice not least among them.

Most Wycliffite writing that seizes on fraternal correction as a fundamental religious practice was composed and was circulating from Wyclif's last several years to just after the turn of the century. Archbishop Thomas Arundel's legislation promulgated in 1409, much discussed by scholars recently, restricted somewhat writing about religion, especially reformist writings, as did the vigorous repression of dissent by the Lancastrian kings. That belongs to the next chapter, but sets a *terminus ad quem* for this. Wycliffite texts in these three decades can rarely be dated exactly. Virtually all are anonymous. Anne Hudson and others have succeeded in dating some texts approximately by internal references. Others can be placed only by scribal hands and so have a range of a quarter of a century. For these reasons, I consider them together as a corpus in this chapter, weaving back and forth between narratives and tractates in the first section, sermons and biblical commentaries in the second.

Fraternal correction was central to Wycliffite identity. That identity was forged, in part and in the beginning, by the persecutions that were built on the papal condemnation of Wyclif's propositions and were initiated by the Blackfriars Council's efforts to silence Wyclif's followers, as well as their master, at Oxford and elsewhere. In Andrew Cole's revisionist reading, the Council documents "constructed Wycliffism as a cohesive body of heretical thought and practice in order to render religious dissent as publicly visible, legally troublesome, conceptually easy to understand, and equally easy to fear." As English ecclesiastical and civil officials tried to grapple with what was proclaimed as widespread heresy, a post-Blackfriars parliamentary statute, coupled with royal letters patent, targeted unlicensed, itinerant preachers, who were said to broadcast Wyclif's ideas.[4] Meanwhile, Archbishop Courtenay directed that every church publish the prohibition against preaching, teaching, or holding the propositions condemned at Blackfriars. Since the teaching that the laity should use fraternal correction to disendow sinful ecclesiastics was among those propositions and was so central to Wyclif's teaching, it is not surprising that Wyclif's followers, lay and clerical alike, came to define themselves, in part, as those who unsparingly practiced fraternal correction of the clergy. Nor is it surprising that powerful lay people are also the targets of the new Wycliffite fraternal correction: The seventeenth Blackfriars proposition condemned by the Council had contended that it was taught that "the commonalty may at their own judgment correct delinquent lords," and lay lords joined the ecclesiastical hierarchy in working to suppress Wyclif's teaching. "Tuo sectis ther ben," claims the tractate *Of Pseudo-Friars*,

& the oon [one] reproveth sinne hardliche [boldly, vigorously], & this secte approveth [attests to] crist in word and dede; the othere secte biddith sinne, as anticrist & hise clerkis, & noo drede [no doubt]. The firste secte is cristis lore [teaching] & the other the fendis; & for the firste secte deiede criste & by him alle hise apostlis, & this they taughten in worde, as we han told ofte bifore. The secounde secte that hidith sinne ...[5]

Wyclif's treatises and sermons had made clerical groups – mendicant orders, monks, the whole English clergy – targets of lay correction, as well as the individuals alone permitted (in most circumstances) by earlier pastoral teaching. And Wyclif had faulted these groups for failing to practice fraternal and prelatical correction of their own members. Now Wycliffite writing distinguishes Wyclif's followers by their commitment to a reproof that follows Christ's laws, and it separates them, in its binary fashion, from those, most often clerics but also powerful lay people, who nourish sin by hiding it. To practice correction is a mark of a "true" Christian life, of membership in the community of the predestined elect;[6] to neglect it, a mark of an evil, "false" (unfaithful and hypocritical) life.

Why else was fraternal correction so central to Wycliffite identity? As the clerical hierarchy and the state worked in concert to repress Wycliffite writing and speech, as well as to proclaim it heretical, fraternal correction became, foremost, a defensive weapon, rather than primarily Wyclif's offensive weapon in the campaign for disendowment. It is true that the Wycliffite tractate *Of Dominion* (about 1400) marshals the "lawe of the gospel," Paul's reproof of Peter, the "lawe of charite," and even the "goostly werkis of mercy" to oblige "lewid" men to correct the priests who sin against them. Priests are then urged to accept joyfully that their "temporal lordscipis" are taken from them.[7] But far more often writers draw on pastoral ethical analysis of the goods at stake in reproof in order to protect and justify reformist speech and writing against attacks. Faithful correctors, they assert, are dismissed as slanderers, whereas, in truth, they strictly hew to the speech of Jesus. (Recall how *Piers Plowman's* Conscience is branded a slanderer by Lady Meed as she resists reproof.) Such claims, of course, do more than exonerate Wycliffite speech and writing. They demonstrate the pastoral power of Wycliffites, their God-given ability to grasp divine law and to discern sin in others. They are the charitable followers of a Christ who reproves sinners; their persecutors, especially ecclesiastical officeholders and "other mightty men,"[8] are those who neither comprehend nor resist sin. The Wycliffites present themselves as the true heirs of the movement of pastoral reform, working to extirpate sin in lay people and clerics alike and to educate them in their fundamental responsibilities, as dictated by scriptural precept.

Fundamentally, of course, Wycliffites worked to defend and propagate fraternal correction because the laity, as well as the clergy, could practice it. They exploited its practice as a leveling action capable even of reversing power, especially if they gutted traditional constraints on how to address clerics. For all of these reasons, fraternal correction became a fundamental cultural resource that enabled Wycliffites to orient themselves toward ecclesiastical institutions, to question them, to expose their ideologies, and to separate from them.

The ways in which Wycliffite writings recast fraternal correction are shaped in part by a public – that is an imagined readership including groups of listeners – and a language usually different from Wyclif's. No writings of Wyclif appear to survive in the vernacular, although he may have issued broadsides in English and certainly preached in it sometimes.[9] The readership he imagines for his *summa* is a University-educated clergy expecting scholastic Latin, elaborate exegesis, ample definition, laborious distinction, precise textual citations – more exclusively academic than the readership of the most expansive pastoral texts. The modes of argument in the later polemics and sermons follow suit. By contrast, save for some texts circulating in both English and Latin, Wycliffite writings are almost always in the vernacular, the language (usually) of lay corrective speech itself. Like *Piers Plowman*, these vernacular texts imagine a public that "would seem to be theologically sophisticated, but debarred from the higher reaches of Latin learning": civil servants, parish priests, merchants, artisans.[10] Some texts, especially biblical commentaries, are designed for use by even less literate people.

Like Langland's speakers, Wycliffite texts of all genres use the mother tongue to raise bluntly basic questions about urgent social concerns, then embrace practical solutions. Their voice is direct, passionate, and admonitory, a voice licensed to correct sin by the scriptures, but threatened by an institutional Church newly bent on suppressing reformist speech and writing, especially in the vernacular. As a result, the writing, like Wyclif's late tracts against the friars, is polemical to the point of invective. The vernacular also "provides an argumentative framework for the struggle to authorize heterodox theological views." In Derrick Pitard's ideological analysis of language practices, to replace Latin, as the long-established language of theology and exegesis, with English is to open the way to subverting academic theology and exegesis, even (more ambitiously for a vernacular) to critiquing it. The vernacular helps establish Wycliffites as a "new class of interpreters."[11] This is especially so when fraternal correction becomes the topic, not only because Wyclif's reinventing of it as a process to disendow the clergy had been branded heretical but also because, from its inception as a universalized Christian practice in the decades after the Fourth Lateran Council, correction of clerics by lay people and higher clerics by lower clerics had the potential to raise questions of pastoral power and moral authority and, from those, questions of fitness for pastoral care, even ecclesiastical office.

These powers of the vernacular in the hands of an oppressed, dissenting "true church" make the stance of its writing even more "extraclergial" than that of *Piers*: Its voices, in Fiona Somerset's conception, "distance themselves from the institutional clergy they criticize and ally themselves with the laity, yet continue to employ the kinds of sophisticated argument that grant them clerical legitimacy."[12] Thus, while blunt, caustic, and subversive to the extreme, the writing also has the resources of Latin learning. Together, this defiant vernacularity, this heterodoxy, and this scholastic learning endow Wycliffite writers with a new power both to alter the practice of fraternal correction and to spell out the political grounding of the different critical understandings of it. For them, fraternal correction is an arena of conflict: what constitutes grievous sin, the ethos of the corrector (especially intention), the corrector's language, the ends and goods involved.

THE TRUE CORRECTOR

Wycliffite narrative and tractate roots resistance to fraternal correction of sin in a culture of slander generated by the fraternal orders. In *Pierce the Ploughman's Crede* (between 1394 and 1401), a satiric narrative in the tradition of *Piers Plowman*, the wandering narrator consults in turn the four orders of friars as he seeks someone to teach him the articles of Christian belief. He fears censure from his parish priest if he enters the confessional dialogue without knowing them. When the seemingly ingenuous narrator tells the first friar, a Franciscan, that a Carmelite has agreed to instruct him, the friar responds with an invective designed to discredit the Carmelites as hypocrites and betrayers of lay people who trust in them. Loose name-calling peppers his account of his rivals: "They ben but jugulers and japers, of kinde, / Lorels and Lechures" [They are only jesters and jokers by nature, / Rogues and lechers].[13] But his accusations are often quite specific: that they sell lace from the Virgin's smock to ease the pain of childbirth and laxly preach only about the Virgin's mercy, not about the penance needed to atone for sin (41–97). The Franciscan then reveals his own hypocrisy by begging for money to decorate his convent "With gaye glitering glas glowing as the sonne" right after praising his order's poverty ("We hondlen no money," a reference to the proscription against handling money in the Rule of St. Francis) (102–23). And he caps the laxity he attributes to Carmelites by giving the narrator absolution without penance (219), even though ignorance of the Creed incurs a penance, as the poem's editor Helen Barr notes. Both "offers" to a layman recall Lady Meed's friar-confessor in *Piers*. The narrator's response to the Franciscan's diatribe is to label it improper correction of sin and slander because it violates the Gospel precept central to the pastoral ethics of reproof (Matthew 7:1, 3 and Luke 6:37, 41–2):

> Thanne saide i to my-self, "Here semeth litel trewthe:
> First to blamen his brother and bacbiten him foule,
> Theire-as curteis Crist clereliche saide,

'Whow might-tou in thine brother eighe a bare mote loken [How could
    you see a tiny mote in your brother's eye]
And in thin owen eighe nought a bem toten [not notice a beam]?
See first on thy-self and sithen [afterwards] on another,
And clense clene thy sight and kepe well thin eighe,
And for another mannes eighe ordeine after" [make provision for another
    man's eye afterwards]. (138–45)

Here the Wycliffite writer's diction neatly invokes traditional pastoral
exegesis of the mote and beam: By reproving the man with the lighter
sin ("bare mote"), the man with the greater sin becomes a hypocrite; he
also simulates righteousness and so distracts attention from his own sin;
he speaks without the charity necessary for proper reproof; he betrays a
lack of spiritual perception and so of pastoral authority ("clense clene");
he violates a biblical imperative, displaying his own lack of "trewthe,"
of religious fidelity. Such speech, later indulged in by a Dominican, an
Augustinian, and a Carmelite, subverts not just the corrector but the act
of correction itself.

Before the generous plowman that is the friars' antitype teaches the
Creed to the narrator, the plowman inveighs against the friars as vigorously and in as much detail as they do against each other (455–790).
However, he anticipates that they will react with the kind of furious
counteraccusations of verbal sins that Wyclif endured (523–43). And he
prepares to be slandered himself by those who are accustomed to slander
their rivals: They will cry out "'thou leiest, and thou lext [lie]'" (542), lies
being one type of slander in pastoral moral theology. In these ways, all of
the exchanges in the poem prepare for the question that finally surfaces
here: How does the plowman's reproof of the friars differ from their slan-
ders? At a remove, how does the writer's fiction that contains all of these
reproofs avoid slipping into slander – or even appearing slanderous?

The writer uses his blunt narrator to bring this question to the fore:

"Sur," i seide my-self, "thou semest to blamen.
Why dispisest thou thus thise sely [innocent] pore freres [friars]
None other men so mychel [greatly], monkes ne [nor] preistes,
Chanons ne Charthous [Canons nor Carthusians] that in chirche
    serveth?
It semeth that this sely men han [have] somwhat the greved
Other [Either] with word or with werke and therefore thou wilnest
    [desire, choose]
To schenden other schamen hem [to destroy or shame them] with thy
    sharpe speche,
And harmen holliche [wholly] and her hous greven." (671–8)

Like a good pastoral moral theologian, the narrator defines slander by its speaker's intention to harm someone by publicly divulging sins behind his or her back.[14] Such is the position of the Wycliffite writer in many tracts, as well: To name the sins of friars or any clerics is to face both their accusations that he has slandered them and, then, their slander of him.[15] For simply broadcasting the truth about clerical sin can elicit the claim that the speaker or writer lacks charity, violating the most essential qualification for fraternal correction and the pastoral power and moral authority that justifies it. In the late-fourteenth-century tract aptly entitled *Hou Sathanas & His Prestis & His Feined Religious Casten by Thre Cursed Heresies to Distroye Alle Good Livinge & Maintene Alle Manere of Sinne*, the third heresy is exactly this friarly claim: "Thes worldly prelatis & peintid religious, beried in here olde sinne, simonye, coveitise & pride & robberye, seyn that it is agenst charite to crye opynly her [their] cursed disceitis to lordis & comyn peple, & namely in here absence." Such claims, the writer states later, further this "ende" of Antichrist: "that in absence of his cursed wordly prelatis & heretikis men schulden not reprove here [their] cursed sinnes for drede of lesingis [lies] of charite & for backbitinge."[16] In the Wycliffite analysis, pastoral ethics of speech becomes the very means by which the friars, like *Piers Plowman*'s Lady Meed, seek both to intimidate would-be reprovers and to retaliate furiously against them, defining their speech as deviant, not virtuous.

This cunning abuse of pastoral ethics springs, in both the tract and the narrative, from a fraternal culture of deceptive speech: lies, flattery of the rich, "glosing" [deceptive glossing or interpretation] of scripture, as well as interfraternal and extrafraternal slander. All of these types of deviant speech do the work of covert sinful desires and intentions, false praise, for example, bringing in extravagant gifts, like the glittering glass of *Crede*.[17] They are thus the habitual speech of hypocrites ("peintid religious") who feign holiness while cloaking sin. True to Wyclif, his disciples' writings trace to the clerical hold on temporal possessions both hypocrisy and the fierce resistance to correction it engenders. That is why this tract links "worldly prelatis" (here, holders of ecclesiastical offices, rather than disciplinary superiors) to the friars, whose communities could be wealthy even if individuals did not handle money. Wealth and its accompanying status lead "possessioners" to seek "more here [their] owene name & honour than honour of god" and to covet "name of holynesse & reverence with this proude worldly lif" (from a tract in the same manuscript).[18] More pragmatically, as *Hou Sathanas* claims, possessioners fear that, if their hypocrisy were known, the laity would take away their vast worldly goods, reducing them to Wycliffian apostolic poverty, as "god techith and here owene profession [their own vows]."[19] Within fraternal communities, Wycliffite writers allege, the fear of disrepute, then dispossession, prompts leaders to discourage fraternal correction of weighty sins, like blasphemous oaths and coveting neighbors' goods, and to promote, as a cover, vigorous policing of minor trespasses against the orders' customs and statutes. This displays righteousness ostentatiously, covering habitual avarice. So, hypocritical friars take refuge in their own disciplinary systems (like the chapter of faults), insisting that the prior or master reproves those within his disciplinary care.[20] Not only is fraternal correction, internal and external, suppressed to preserve the orders' good repute, but the friars also dare not reprove the sins of lay people "les ther ordre leese [lose] worldly helpe."[21] In all these ways, the orders join secular priests and bishops in resisting Wycliffite fraternal correction, with its disciplinary power to remove clerics from office and to seize their temporal goods.

Against these threats and claims, Wycliffite writing counterposes the simple imperative at the root of fraternal correction: "*Iesu, biholding his disciplis, seide to Simound Petre,* and in him to eche cristen man, '*If thy brother sinne agenus thee, go thou and snibbe* [correct, rebuke] *him.*'"[22] Citing this evangelical law so prized by Wyclif, *Of Pseudo-Friars* opposes popular revulsion at Wycliffite polemic against the friars with the ringing claim that "fro the biginning of the world til this time was it usid [customary] that men shulden reprove sinne for love and worship of god." To reinforce this, the writer takes a potent line of defense new to writing on fraternal correction (save for Wyclif's later works): Jesus' own correction of sin, especially when "spak crist sharpliche agen the secte of pharisees" in Matthew 23:13–33 ("Woe to you, scribes and Pharisees, hypocrites").[23] In discourse on fraternal correction before 1380, Jesus' language itself had never been a model for how to word a reproof, perhaps because Jesus reproved groups, as well as individuals. Now, plucking out one strand of traditional pastoral debate on proper corrective speech, the Wycliffite tractate cites the common pastoral *exemplum* of Eli, "dampned for he reproved hise sones but to softliche & slowliche." Tossed aside is pastoral concern for the reproved persons' responses: Will shame or fury drive them to reject harsh reproof as deviant chiding? Tossed aside, too, is the clerically inculcated reverence for social superiors, especially disciplinary authorities. Rhetorical effect and Christ's example overbear all competing claims for courtesy and balance: Since Christ reproved even his own disciples as "foolis and slow to trowe," "why may not men by lore of crist reprove more foolis for more perile? & this men shulden do sharpliche for

softe wordis moven not thise men."²⁴ In the tractate, examples of Jesus'
denunciations – even of his own disciples – demonstrate that to sharpen
correction with insult, threat, and chiding is to imitate Christ. So, the
Gospel-minded Peres is authorized to match name-calling and lively specific accusations with the worst of the friars in *Crede*: "'A, brother!" he
says to the narrator,

"Beware of tho foles [those fools]!
For Crist seide him-selfe, 'of swiche [such] I you warne.'
And false profetes in the feith he fulliche hem calde,
'*In vestimentis ovium* [in clothing of sheep] but onlye with-inne
They ben wilde wer-wolves that wiln the folk robben.'
…. …. …. …. …. …. …. …. …. …. …. …. …. …. …. …. …
They coveten confessions to kachen some hire [gain some payments],
And sepultures [burials] also some waiten [look] to cacchen."
   (455–9, 468–9)

Imitation of Christ also justifies correction of a group, ignored or marginalized in pastoral discourse before 1375. For the Wycliffites, friars and
bishops are descendants of the New Testament's scribes, Pharisees, and
high priests. Moreover, Wycliffite writing makes explicit the implications of
Lewte in *Piers Plowman*: All individuals in a religious group sin by participating in communal practices. For Wycliffites, simply to wear a habit was
to claim holiness wrongfully, to become a hypocrite, because Jesus never
prescribed particular clothing for the faithful.²⁵ To reverence a Francis or a
Dominic, let alone a current Minister General, was to scant reverence for
Paul or Christ. The Wycliffite term "sect" for Pharisees and for the fraternal orders conveys that the group is defined by aberrant practices. It also
suggests that the individual, characterized by those practices, disappears
into the group. As a result, the Wycliffite corrector is freed from one of the
central claims that correctors of individuals were bound to negotiate: protecting the sinner's reputation, usually by speaking privately at first. Surely
this is why Wycliffite writing almost wholly ignores the four-part procedure of Matthew 18, so central in pre-1375 pastoral writing about the ethics
of correction and equally central in Wyclif's disciplinary process.

The Wycliffites' embrace of jeremiad raises even more acutely in their
own writing the narrator's question in *Crede*: What distinguishes proper
corrective speech from the slander of pharisaical possessioners? Like pastoral writing before Wyclif, *Of Pseudo-Friars* insists that God demands
"order" in correction. Central to this "order" is the expected charitable
will of the pastoral tradition, even more important to Wycliffites because
their Wycliffian use of correction to threaten to disendow clerics left them

open to charges that lust for clerical goods and power fueled their reproof. The friars, the tractate acknowledges, constantly accuse Wycliffites of having a vicious intent. In response, one of the tractate's two "condicioun[s] of blaming that cristen men shulden holde is that they shulden blame no men by envye or coveitise, but algatis [always] by charite that they haven to god & to his chirche – yhe [yes, indeed] to tho [those] persones that they snibben al if [although] they shal be dampned aftir."[26] Wycliffite tract and narrative claim both charity of will and the intent to amend the lives of sinners that charity engenders. "For amending of thise men is most that I write" protest the conflated voices of Peres, the narrator, and the writer at the end of *Crede* (838).[27] Thus, they claim that their speech/writing cannot be slander, defined by a malicious will and the intention to injure another. But how could writers make that will and intention manifest when, as *Of Pseudo-Friars* admits, no human can judge another's intents, hidden as they are?[28]

In Wycliffite narrative deeds can embody charity. So, the Peres of *Crede* offers to give the sighing, wandering narrator "liiflode," what is necessary to sustain life, even though he is plowing in the icy muck and his three children are crying with hunger and cold at the field's end: "lene the ich will [I will give you]/ Swich good as God hath sent. Go we, leve [dear] brother" (445–6). So, too, does his obedience to the literal sense of scripture enact charity: He does not set his hand to the plow and look back, but leaves plow and family behind to teach a stranger the Gospel (Luke 9:62).[29] *Crede* creates an authoritative speaker as the English Wycliffite sermon cycle does, in Kantik Ghosh's reading: "the interpreter who realizes in his life the art of *recte vivendi* becomes in effect a transparent mediator of God's Word."[30] In Wycliffite writing, a rightly ordered inner life is reflected in action, and it – not the traditional adherence to the constraints set forth by the higher clergy – guarantees pastoral power and moral authority, validating corrective speech.

But how can the writer of a tractate make will and intention manifest, especially when the friars cleverly charge that, when Wycliffites call them Pharisees, "we maken us evene with [equal to] crist & trowen [believe] oure wordis as we were god & forsaken [forget?] that we erren in entent as seintis in hevene, but our dedis & oure life shewen openliche the contrarye"? Their very following of a Christ given to denunciation opens them to being discredited. For a defense, at least one Wycliffite, the writer of *Of Pseudo-Friars*, reverts to traditional pastoral discourse on the question of whether sinners can correct. In the voice of his fellow Wycliffites, he confesses that "we erren ofte & failen in the heighnesse [highness] of

charite, & herfore we weilen [wail] here … And ofte we erren in entent
& desiren veniaunce [vengeance] in rancour." This confession of a partly
uncharitable will and a partly vengeful intent demonstrates some of the
ethical reflexivity of the pastoral tradition. It also evades neatly the friars' accusation of hypocrisy because the writer does not mask his own
vengeful intention behind the reproof of others, that abuse of correction
denounced by pastoral writers since the mid thirteenth century. However,
does not his confession also impugn the validity of his writing, especially
when he is exposing the friars' acts of vengeance, like slander itself? He is
hardly hewing to the traditional pastoral criterion of withholding reproof
for sins of which he is guilty, grieving instead with a fellow sinner. Pre-
1375 pastoral writing, however, continues to fuel his defense: "by process
of time we trowen [trust, believe] that god wole clenese oure entent &
thus when we ben in quiete [at rest], we don this moost for goddis worship, & also for profit of his chirche & for good that freris may have."
Like early pastoral writers, this Wycliffite believes God will infuse charity into his heart, ensuring a properly ordered and directed will in correction (although he does not embrace the sacrament of penance as
a means to move the will from love of sin to love of God, clearing the
way for the action of God's grace). Unlike them, however, he insists that
he must continue correcting sin in the meantime, despite such a sinful
intention: "when that god giveth us grace, we leven errour of this entent
& witen [know] that we shulden not leve here [corrective writing] for
creping in of siche sinnes sith [because] we shulden sinne more, levinge
to speke sharpliche this."[31] The pastoral "order of charity," in which the
would-be corrector is first restored to charity with God, is discarded. The
good of following the biblical precept to correct sin outweighs the contrary good of a fully charitable will. So do the charitable ends and goods
to which the words are directed: not only the traditional spiritual welfare
of the corrected, but also the radical, largely new end that "the pepil shal
knowe hem [the friars] betere," knowledge Wycliffites are certain will lead
to dismantling the religious orders altogether.[32] Wycliffite fraternal correction, in line with Wyclif, is written and spoken for the good of the whole
community. It sets the Church right by undeceiving it (which might be
seen, in part, as an extension of one old end and good of fraternal correction: unmasking heresy).

Central to this Wycliffite mission is the truth of what is written or
spoken in correction of sin. The other – in fact, the first – condition that
Of Pseudo-Friars lays down for corrective speech is "that men that blamen
hem [the friars] shulden holde treuthe & not gabbe [tell lies, deceive] on

hem," and the tractate's writer also justifies correcting when his intention
is partially sinful by trumpeting "we ben war that we seyn soth [truth]."[33]
What does this tract mean by "truth" and why is it so crucial to Wycliffite
polemic?

In pastoral writing before 1380 truth was only rarely given as a condition of proper reproof. The object of reproof was clear and incontrovert-
ible, at least in the eyes of pastoral writers: a sin as defined by pastoral
texts and as witnessed by the reprover, who was to correct only individuals who had sinned directly against him or her by injury or destructive
example. In Wycliffite writing, the truth status of reproof becomes newly
important because what Wycliffites claim to be a sin had not always been
understood as sin before (at least by many) and was often vigorously contested by their opponents: parish clergy living off tithes, for example, or
clerics pronouncing sentences of excommunication. Truth they define
emphatically as what is consonant with the Christian scriptures – as, of
course, they interpret them. Certainly they do insist on accuracy, as well.
Peres concludes his denunciations of the friars with an emphatic "But all
that ever I have seid soth it me semeth, / And all that ever I have writen
is soth, as I trowe" (836–7). In the late fourteenth century, "soth" was an
old (Anglo-Saxon) word with the primary sense of factual statement or
correspondence to reality – something subject to objective verification.[34]
What Peres has reproved in the friars he has observed: the elaborate silvery
stitching on their habits, the grand tombs in their convents. But when he
judges these to be sinful, he does more than appeal to experience: He
cites words of Jesus that literally condemn them ("'Wo mote you worthen
[happen, be], / That the toumbes of profetes tildeth [build] up heighe!'"
[493–4]) or that enjoin goods contrary to them ("'Y-blessed mote [may]
they ben that mene [poor] ben in soule'" [520]).[35] So, Wycliffite truth carries the related sense of Christian doctrine, and that which undergirds
it: God or Christ as what is real ontologically.[36] Christ, *Of Pseudo-Friars*
proclaims, is "the first treuthe."[37] So, Christ's words, as the tractate cites
them, disclose the doctrinal errors of the friars. In this way the Wycliffite
polemic *Jack Upland* (between the early 1380s and early 1390s) uses the
very precept establishing fraternal correction – plus, interestingly, the
Augustinian Rule adopted by several fraternal orders – to discredit the
practice of imprisoning sinful brothers: "Frere, where find ye by Goddis
law that preestis schulden prisoun her [their] britheren and so distroye
hem, sith [since] the Gospel techith to undirnime [rebuke, correct] hem in
charite and so to winne hem? And if he wole not be wonne by you, ne by
the Churche, Goddis lawe and Seint Austins rule techith us to putte him

from thee as a hethen man. This is not to prison hem."[38] In this way, truth trumps intent, as *Of Pseudo-Friars* makes clear: "We seyen the trewthe that he hath taught & ofte we erren in entent & desiren veniaunce in rancour, but we ben war that we seyn sothe."[39] What Wycliffites say is both doctrinally reliable and accurate.

The truth of such rebukes also has an ethical cast. "Truth" in *Crede*, *Of Pseudo-Friars*, and other Wycliffite writing means to be loyal, to be faithful – its primary sense in the fourteenth century.[40] Wycliffites called themselves "trewe precheours" or "trewe men," Englishing, as Anne Hudson has demonstrated, Wyclif's *fideles*.[41] What they are faithful to is religious truth in the person of Christ and in the literal sense of the scriptures. So, in the second condition of proper reproof in *Of Pseudo-Friars*, to "hold treuthe" is faithfully to judge by the plain statements of Christ what is observed, while "to gabbe" is to speak disloyally what contravenes scripture, to lie.[42] Behind this contrast lies what Kantik Ghosh finds most distinctive in the Wycliffite sermon cycle: "an extreme and categorical disjunction of God's Law and man's."[43] For example, the friars cunningly follow the latter when they legislate discipline centered on their master or prior, instead of disciplining each other in obedience to Christ's injunction in Matthew 18:15. Ultimately, the ethos of Wycliffites faithful to scripture and so to God validates Wycliffite speech and writing, distinguishing it from slander, especially in the form of lies. What matters is not their will and intention toward those they reprove – so central in traditional pastoral ethics – but that "have we evere oure hertis to him and comune entent to plese him."[44]

At the end of *Pierce the Ploughman's Crede,* the voices of the questioning narrator, who has heard friarly hypocrisy, of Peres, who has observed and rebuked it, and of the writer merge in the double validation of all three in terms of charitable will and intention and of truth. The whole text's bitter contrast of Peres's truth with the friars' hypocrisy and slander does, as Helen Barr writes, wrest authority "from the representatives of the institutionalized church" and vest it "in the words of a member of the laity."[45] Like *Piers Plowman*, Wycliffite narrative and tractate work to license lay corrective speech. However, the merging of Peres, the narrator, and the writer accomplishes something much more. Wycliffite texts are bent far more on authorizing their own polemic than is *Piers Plowman*. The two opening chapters of *Of Pseudo-Friars*, as we have seen, are constructed to counter popular sentiment in favor of the friars, as well as friarly slander, and this defensive rhetoric shapes every chapter that follows. The corrector envisioned by pre-1380 pastoral discourse, cleric or lay person, validated his or her speech by hewing to the constraints laid down by pastoral writers and by negotiating contrary goods in specific circumstances; this is what the Lewte of *Piers Plowman* urges Will to do. Wyclif and his followers loosened or voided traditional constraints on reproving groups, speaking insults, and exposing sin publicly before private admonition. Without ostentatiously following these constraints in order to testify to their pastoral power and authority, Wycliffite writers laid on themselves the burden of demonstrating in their writing that they were of the "true" church. From its inception, pastoral discourse on fraternal correction, as chapter 1 argues, is insistently ideological, explicit, and argumentative about the claims it makes on people because it does not take for granted that people desire to correct others' sins or that, if they do, charity is what fuels their words. Wycliffism, in general, was "ideologized religion," in the sociologist Ann Swidler's sense: It defined itself by required, explicit, reasonably coherent, and constantly articulated language, beliefs, reasoning, and practices. This is hardly surprising in a group branded as heretical and subject to persecution, bent on defining its identity in writing intended, in part, and perhaps even largely, for a Wycliffite public, rather than the friars and priests it castigates and the large populace it sometimes invokes. As Swidler concludes, the more unsettled people's lives and cultures are and the more they must "construct new lines of action," the more they "elaborate self-conscious … meanings."[46] Hence Wycliffite writers on fraternal correction were preoccupied with manifesting their charitable will and intention, with asserting the experiential, scriptural, and ethical truth of their writing, and, within their narratives, with authenticating characters' polemics with charitable, Christ-imitating action. In Wycliffite fraternal correction, as in William Thorpe's *Testimony* as interpreted by Emily Steiner, "authority can be supported only by the truth of Scripture and the witnessing of true Christian men."[47]

WRESTING PASTORAL CARE FROM THE CLERGY

Defended against slander and freed from many traditional constraints on corrective speech, the Wycliffite polemicist licensed himself to expose harshly the sins of his opponents and persecutors in the institutional Church. The defensive weapon into which he had recast fraternal correction could now do more than parry strokes. It could go for the institutional jugular: the clergy's failure to provide adequate pastoral care – particularly the efficacious reproof of sin – that *Piers Plowman*'s Clergie fears the laity will detect and mock. Nothing makes this Wycliffite offensive clearer than commentary and preaching on Luke 6:36–42 ("Estote misericordes"), the biblical text traditionally used in pastoral writing and sermons to explore the question of whether a sinner should correct another sinner, sometimes specifically whether sinning clerics should correct the laity, not least of all in confession.

This polemical offensive is manifest even in the Wycliffite academic enterprise of commentary on the Gospels. Compiled before 1407, the *Glossed Gospels* were, in Anne Hudson's words, designed "to make available in the vernacular a bulk of traditional exegesis of a kind that would facilitate the understanding of the literal sense at the centre of the biblical message."[48] The long commentary on Luke interprets the central metaphor of the mote and beam in a way quite similar to early-fourteenth-century exegetes like William of Nottingham and Nicolas de Lyre. (The literal sense included figurative meaning in Wycliffite exegesis, as in that of the thirteenth and earlier fourteenth centuries.[49]) The mote is the brother's "litil sinne"; the beam, the corrector's "grettest sinne," settled vices of pride, hatred, and avarice. Nevertheless, the commentary acknowledges, sometimes "nede constreineth to reprove ether [or] to chide" others. Traditional exegesis, rooted in patristic glosses, leads to two usual pastoral resolutions for this situation: People can correct others if they can show that they are clean from sin (no advice on how to achieve that state!) and if they temper reproof with mercy.[50] Sharp reproofs should be given seldom, only in the cases of greatest need.

In the midst of this commentary, between the exegesis of the central metaphor and the resolution, comes a significant shift: The commentary turns its eye from "alle men" and focuses on clerics as teachers and disciplinary agents "whiche leven ther owne sinnes unpunischid whanne they punischen the leeste sinnes of sugetis [subjects]." These priests it identifies as the hypocrites Christ denounces with the metaphor of the mote and beam. Their lives of "greete sinnes" give the lie to their pastoral reproofs of sin, which become sinful in themselves.[51] This reading of Luke in terms of power relations between sinful disciplinary agents and their subjects is rooted in traditional commentary and preaching, especially sermons directed to a clerical audience. Often these pre-1375 texts draw on the exegetical sermons on Matthew by Pseudo-Chrysostom, favored by Wyclif and his followers. The Wycliffite short commentary on the parallel passage in Matthew is shaped by Pseudo-Chrysostom's insistence that Jesus' command "Nile ye deme" [Judge not] is given especially to teachers, for whom even a little sin becomes great because it offends those "lewide men," the lay and often less learned, whom they are reproving and so obstructs amending their lives. Clerics' sins indicate that their reproofs are driven by malice and by seeking "of men the praising of kunning" [people's praise for learned skills].[52] All of these consequences of sinful priests correcting disciplinary subjects are present in traditional pastoral exegesis, treatise, and sermon, but for the Wycliffite, all priests, as tithe collectors, property occupiers, and fee collectors, were guilty of vice: settled, habitual, grievous. Their very institutional positions make their corrective speech ineffective and sinful in itself. In Wycliffite writing, the ethical worries developed by the higher clergy to reform sinful clerics (remember Langland's Clergie) become the very means of discrediting those to whom the institutional Church had entrusted the work of pastoral care.

While strands of patristic exegesis preserve many traditional constraints on corrective speech in Wycliffite vernacular biblical commentary, sermons on "Estote misericordes" abandon them altogether as the "true" preacher turns his exegesis of Luke 6 entirely against the clergy. Preaching, of course, was the central means of disseminating Wycliffite thinking, whether sermons were preached at the traditional time and place (after the reading of the Gospel at Mass) or read aloud in Wycliffite study groups – or both, as is likely. The *English Wycliffite Sermon Cycle* (*EWS*), mostly likely composed at Oxford in the late 1380s and the 1390s, assumes a lay audience and was widely disseminated (thirty-one manuscripts of all or parts survive).[53] While its author or authors may very well have been clerical, perhaps even academic, the preacher's voice is "extraclergial," transmitting Latinate learning to the laity in the vernacular. Thus, the preacher can work a basic contrast between unmerciful "clerkys" who sell the works of mercy by charging fees for pastoral acts and himself, who offers, free of charge, merciful reproof to these "false pharisees."

Central to the *EWS* sermon on "Estote misericordes" and to its reworking in Cambridge University MS Sidney Sussex 74[54] are the works of spiritual mercy, including, of course, chastising sin. Although Wycliffite preaching shunned traditional catechetica, the topos provides an occasion to denounce those "cursiid of god" who "taken much mede" [wages, fees] to do "these werkes of gostly mercye, as do curatis & prelatiis." Clerics often farm out these obligations to other men "by feined jurisdiccion" because of their own sloth. By either route, they become simoniacs, selling spiritual offices.[55] (The "mede" Wycliffites denounced certainly includes tithes as support for pastoral work and probably also oblations at funerals, gifts at major feast days, and offerings at the purification of women.[56]) Thus, the institutional clergy, in Katherine Little's penetrating reading of the *EWS* sermon, sin by "their position in the church," not by "faults within," the kind of sins (I would add) that pastoral discourse gives sinful correctors (hatred, adulterous thoughts). Gone is traditional exegesis of the mote and beam as an incitement to self-examination, as Little argues, or even to a shared relationship between the would-be corrector and the sinner. "This accusing eye is looking outward and is not at all encumbered by its own sin." Gone, too, is penance as a will-transforming, grace-inducing, and cleansing prelude to charitable correction. "Instead, the Wycliffites transfer the language of sin from the listeners to the institutions in order to emphasize structural sin, to claim that institutions create sin in as powerful and significant ways as an individual's choice to commit adultery or kill a friend."[57]

The *EWS* sermon is cast differently from the *Northern Homily Cycle* vernacular sermon on the same passage, examined in chapter 2. The Wycliffite blind leading the blind who cannot see the beam in their own eyes, neglecting to correct their own sinful dispositions of will, are not the *NHC*'s all Christians, but clerics alone, who, by their office, inevitably "weien her winning [value their profits] more than ther God," neglecting God's precept to be merciful to all.[58] The *NHC* stresses the sinful corrector's misperception, his erring judgment of himself and the other person he desires to correct. The *NHC*'s monk is given to rash judgment: He judges the working man guilty of the light sin of eating on a fast day, in contrast to his heavy one of self-righteous anger. He also judges the act on the surface, not discerning its cause. In *EWS* it is clerics who judge falsely, and they do so by excommunicating those whose inner state they cannot judge, instead of discerning whether or not they are acting by God's law (a common Wycliffite complaint).[59] Indeed, Wycliffites restrict excommunication to the whole Church, insisting that the last step in correction (Wyclif's fourth) is to be taken by "the congregation of the faithful, the predestinate, and the justified" ("congregacio fidelium predestinatorum et justificatorum").[60] This analysis of corporate false judgment extends beyond the clergy. Lords, the *EWS* preacher insists, often misjudge those who cross their wills. Although he illustrates this claim first with the English bishops' excommunication of the anti-pope Clement VII, a Frenchman, when England was at war with France, he then turns to kings who damn their adversaries.[61] Such false judgments disqualify these groups as correctors; they are mere abusers of corrective speech.

The Wycliffite preacher escapes this false judging of the opaque human heart and the equally foolish alternative of tolerating clerical hypocrites by simply reproving clerical hypocrisy in the manner of Jesus. And, of course, like *Piers Plowman*'s Lewte, he also places the responsibility for practicing this kind of corrective speech in the hands of the laity: "sugetys schylden [subjects should] blame prelatys [disciplinary superiors] whan they sen opynly greet defawtys in hem [them]." The old pastoral requirement that the sin to be reproved must be open and observable is easily met, as it is in Wyclif's writing: The clergy's very institutional position is in "defawte of Godus lawe" because it involves "keping and teching" – that is, making money from pastoral care instead of freely offering it to all as an act of mercy. Gone with self-examination are mild speech and mutual condolence as forms of mercy in the corrector, even though they are advocated in the academic *Glossed Gospels*. Set against these clerics is the Wycliffite preacher who judges rightly and reproves with a will "clothid with mercy" simply by preaching against "ypocrites" without taking money for it. The corrector's mercy does not lie in how he or she treats the sinful other, but in the act of correction itself. Thus, the Wycliffite corrector of sin follows his "goode maistur," who "may not leve trewthe, ne [nor] failen in teching of trewthe": the propertyless and anticlerical Jesus who reproved the Pharisees as an institutionalized religious group in this Gospel lection.[62] And so the preacher "tempre[s] iugement aftir God,"[63] preaching evangelical law and modeling Wycliffite correction for lay subjects of a hypocritical clergy. His will, his intent, his perception of sin and of others, and his speech are correctly directed because they are melded with those of Jesus and open to his directive grace. As Kantik Ghosh says of the hermeneutics of the sermon cycle as a whole, "The conviction of a direct, 'ecstatic,' access to God can result only in a critique of other ideologies, not one's own."[64] In this way, too, this Wycliffite preacher escapes the old pastoral requirement of ethical self-reflexiveness (though some writers of tracts and exegetes, as we have seen, retain some measure of it).

Behind Wycliffite preaching on fraternal correction of sin lies Wyclif's own sermon of 1382 on this lection, preached just a few weeks after the Blackfriars Council. Wyclif's analysis of clerical false judgment, clerical hypocrisy in correcting sin, and clerical failures in pastoral care is substantially the same as the Wycliffite preacher's.[65] He puts that analysis to quite different uses. He condemns corrupt patrons for appointing such worldly and ignorant spiritual guides in the first place. Then he urges lay people to withhold financial payment from any notoriously sinful disciplinary agent lest they consent to his sin, to shun him as excommunicated by God (the fourth stage of Wyclif's fraternal correction), and to prevent him from administering the Church's temporal goods, given in trust for the poor. Thus Wyclif advocates specific political and economic solutions

to the problem of clerical sin. But like Wyclif, the Wycliffite preacher
advocates – and practices – polemical exposure of institutional sin. Both
entrust – no, both oblige – lay people to practice this corrective speech
and corrective action.[66] While Wyclif and Wycliffite sermons still occasionally envisage individuals reproving individuals, their emphasis lies on
correcting institutional groups. The *EWS* sermon on "If thy brother shall
offend" ["Si peccaverit"], for example, begins by acknowledging individual reproof, but shifts, by the fourth sentence, to the "new lawis" made
by the religious orders to hinder reproof.[67] The practice constructed elab-
orately by the high clergy to enlist individuals in realizing its pastoral
initiatives has now been seized by Wyclif and his followers to deprive all
institutionally formed clerical groups of the very practice of pastoral care.
Pastoral power and moral authority have passed to the Wycliffite, clerical
or lay, who alone knows and lives by the scriptures and the example of
Jesus and so can alone judge what is necessary for the salvation of others.

CHAPTER 6

Lancastrian reformist lives: toeing the line while stepping over it

Despite John Wyclif's radical, unprecedented conversion of fraternal correction into a tool for disendowing the English Church and despite the grounding of Wycliffite anticlerical polemics in the key Gospel texts (Matthew 18 and Luke 6), non-Wycliffites continued to advocate the practice of fraternal correction. Between Pope Gregory's branding as erroneous Wyclif's teaching on fraternal correction (1377) and Archbishop Thomas Arundel's Constitutions of 1409, pastoral literature and sermon cycles present discourse on fraternal correction in the usual places and in the usual ways. (New manuscripts of pre-1375 preaching materials, exegetical works, and sermons promulgating fraternal correction as part of the pastoral program of reform also appeared in these decades, of course.[1]) For example, in the entry on fraternal correction in his *Florarium Bartholomaei*, the Augustinian canon John of Mirfield proclaims repeatedly that subjects are bound to admonish their disciplinary superiors, although he insists that such speech always be delivered in private – a fairly restrictive position.[2] Throughout these years, exegesis of Jesus' metaphor of the mote and beam – in sermon and biblical commentary, in Latin and English – argues that sinners may correct others' sins if they examine themselves, correct their own sins first, and admonish others mercifully.[3] Even the much studied *quaestio* "Whether it is fitting for women to teach men gathered together in public" resorts to fraternal correction as a work of spiritual mercy required of all Christians in order to refute the claim that women may preach and teach publicly.[4] In all the forms of pastoral writing and preaching, I can find only one possible pervasive reaction to Wyclif's and Wycliffite recasting of fraternal correction: The old note that correctors must avoid slander may be sounded with even greater insistence and frequency.[5]

The climate that produced writing advocating and delivering corrective speech was somewhat transformed by Archbishop Arundel's Constitutions, just as it had been by John Wyclif's reformist theology of the 1370s and early 1380s. Two years after Henry IV had assumed the throne, Parliament permitted the burning of relapsed heretics for the first time in England – to be done in a high place "that such punishment may strike fear into the minds of others."[6] That year (1401) the Wycliffite William Sawtry was burnt at Smithfield. Quick to associate opposition to his contested rule with heresy, the new king was only too eager to turn the apparatus of state power against those accused.[7] Drafted six years later at Oxford, that notorious center of Wycliffite writing and teaching, and promulgated in 1409, the Constitutions were intended by Arundel and his lawyers to defend the faith and extirpate heresy, particularly Wycliffism. To that end, they proposed to regulate religious speech and writing throughout the province of Canterbury in sweeping, though not wholly unprecedented, ways. (We need to keep in mind throughout this chapter that the Constitutions were enforced only sporadically and were often evaded.)

Several constitutions threatened to circumscribe either teaching fraternal correction of sin or practicing it, especially if the sins of clerics were the targets. Nevertheless, sermons, pastoral compendia, and narratives continued to advocate the practice – in the case of narrative, to model it, as well – from 1409 itself down into the late 1430s. *The Book of Margery Kempe* marks the terminus for this study. No new English pastoral texts or narratives dealing extensively with fraternal correction appear in the last six decades of the century (I have not read widely enough in polemical texts to make a judgment).

The first constitution restricted parish priests and the unbeneficed to preaching only the rudiments of religious knowledge listed by Arundel's predecessor John Pecham in the well-known constitution of 1281 (the Seven Sins, the Decalogue, the Creed, and so on). As Nicholas Watson has underscored, Pecham's syllabus, a "*minimum* necessary for the laity to know if they are to be saved," becomes in the Constitutions "the *maximum* that they may hear, read, or even discuss." Far from reviving the pastoral reform and education of which the syllabus was a key tool, Arundel, he argues, builds on Pecham to rein in "the laity's too eager pursuit of knowledge."[8] The seven works of mercy appear in Pecham's list of fundamentals, although the spiritual works, of which chastising or correcting sin was one, are not listed.[9] However, the works of spiritual mercy are frequently expounded alongside the corporal ones in fourteenth- and early-fifteenth-century pastoral texts, Latin and vernacular, in many genres. So, fraternal correction could still be a catechetical topic for preaching after the Constitutions.[10] More importantly, the set Gospel readings of Matthew 18 and Luke 6 still provided, as they had throughout the thirteenth and fourteenth centuries, the main occasions for extended preaching/teaching on fraternal correction. Although the Constitutions had "a marked repressive effect" on sermon collections in English, Siegfried Wenzel finds that they "had no immediate negative effect on making and collecting [Latin] sermons."[11] Moreover, manuscripts of already circulating collections in both the vernacular and Latin could still be read, and new ones were produced (of Jacopo da Varazze's *Sermones quadragesimales* and the *Northern Homily Cycle* – to take only two examples with extended sermons on the two Gospel readings[12]). Therefore, preachers could still find model sermons for both set readings, and while sermons could treat Luke 6 without dealing with fraternal correction, it would have been a stretch for any kind of sermon on Matthew 18 to avoid it, given its *thema* and the elaborate four-part procedure at the outset of the short reading.

Beyond sermons, always a main means for conveying the obligation to practice fraternal correction and at least some norms for corrective speech, the Constitutions may have limited somewhat new comprehensive pastoral writing about correction. The eighth constitution, which forbade everyone propounding positions in the Catholic faith or ones adverse to good morals (except in the universities), certainly was designed to inhibit and control theological discussion, especially scholastic argumentation in Latin and the vernacular.[13] While fraternal correction was a well-established topic in moral theology, as our first two chapters demonstrate, this constitution could have inhibited teaching it insofar as it inhibited theological debate and writing in general. Nevertheless, two substantial Latin expositions of fraternal correction appeared, probably in the 1420s. The *Speculum spiritualium* draws heavily on Thomas Aquinas to examine the proper procedure for correcting sins, especially within monastic communities. Far more probing, universalized, and comprehensive is the entry "de correctione fraterna" in Alexander Carpenter's *Destructorium viciorum* (by 1429), an encyclopedia of preaching materials that does not hesitate to tackle power relations head on. As H. Leith Spencer has observed, Carpenter did not "favour a strict interpretation of the Constitutions"; he insists that lay people must not be ignorant of the Gospel, that priests must prepare them to listen to scripture, and that "they may talk about what they have heard."[14] With greater explicitness than most earlier pastoral writers, Carpenter marks out the kinds of corrective speech that different social groups are obligated to practice: priests as disciplinary agents, judges in secular courts, lay people witnessing the sins of others. Rather than resting with the general term *subditus*, he specifies *laici* as agents bound to reprove disciplinary superiors in the Church, not just their own superiors but any egregiously sinful *pastor*, because the example of sinning clerics draws others to sin ("prelatos suos et alios eccles[i]e pastores enormiter peccantes"). Therefore, the learned may be reproved by the unlearned, clerics by lay people, just as Balaam was reproved by his ass. Carpenter even takes pains to distinguish slander from fraternal correction, pointing out that a fraternal corrector may justly take away a person's reputation if an obdurate sinner pushes through to the fourth step. In addition to the *Destructorium* and the *Speculum*, manuscripts of earlier pastoral works teaching fraternal correction, like John of Mirfield's recent *Florarium*, continued to be made and circulated during the first half of the century.[15]

Perhaps more pivotal in curtailing daring writing about correction was the seventh constitution, which forbade anyone by his or her own authority to make a written translation of a text of holy scripture – even a single passage or phrase – or to read a work containing one.[16] Because fraternal correction was founded in a biblical text (Matthew 18:15) and regulated by others (like Luke 6 and Galatians 2), this part of the legislation could make it difficult to expound fraternal correction in the vernacular. The reference to Wyclif in this constitution might also discourage discussion of fraternal correction in English, associating it with Wyclif, whose teaching about correction, after all, had been branded contrary to the faith by Pope Gregory and English doctors.

The one constitution that might actually discourage corrective speech itself prohibited clerics preaching to the laity about clerical sins. Such a restriction might deprive the laity of ammunition – the habitual clerical sins retailed by clerics – and remove a reformist model for how to address clerical sins. In addition, resisters of correction, especially among the clergy, might attempt to silence lay correctors by labeling their speech as preaching, limited by the first constitution to licensed clerics – a tactic used by the York opponents of Margery Kempe. Certainly a subject's reproof of a disciplinary superior could be seen as more dangerous after 1409 (and, before then, after the branding of Wycliffism as widespread heresy), just as, Watson has argued, the writing of complex (let alone daring) theology in the vernacular could be.[17]

For all that the Constitutions and the general Lancastrian climate of surveillance may have done to damp down corrective speech and writing advocating fraternal correction, two different and usually unassociated vernacular texts advocate – indeed, model – the practice in bold, somewhat new reformist contexts, while warding off the specter of Wycliffism.

The anonymous *Mum and the Sothsegger* (after March 1409), written by a Bristol native familiar with legal and parliamentary affairs, invokes the originary grant of Matthew 18:15–17 to authorize both truth-telling counsel by advisors to King Henry IV and its own blunt rebukes of political, friarly, academic, and priestly vices.[18] (*Pace* Arundel, he quotes the beginning of the text in Latin, then translates expansively the first two verses.) Although the *praelates* whom pastoral discourse always presented as legitimate targets of correction could include those national and local office-holders responsible for regulating the conduct of citizens, until *Mum* no Middle English text that I know of advocates extensively and explicitly practicing fraternal correction within the political arena, even within its institutional channels. And we come finally to the long-promised bookend of this study, *The Book of Margery Kempe*, which probably took its final form in the late 1430s. For the first time, an English text presents a contemporary Englishwoman whose life is defined in no small part by correcting the sins of others: male and female social equals, male clerics, and, most notoriously, the two English Archbishops, Arundel himself and Bowet. Although discourse on fraternal correction certainly could be seen as opening the practice to women (the generic "whoever has charity" may correct as a "brother," a fellow Christian) and although some pastoral texts contained a few embryonic *exempla* of female correctors, all well-developed correctors we have examined, both fictive figures within texts and writers, have been male: Will, the Peres in *Crede*, John Wyclif, and Wycliffite polemicists.

Despite the obvious differences in genre, date (nearly thirty years apart), the corrector's gender and social position, and the arena of their corrective speech, *Mum* and the *Book* employ surprisingly similar strategies for conveying the need to practice fraternal correction in this age of repressive maneuvers. Both texts are lives. That is, they present a model way – a correct way – of moral living in a central figure who encounters radically opposite ways of life that fiercely challenge hers or his.[19] In both, the good life for the central figure and others is marked prominently by fraternal correction of sins, not as an isolated act, but as a habitual practice so rooted in emotion, mind, and memorized texts that it springs forth even in the most dangerous situations. In both, the truth-telling corrector of entrenched evils, the "sothsegger" and Margery Kempe, struggles against, matches wits with, and is almost overborne by hosts of deviant speakers: flatterers of the powerful in *Mum* and slanderers and false accusers in the *Book*. As in Wycliffite texts (and *Piers Plowman*), the corrector is branded as a deviant speaker who ought to be silenced by authorities.

Unlike Wycliffites, these correctors defend their lives – that is, their habits of living, the ideal pattern they offer society, and life itself – by strictly and explicitly cleaving to the norms and constraints demanded by pastoral writers and preachers before 1375 and by non-Wycliffite texts in their own time. They toe ostentatiously the old pastoral lines. They mount and deliver impeccable reproofs, modeling how to manifest moral authority, charity, and pastoral power, how to invoke the clerically created practice against the lives of resistant clerics, and how to employ pastoral discourse to subvert traditional pastoral limits on reformist speech, even in an age of vigilant ecclesiastical and political policing. In all this, *Mum* and the *Book* invite their reform-minded readers to sympathize with, admire, and imitate the correctors their narratives shape. Their end, like that of exemplary rhetoric in general as J. Allan Mitchell reads it, is "to discover how to lead a moral life," and, therefore, as exemplary texts they give readers "practical guidance concerning future action."[20] In the process, as we would suspect from *Piers Plowman* and Wycliffite texts, they also validate their own corrective writing, their setting straight of individuals and social groups.

THE TRUTH-TELLER IN POLITICAL LIFE: *MUM AND THE SOTHSEGGER*

Baffled but driven, the narrator of *Mum and the Sothsegger*, like *Piers Plowman*'s Will and the narrator of *Crede*, is searching for someone who can answer his insistent question:

> And therfore my wil is to walke more at large
> Forto finde sum freke [man] that of feith were
> Not double [deceptive], but indifferent [unbiased] to deme the sothe
>   [truth],
> Whether Mum is more better or Melle-sum-time [Speak-some-time]
> Forto amend that were amisse into more ease.[21]

Is self-interested silence in the face of social evils the better way of life? Or is it truth-telling that can rectify somewhat those evils, the life of a "sothsegger," as the poem most often terms it? In the course of the narrator's journey, as he surveys social estates, debates allegorical figures, has a dream vision (all in the manner of the *Piers Plowman* tradition, often highlighted by specific allusions to *Piers*), his question shifts significantly to "who shuld have / The maistrye?" (574–5). Who ought to rule or control life by offering a model to which others aspire? Which will prevail over the other in their fierce struggle to set the terms of Lancastrian public life? Far more than the quests of *Piers*, this quest is driven by political concerns, concerns that dominated the first decade of Henry IV's reign (1399–1409): the new king's lavish grants to nobles who had supported him against Richard II; his unending expenditures to maintain a grand court that might legitimate his rule; military action against the French, the Scots, and the Welsh; the burden of taxation on the commons and the regular requests for new taxes; the inability of the poor to initiate proceedings in royal courts; the violent oppression of religious and political dissent.[22] As the last suggests, the poem's reformist scope is ecclesiastical as well as political. Both areas, after all, interlocked in this decade (to put it mildly), and, in the poem's vision of both, institutions are used for the benefit of the powerful and privileged (nobles, beneficed clerics), who oppress poor laborers and deprive them of goods and sustenance. *Mum* bears witness, in the words of its recent editor, Helen Barr, to "those literate members of society who may have been excluded from key positions of sacred or secular authority, but who were keen, in this time of flux and unrest, that their voices be heard."[23] Fraternal correction of sin becomes the means the poem advances to make those voices heard: to awaken them, to authorize rebuking those in power, to guide them so that corrective speech has a chance of reforming individuals, estates, and institutions.

The cruel paradox that runs through the whole poem is what introduces pastoral discourse on fraternal correction. Of all the officers, the narrator proclaims at the outset,[24] the king and lay lords need most a "sothsegger" who will present the grievances of the commons, but that truth-teller is the first to be loathed, rebuked, rejected, and ejected from any court because of his "feithful tale," the accurate quasi-legal complaint of a loyal citizen who keeps faith with both his king and the commons.[25] (The narrator is quick to praise King Henry IV, to lay the blame for misrule on his covetous, deceptive advisors and on the nobles. The king would address the grievances, if he only knew of them.) To remedy this situation, replayed over and over again, the narrator counsels as he shifts from social survey to an intimate direct address to his readers, the truth-teller must distinguish his speech from the deviant unrestrained talk, especially slander, that his enemies are quick to accuse him of (49–50, 72–3). The truth itself is not enough to defend corrective speech. The truth-teller must establish that his intention is not malicious by adhering to the "gospel that ground is of lore" (76). The narrator's paraphrase of Matthew 18:15–16, underscored in the manuscript margin by its Latin first line,[26] the *thema* of sermons on the lection, drives home what validates corrective speech:

He [the Gospel, Jesus] seith that thou shuldes the sinne of thy brother
Telle him by time and til himsilf oon [to him alone],
In ful wil to amende him of his misse-deedes.
Si peccaverit in te frater tuus corrige etc.
And if he chargeth not [doesn't regard] thy charite but chideth the
    againes,
Yit leve him not so lightly though he loure oones [lower once]
But funde [try] him to freine efte of the newe [to question him again],
And have wittenes the with that thou wel knowes,
And spare not to speke, spede if thou mowe [if you will prosper]. (79–86)

The narrator's verbs ("shuldes," the imperatives) stress that this is a precept
that, as *Piers Plowman*'s Lewte says of Leviticus 19:17 and the Wycliffites
of Matthew 18, obligates all Christians to practice correction of sin.[27]
But unlike the Wycliffites, *Mum*'s narrator suggests that individuals (not
groups) are the subject of correction and he insists that strictly following
Gospel procedure (its first two steps) is also obligatory: Delivering admonition first in private, then persisting by returning with witnesses, makes
apparent the correctors' charitable will and intention to help amend their
brother's misdeeds. To do so is to achieve what pastoral discourse promises: escaping any accusation of slander, succeeding at amending lives (if
the sinner is prudent), and gaining the sinner's thanks:

For whenne thy tente [intention] and thy tale [complaint] been temprid
    in oone,
And menys [you intend] no malice to man that [to whom] thou spekys,
But forto mende him mukely [meekly] of his misse-deedes,
Sory for his sinne and his shrewed taicches [cursed vices]
And the burne [man] be y-blessid and balys cunne eschewe [knows how
    to avoid sorrows]
And thrifty and towarde, thou shal thanke gete. (90–5)

While this emphatically biblical and ethical passage does authorize the
narrator's satiric verse, as scholars have stressed,[28] it does so at a remove. Its
intimate voice, its traditional pastoral focus on the two individuals (and
the witnesses), and its preoccupation with ethical intentionality (and will)
more directly instructs the poem's readers how to tell the truth about sin
in a way that most deserves a hearing, most promises success because it
establishes that each is a "siker servant" (97), steadfast, reliable, and worthy of trust. It advises them how to become desirable servants to a king or
noble. Yet its ostentatious textuality cloaks a textual sleight of hand. Like
Lewte – and moral theologians, canonists, and pastoral writers – the narrator adapts his biblical text to contemporary needs. He does not English

"in te," making anyone's misdeeds the subject of correction. In the public domain of Church and state, any prominent person's misdeeds, the "soth" the "sothsegger" declares, are likely to be known by all. In this way, *Mum*'s author carries the fundamental pastoral ethics of correction – with its concerns for fulfilling obligations, for the welfare of others, for amendment of life, for a virtuous will and intention, for proper procedure – into the public realm, authorizing and guiding reformist speech. Grounding correction in Matthew 18 also enables him to designate as sins political, economic, legal, and ecclesiastical actions by the powerful; thus, courting lavish royal gifts, exacting higher rents from tenants, devising ruinous taxes, and not carrying out episcopal visitations become violations of divine law, rebellion against God's order, and a refusal to give others their just due. The amendment of life that correction seeks thus becomes reformation of individuals' political (or ecclesiastical), legal, and economic practices. Moreover, the biblical text's leveling language of brother or fellow Christian elides social and institutional status, clearing the way for someone of lesser political position, like the narrator, to reprove the greater.

While the truth-teller's way of life is marked throughout the poem by his habitual practice of fraternal correction, it is defined even more sharply by a running contrast with Mum, who practices self-interested silence in the same situations in which the truth-teller speaks out. Mum breaks into the poem just as the narrator is worrying that Henry IV's councilors, driven by greed, will deter him from acting for the common profit. "Nomore of this matiere," he commands, proclaiming himself the narrator's master, master both as the spyer-out of all his dissenting speech (yes, Lancastrian surveillance!) and as the model of a life the narrator should lead:

> "I am Mum thy maister," cothe [said] he, "in alle maniere places,
> That sittith with souverains and servyd with greete.
> Thaire will ne thaire wordes I withseye [contradict] never,
> But folowe thaym in thaire folye and fare muche the bettere,
> Easily for oile, sire, and elles were I nice [foolish].
> Thus leede I my life in luste [pleasure] of my herte,
> And for me wisedame and witte won [dwell] I with the beste;
> While sergeantz the sechith [seek] to saise by the lappe [arrest]
> For the wilde wordes that maken wretthe [cause anger] ofte.
> Thow were better folwe me foure score winter
> Thenne [than] be a soeth-sigger." (243–53)

Thus Mum defines himself as the opposite of the truth-teller. He never speaks out against the folly of the powerful; his intention is to live for pleasure among those of high status; he is guided not by scripture but by prudential wisdom.

Here and throughout the narrator's two disputations with Mum (232–76 and 674–787), the poet subverts Mum's self-characterization by riddling it with unacknowledged contradictions, which contrast with the integrity of the truth-teller. While he praises silence in the households of the great, Mum lives equally by a very different habit of speech: unrestrained flattery. Mum's metaphor, the oil that profits him, conveys in pastoral discourse on flattery and political satire the false praise that, anointing the powerful as if they were kings, tempts them to see themselves as gods, able to transgress social boundaries, as they do in Mum's vision of the life of magnates. Silent only about misdeeds and misrule, Mum is loquacious in flattery, which pastoral discourse presents routinely as the antithesis of corrective speech. As oil does too, flattery promises to comfort and heal, but only correction of sin (in the usual metaphor of disease) does that. Further, the oil of flattery so softens people's minds that they reject truths about themselves as hard and inflexible, while embracing destructive acts.[29]

Mum is equally loquacious in disputation. Ironically he reduces the narrator to silence, condemning himself with his own words. In his second disputation with the narrator, Mum veers from his advice that the narrator imitate Mum by winning silver through tricks and bribes to quote the canon law maxim *"qui tacet consentire videtur"* [whoever keeps silent seems to consent] (745) – a move that has puzzled scholars. Mum uses this maxim as pastoral writers do similar phrases: to insist that anyone who observes sin is complicit in it unless he or she corrects it.[30] Mum's inconsistency here, just like his advocacy of both silence and flattery (and disputatious babbling), stems from self-interest. He worries that violent conflict between magnates, even to the point of manslaughter and murder, threatens his stratagems and his place among them. And he limits admonition of the angry magnates to prelates – in this context, bishops and, perhaps, abbots (fellow magnates, in effect). Nonetheless, his consistent inconsistency condemns him, especially as he expounds the maxim in pastoral terms:

> And who-so hath in-sight of silde-couthe [seldom known and marvellous]
>   thingz,
> Of sinne or of shame or of shonde outher [disgrace either],
> And luste [desires] not to lette [prevent] hit, but leteth [allows] hit forth
>   passe,
> As clercz doon construe that knowen alle bookes,
> He shal be demyd doer of the same deede. (746–50)

He reverts to a traditional moral discourse about social responsibility when it advances his own fortunes, made at the expense of others.

Mum's very "flexibility," of course, enables him to thrive in every estate the narrator surveys, while the "sothsegger" licks his wounds in solitude: amid monks, canons, friars, the secular clergy (especially parish priests pocketing tithes), academics, civic officials, royal officers (321–673, 788–868). That Mum appears abruptly wearing a miter at one point in order to menace the narrator (579–81) underscores his alliance with the powerful in the Church under Henry IV and so his ability to spy on, to silence, and to threaten to execute dissenters.[31] Distressed "That Mum shuld be maister moste uppon erthe" (868), the narrator falls into a dream that renews his commitment to truth-telling as a way of life. In an idealized medieval landscape, a beekeeper bears up the king bee when he weakens and keeps parasitical drones from entering the hive to devour the honey of the workers. A figure for the model royal advisor and the reformist truth-teller the narrator has been seeking, the beekeeper rails against prelates and members of Parliament who fail to voice the wrongs done to commoners, as scripture and canon law enjoin. Exposing Mum's way of life as the cause of misrule, he exhorts the narrator to adopt the life of the "sothsegger" as the best form of life, filling with his "boke-making" the void created by the failure of prelatical and fraternal correction: "thow mays do no better. / Hit may amende many men of thaire misdeedes" (1,279–80).

Although the poem breaks off with the narrator, now awake, pulling different kinds of documentary writing out of his bag in order to counsel the king,[32] pastoral discourse does not recede in this final section of the poem as we have it. Reformist writing is to be governed by the same norms as reformist speech ("write" and "seye" are used interchangeably at this point). The beekeeper warns him, just as the dream ends, against shaming his brother in the process of telling the truth, shaming that will cause him to reject angrily the truth about himself. He counsels mild words. He urges him to wait for a suitable time ("And not eche day to egge [urge] him, but in a deue time" [1,274]) . All of these norms, we have seen, had been constructed by pastoral writers from the mid thirteenth century on, as they worked out how practical reason guides charity into effective speech. They are of a piece with the *Mum* author's concern throughout the poem with how the marginalized truth-teller may gain the moral authority to make his voice heard by the king, the royal Council, and magnates and how he can make his harsh truths acceptable. However, this licence for the poem and for fraternal correctors of individuals does not extend to just anyone's political speech. Neither does the originary grant of Matthew 18:15–16 as the author construes it. The poem condemns as "grucching" complaints against the king and nobles by the commons themselves (1388–1488); as a Sin of the Tongue, "grucching" or murmur is the ungoverned speech of those who are ignorant, prone to lie, and insubordinate to proper authority.[33] Working to constrain any *vox populi* that discourse on fraternal correction might unleash through its proclamation that anyone having charity may rebuke the sins of disciplinary superiors, the author insists that truth-telling political speech must operate in proper institutional settings: in King Henry's Council, in Parliament, in the households of magnates, secular and ecclesiastical.[34]

Within those settings, the author envisions the reciprocity of fraternal correction operating as part of his contractual conception of political and ecclesiastical life. The king or other person of power recognizes his responsibility to listen to, even to seek out, good counsel; the truth-teller in office (knight of the shire, rural dean, ecclesiastical lawyer, steward, chancellor, judge) conforms his speech to pastoral norms and constraints. Thus the good counselor demonstrates a moral authority in politics akin to that of the charitable corrector in interpersonal relations: concern for the common profit (including that of the king), powers of ethical analysis and reasoning, practical reason, and the intention to amend what is amiss in England. Outside these offices, the poem makes room for "extra-parliamentary, informal counsel," especially from the clergy "as guardians of the morality upon which all human relationship depends."[35] When the clergy remains mum, failing to practice either prelatical or fraternal correction,[36] the poet who shares clerical learning may reprove the sins of social groups, both for their oppression of the commons and for their failure to embrace the life of truth-telling – sometimes even to grasp the significance of the narrator's question about Mum and the "sothsegger." Narrative poetry that is built out of the discourses of correction and normative/deviant speech, as it is also out of civil law and of estates satire, steps into the gap. But the author does not imagine that it can fill the gap. While *Mum* may reprove the sins of violent nobles, self-serving advisors, and avaricious clerics (among other groups), extending fraternal correction to groups in ways anticipated by *Piers Plowman* and the Wycliffites, it entrusts the correction of individuals necessary for political, economic, and ecclesiastical reform (except, gingerly, King Henry IV) to the readers it aims to persuade to a life of truth-telling as agents of reform. Not so *The Book of Margery Kempe*, where Kempe resourcefully corrects at once individual sin and the groups and institutions that foster it.

THE HOLY WOMAN: MARGERY KEMPE
THE IMPECCABLE CORRECTOR

However great its social and political scope, the arena of *Mum and the Sothsegger* is populated only by men: Mum as bishop, the "sothsegger" in his corner, the chancellor, magnates, prelates, mayors, and aldermen. Yet in our second Lancastrian life, Margery Kempe not only practices fraternal correction but defines herself as a corrector in Archbishop Bowet's household and during her interrogation by licensed, ordained, Latin-educated men. Throughout the *Book of Margery Kempe* it is largely in the arena of the Church, especially in encounters with clerics, that a woman blossoms as a reprover of sin – and that in spite of well-known arguments for why women should not preach and why they should see their bodies, not least of all their tongues, as disruptive, discordant, fickle, and untrustworthy.[37] How did that come about, given the predominance of men in *exempla* of correction and the pastoral language of "fraterna correctio" (by a "brother," as well as by a "fellow Christian")?

First the situation. Margery Kempe's definition of herself at York is reactive, as it is so often in the *Book*, where prelatical correction lies cheek by jowl with fraternal speech. She is resisting other current, life-threatening definitions imposed on her by the Archbishop's retainers: "loller" (vagabond, Wycliffite) and "heretyk" (pp. 124–5). In fact, they swear the oaths she reproves as they threaten her with the heretic's fate: burning. Margery Kempe's very habit of rebuking the blasphemous oaths of men allows them to construe her identity in this way because, as scholars have often remarked, Wycliffites were marked in the popular imagination by two of their practices: rebuking those who swore and allowing women to instruct men. Wandering teachers also propagated Wycliffite teachings, and she has been moving across the Midlands and Yorkshire, engaging in conversation with sympathizers as she has visited shrines. The Archbishop signals that she is, in his words, "a fals heretyke" by commanding his men to fetter her before he interrogates her. But she sets out resourcefully to challenge his definition of her: "I am non heretike, ne [nor] ye xal [shall] non preve me" (p. 124). While her faultless answers to his questions about the Articles of Faith manifest her orthodoxy, her proof also involves reconstructing the inquisitors' definition of her. She does so by boldly referring to the very speech acts they have used to label her as heretic: "for I xal spekyn of God & undirnemyn hem [correct them] that sweryn gret othys wher-so-evyr I go" (p. 126). She does not invoke other culturally constructed selves that she might here and, in fact, does elsewhere invoke: pilgrim, for example, or mystic. In defining her speech in the household and through the archdiocese as fraternal correction, she becomes an institutionally sanctioned critic of institutionally proscribed speech (and acts) and, more generally, an agent in the pastoral program of combating sin that the clergy, especially the Archbishops of York, had vigorously promoted (as we know from Jonathan Hughes's *Pastors and Visionaries*).[38] The role of fraternal corrector thus at once plausibly licenses Margery Kempe's dangerous speech, defanging her accusers, and enables her to assume a social self that involves moral action, that insists on her sense of what is good for herself, her oppressors (not committing blasphemy, for instance), and the Church at York.[39]

As a cultural resource constructed by pastoral texts and sermons, fraternal correction was, in the realm of discourse at least, open to women as well as to men, as I argued in chapter 1. Pastoral writers (most recently Alexander Carpenter) continued to present women as exemplary fraternal correctors of men with power over them, most often Abigail, who rebukes her husband Nabal for not receiving David hospitably, then does what her husband refuses to do.[40] Outside the household, more apt for Margery Kempe's situation at York, was Judith, who, as we saw in chapter 1, rebukes the elders of her city and changes their plan to surrender to the Assyrians. Although the voices of female saints in Latin and vernacular collections are not labeled fraternal correction because they address pagan officials, not fellow Christians, they nonetheless exemplify female correction of male misliving, correction that seeks amendment of life – and sometimes achieves it.[41] Even closer to the *Book of Margery Kempe* is the newly canonized Birgitta of Sweden (1302/3–73), whose revelations Kempe often begs to have read to her. While scholars have unfolded how Birgitta's affective and visionary piety shapes Kempe's, Birgitta is also instructed repeatedly by God to correct nobles and prelates. Latin and English versions of her revelations were read widely in the early fifteenth century; I will cite one of them recurrently, the *Liber Celestis* (manuscript *c.* 1410–20), to mark rhetorical strategies shared by her English admirer and imitator. Birgitta's revelations stand in a long and broad Continental tradition of lives of holy women who are skilled in detecting and voicing the sins of clerics (and others), a tradition several centuries old by the time the *Book* was written.[42]

The role of corrector is an easy one for the *Book*'s Margery Kempe to adopt in her crisis at York because she had reproved male authorities' manifest sins for years wherever she had encountered them: the blasphemy of Cistercians at the shrine of the Holy Blood at Hailes, the extravagant dress of Bishop Thomas Peveral's retinue at Worcester; the negligent household governance of Archbishop Arundel himself. Except for the correction of Arundel, however, her life before and during her pilgrimage to Jerusalem is marked by her being the subject of correction, not the corrector. Her own unimpeachable practice of correction emerges out of a matrix of deviant correction by lay people and clerics alike, certainly the harshness of her first confessor, but, more extensively, the three types of speech that Lady Meed accuses Conscience of (and she herself practices), the very abuses of correction pastoral writers had warned against since the 1230s: slander, uncharitable reproof, and chiding. The *Book*'s first preface introduces this major strand in its tapestry of speech: "Sche was so usyd to be slawndred & repreved, to be cheden & rebuked of the world" (p. 2). Throughout, the *Book* discredits these "wicked tongues" because they violate the basic norms and constraints pastoral discourse established to regulate reproof. They assault Margery Kempe's *fama* as a holy woman.

The *Book* constructs Margery Kempe initially as a bourgeois wife whose social self is defined by the "worship" – the esteem, the good name, the social worth – that others confer on her in response to her standing in a mercantile community focused on material profit. "Worship" in the *Book* is Janus-faced, as Derek Brewer finds honor to be in Chaucer's poetry. One of honor's faces is the citizen's status as determined by lineage and by achievement in the mercantile world; the other, the response which that deserves (adapted from *OED* 1a and b).[43] When Margery Kempe emerges from the madness provoked by her confessor's overhasty rebuke, she is driven to reassert her claims to "worship" through elaborate clothing and her much studied domestic industries of brewing and milling. When these inexplicably fail, she becomes the subject of gossip, which, like the bourgeois "worship" conferred on her in response to a clearly marked status, reads these failures as signs of a deficient inner life:

A-noon as it was noised a-bowt the town of N. that ther wold neithyr man ne best don servise to the seid creatur, than summe seiden sche was a-cursid; sum seiden God toke opyn veniawns up-on hir; sum seiden o [one] thing; & sum seid an-other. And sum wise men, whos mend was mor growndyd in the lofe of owyr Lord, seid it was the hei [high] mercy of our Lord Ihesu Crist clepyd and kallyd hir fro the pride and vanite of the wretthyd [wretched] world. (pp. 10–11)

The repeated "sum seiden" constructs gossip as it appears throughout the *Book*, as variable and usually unreliable responses to the same event, really determined by the gossipers' wills and intentions.[44] This talk remains simply gossip, "talking about other people behind their backs," until it turns to her new ascetic and affective practices: daily confession, "to [too] grete fasting & to grete waking," and public weeping. Then the *Book* labels this talk slander and improper (uncharitable) reproof, speech that assaults her reputation maliciously.

Pastoral texts, writings in the tradition of *Piers Plowman* (and *Piers* itself), and Wycliffite texts, as we have seen, all deal openly with the kinship between slander and fraternal correction as types of social blame: Speakers of both impute evil to others, sometimes even exposing "hidden evils." The speaker's will and intention is what differentiates slander from fraternal speech, but others cannot know those directly, or perhaps even have any sense of them at all. In the penultimate incident in the *Book*, Margery Kempe is reproved mockingly by "sum dissolute personis," repeating words falsely attributed to her: "'A, thu fals flesch, thu xalt [shall] no good mete etyn.'" The *Book* traces those words back to a false story contrived by neighbors in response to her early ascetic practices, some forty years before. In their tale, she was dining on a fast day with a prosperous man who served his guest a plate of ordinary red herring and one of excellent pike. Setting aside the herring ostentatiously, she loudly proclaimed "'A, thu fals flesch, thu woldyst now etyn reed hering, but thu xalt not han thy wille.'" Then she feasted on the pike. The *Book* attributes the staying power of this slanderous story to those envious and angry at "hir vertuows levyng, not of powyr to hindryn hir but thorw her [their] fals tungys."[45] By urban networks of gossip the words were transmitted over forty years or so in "many a place wher sche was nevyr kyd ne knowyn," and were used to give her "grete repref" time and again (pp. 243–4). So, words generated and transmitted as slander, spoken out of her hearing ostensibly to expose her "hidden evil" of hypocrisy, but really to damage her *fama*, become the stuff of uncharitable reproof, uttered to her face to cause her pain. A pastoral Sin of the Tongue, uncharitable reproof (*convicium*) is akin to slander in divulging blameable failing (*defectus culpae*), but different because it aims to openly rob her of her honor, the public repute given her in response to her virtue (as differentiated from *fama*, which may be good or evil – and, of course, mixed).[46] More often than retailing false stories, Margery Kempe's slanderers and uncharitable reprovers alike attribute her affective practices to evil intentions, especially her public weeping, said to be "for the world for socowr & for worldly good" (p. 13).[47]

Like pastoral discourse on fraternal correction, the *Book* is keen to trace the destructive consequences of slander and uncharitable reproof: what loss of good name (*bona fama*) involves. In pastoral writing, *fama*, as chapter 2 explains, was commodified, made an object valuable in personal relations. Slanderers sin more grievously than thieves because they rob people of *fama*, a greater good than temporal riches – indeed the greatest of earthly goods.[48] With her good name lost, the *Book*'s Margery Kempe loses the trust of others who aspire to holiness, much as a man of ill repute loses the trust of court officials. As a result, she is abandoned by former confreres, whom she desperately needs on her many pilgrimages for food, for spiritual conversation, for protection from rape, robbery, and hostile officials. The loss of good name also inflicts pain in itself for this bourgeois woman acculturated to the value of "worship." When Margery Kempe worries that virgins in heaven will dance more merrily than she, the voice of Christ promises "[thou] xuldyst noon other Purgatory han than slawndyr & speche of the world" (p. 51).

Chiding (*contentio*), the other Sin of the Tongue that the *Book*, like pastoral writers and Langland's Lady Meed, couples with uncharitable reproof, accuses another person of sin, as does slander, but it does so directly in the course of a dispute out of pride or anger.[49] The *Book*'s incidents of chiding are pivotal in Margery Kempe's life because they bring her into conflict with quarrelsome males of beyond-the-ordinary authority and power, not the lay people, friars, and parish priests who tend to slander her. The chiders react against her assumption of religious authority as teacher, scriptural expositor, and corrector of sin. In the most vehement conflict with clerics in her early life of wanderings, when she is visiting monastic houses for her spiritual benefit, her chiders are none other than the monks of Christ Church, Canterbury.

"What kanst thow sein of God?" "Ser," sche seith, "I wil bothe speke of him & heryn of him," rehersing the monk a story of Scriptur. The munke seide, "I wold thow wer closyd in an hows of ston that ther schuld no man speke with the." (p. 27)

Thanks to several decades of scholarship on women and clerics, the social dynamic of this exchange needs little gloss: The supposedly unlettered bourgeois wife whose mastery of scripture leads a lordly man, most likely a cleric, to desire to isolate and silence her – whether the house of stone be a prison or an anchorage (perhaps, also, a community of nuns). Margery's response in the *Book* is a direct, spirited, and public act of fraternal correction designed to amend his error: "'A, ser,' sche seid, 'Ye schuld meintein Goddis servawntys, & ye arn the first that heldyn a-gens hem. Owyr Lord amend yow'" (pp. 27–8). This further assumption of religious authority provokes a young monk to claim that she speaks scripture by agency either of the Holy Ghost or of a devil because, as a woman, she could not have it "of thyself" (p. 28). Looking back on the incident at the beginning of the next chapter, the *Book* retrospectively reads the monks' chiding as their response to Margery Kempe's speaking about scripture and practicing fraternal correction. It resists the truth about her speech, her obedience to pastoral (and, therefore, male) injunctions, and her orthodoxy; it also does so harshly (also a characteristic of chiding, which Lady Meed does not forget when she accuses Conscience). Moreover, as falsehood spoken openly and harshly, it, like the Mayor of Leicester's violent claims that she is a "fals strumpet" and a "fals loller" years later (p. 112), takes on the nature of uncharitable reproof, intended to rob her of her honor, her standing as a holy woman.

Now we come to the question pastoral writers and Langland explored so urgently and extensively: How can we distinguish charitable correction from chiding and uncharitable reproof? No doubt the Canterbury monks thought of their own speech as fraternal correction, Margery Kempe's as chiding. Similarly, the incident in London near the close of the *Book* raises the equally vexed question of how to distinguish correction from slander, again an old pastoral issue – and one made urgent by Wycliffites. Since inner desire and inner-directedness cannot be known by others directly, how can the *Book*'s holy woman assume the mantle of fraternal corrector without being accused of the deviant speech of which the *Book* accuses her adversarial townsmen, her fellow pilgrims, the Mayor of Leicester, and the Canterbury monks (among others)?

The great initial test of Margery Kempe's speech as a corrector of sin comes during her encounter with Archbishop Arundel himself, just four years after the Constitutions were promulgated (1413). Waiting in Lambeth's great hall to petition him to take communion weekly and to name her own confessor (both unusual practices), she overhears his retinue (as she would Bowet's years later) swearing "gret othis." Her response is the same as that at York, which opened this book: She rebukes the men boldly, priests among them, claiming that they will be damned unless they forsake the practice. (Notice that she does not seek out sinners; they sin against her by swearing in her presence, offending her and giving scandal.) When she meets the Archbishop in his garden, she "boldly spak to him for the correccion of his meny [household, retinue]," accusing him of abusing his office by maintaining traitors to God and then claiming that he is responsible for their sins: "Ye schal answer for hem les than [unless] ye corre ctyn hem or ellys put hem owt of yowr servise" (p. 37).

What makes proper this bourgeois woman's astonishingly forthright correction of this formidable nobleman, Lord Chancellor, Oxford graduate, leader of the rebellion against Richard II, judge of Wycliffites, is, first of all, that blasphemy was widely condemned by the movement of pastoral reform, as I demonstrated at the outset of this study. There are no ambiguous, disputable words here, marking her words then as fraternal correction, instead of slanderous lies or chiding. Moreover, canon law specifically licensed correcting a bishop who neglects to amend such swearing: "si episcopus ista emendare neglexerit, acerrime corripiatur." A bishop, as head of a *familia*, was particularly bound to correct the sins of those belonging to his household. According to John Bromyard, the *familiares* of great prelates tend to sin quite freely because they believe that bearing a prelate's livery protects them from correction like a shield or letter of safe conduct. Prelates who neglect to correct their *familiares* will be punished severely by God: temporal suffering, *infamia*, and eternal damnation.[50] Thus even Margery Kempe's stress on prelatical accountability to God is authorized by canon law and pastoral writing. As Jeffrey Cohen writes generally of this episode and that at York, her "reproach enables her to master authority in its own arena of performance, catching up those who were supposed to represent Law by invoking its strictures against them."[51]

Margery Kempe also validates her practice of correction by following pastoral norms and constraints as strictly as any pastoral writer advocated.[52] She clearly seeks what makes corrective speech virtuous: the end of amending sinners. In the reproof itself she suggests two remedies for the Archbishop's complicity in his retinue's sinful acts, and for the acts themselves: correcting the men successfully or dismissing them from his service. The very same remedies for a sinning bishop and his retinue are advanced by her beloved St. Birgitta: "For, if he [a bishop] knawe one of his meine sin dedely, he suld stir him to amendment. And, if he will noght amend him, he suld put him away fro him."[53] Margery Kempe also follows strictly the particular norms governing disciplinary inferiors who correct disciplinary superiors. The *Book* takes pains to note that she addresses the Archbishop "with reverens." She rebukes him in the privacy of his garden. His toleration of blasphemy in his own great hall might be construed as manifest sin that, like Peter's at Antioch, justifies public reproof because it scandalizes others, but she chooses tactfully to rebuke him in the manner of Matthew 18:15, "inter te et ipsum solum." Thus she preserves his *fama*. Scrupulously adhering to these constraints also stands her in good stead as a bourgeois woman rebuking the most powerful male in the English Church at a time when corrective speech was fraught with danger. It manifests her charity as she negotiates contrary goods, like speaking firmly but acknowledging institutional status, just as protecting a good like reputation does. In the whole *Book*, her correction contrasts sharply with prelatical correction that violates constraints and so fails in its end, beginning with the overly harsh confessor of the first chapter who drives her to despair.

Although Margery Kempe must react to inquisition by a whole phalanx of clerics with great institutional power at York, rather than initiating correction of one person herself, at York the rhetoric of fraternal correction allows her to achieve ends distinctively her own, as well as the traditional ends of correction.[54] She protects her very life by observing clerical norms, while at the same time subverting some of them, including not correcting groups and not carrying out revenge. Like the author of *Mum and the Sothsegger*, John Wyclif, and Wycliffite writers, she redefines what is good for the corrector, the corrected subject, and the Church. Unlike them, however, she does so in a specific situation by resorting to that clerically recommended resource for rebuking a sinner of greater institutional power: the *exemplum*.[55]

Margery Kempe is adhering to more than pastoral discourse by employing an *exemplum* to reprove powerful men. She is imitating her beloved Birgitta. After retelling briefly how King Ahab and Queen Jezebel were punished for seizing Naboth's vineyard (1 Kings 22), Birgitta reproves a lord for wrongfully acquiring others' goods: "And tharfor be ye wele ware that ye have noght of any mannes thinges with wronge, or agains his will, or stressand him to selle, or noght to pay him, that as fell a dome sall be on you as fell apon the qwene."[56] In this episode Birgitta has sources of authority that Margery Kempe lacks at York: aristocratic status, a biblical story, and a visionary message (from an angel). Indeed, the *Book* depicts Margery Kempe turning to an *exemplum* after the Latin-educated Church officials use their powers to attempt to silence her in ways much studied of late: Her inquisitors, we have seen, have labeled her a heretic; the Archbishop has forbidden her to teach or preach in his archdiocese; one of her inquisitors has toted out the Bible to theatricalize the Pauline prohibition against women speaking in church. The men display the sources of their authority, sources women could not share: ecclesiastical office, episcopal injunction, Latin book. So, they define Margery Kempe's subject position: female, lay, illiterate (in their eyes), unlicensed by the Church.[57] What provokes Margery Kempe to tell the *exemplum* is the clerics' very attempt to discredit the non-heretical speaking position she has just deftly marked out for herself: a mere speaker of correction and "good wordis," not a preacher. One of her learned inquisitors informs the Archbishop that she has told him "the werst talys of prestys that evyr I herde" – that is, she speaks ill of a whole social group. In the context of her interrogation, this accusation also works to align her with the Wycliffites, famous for their anticlericalism, particularly, as the previous chapter argues, their criticism of whole clerical communities or orders. Margery Kempe's sure response identifies her as an orthodox fraternal corrector. She "spak but of o preste þe the maner of exampyl" (p. 126), addressing only an individual's sin and doing so by means of John Bromyard's "cautum exemplum," which does not directly reprove another but invites him to transfer judgment from a figure in the narrative to himself.

As the *Book*'s Margery Kempe tells the tale at the Archbishop's command, it has exactly this effect on her clerical accuser. In the tale, a priest observes a bear pull down a lovely pear tree, devour its white blossoms, and defecate. An aged pilgrim then interprets the events for the confused priest. He, as priest, is the flourishing pear tree, but he, as sinner, is the bear, guilty of avarice, lechery, negligence in reciting the liturgy, gluttony, lies, and slander – sins traditionally identified by reformist pastoral writers worrying about corrupt and ineffectual priests. At the tale's close, Margery Kempe has the pilgrim speak as a fraternal corrector, using the events to move the story's sinful priest to amend his life: "Thus be thy misgovernawns, lich on-to the lothly ber, thu devowryst & destroyst the flowerys & blomys of vertuows levyng to thine endles dampnacyon & many mannys hindring lesse than [unless] thu have grace of repentawns & amending" (p. 127). Like the pilgrim whose voice she adopts here, Margery Kempe is the charitable corrector envisioned by pastoral discourse: Her speech combats clerically identified sin, and, concerned for the spiritual welfare of others, she seeks their amendment. Her very choice of an *exemplum* enacts this pastoral role because, as fiction, it creates the distance that prevents angry rejection, while, as similitude, it moves any sinful priest in hearing to see himself in the fictive priest. Her accuser then confesses to the Archbishop, as David confesses to Nathan in John Bromyard's entry on "correctio": "Ser, this tale smityth me to the hert." In response, she addresses him as "worchipful doctour," neatly displaying the reverence, the acknowledgment of high position and status expected by the *subditus* correcting the *praelatus* – here not just a cleric with the care of souls, but one who has exercised disciplinary authority over her by examining her for heresy and by accusing her of spreading vicious tales about the clergy. But she uses that very reverent address to drive home her rhetorical advantage (again indirectly) by reporting the saying of a favorite reformist preacher, "whech boldly spekyth agein the misgovernawns of the pepil & wil flatyr no man." "If any man," she reports him saying, "be evyl plesyd with my preching, note him wel, for he is gilty." "And rith so, ser," she says to her accuser, "far ye be me, god forgeve it yow" (pp. 127–8), suggesting that his early objections to her *exemplum*, and more broadly his opposition to her speech, springs from reluctance to face his own sins.

Margery Kempe negotiates the power differential in this specific situation in the approved pastoral manner – *exemplum*, reverence, concern for amendment, all displaying charity as the virtue governing her speech and gaining the approved end, the cleric's repentance. But she accomplishes much more. "Aftirward the same clerk cam to hir & preyid hir of forgefnes that he had so ben a-gein hir. Also he preyid hir specialy to prey for him" (p. 128). He not only reconciles himself to her and seeks forgiveness, that ancillary good of fraternal correction, but he is removed as an opponent. Moreover, this ecclesiastical authority – learned, male, priestly – acknowledges her pastoral power as manifested in the way she corrects.[58] He asks for her prayers, the sinner sensing her knowledge of his conscience and her skill in directing it toward salvation in accordance with religious law and pastoral teaching.[59] (That knowledge, of course, contrasts sharply with her slanderers' and scolders' inability, and unwillingness, to grasp her inner life.) Pastoral teaching has so informed Margery Kempe that she can exploit it, calculatedly, in this specific situation, in ways that appropriate clerical pastoral power and challenge clerical moral authority, all the while observing institutionalized power relations (akin to the way she appropriates pulpit rhetoric in Genelle Gertz-Robinson's subtle analysis of this episode).[60] The constructed subject becomes the constructing agent, using the practice of fraternal correction to resist oppressors, escape their nets, convert a prominent one of them, and enact what she sees as good for her, for them, and for the Church at York: reform of clerical sins. And was not that *exemplum*, which, after all, retails common complaints about clerical immorality and laxness, really aimed at all the clerics present, including the Archbishop? The priest in it does not repent at its close, leaving any cleric within earshot to be corrected by the pilgrim/Margery Kempe and to see his need to amend his life. Moreover, the *exemplum* makes her whole audience aware of the communal nature of sin, how the social conditions of priesthood – the regular reciting of liturgies and celibacy, for example – prompt priests to sin in certain ways, like mumbling the liturgy or fornicating. Thus, the exchange functions as part of an episode that discloses clerics' habitual, corporate (the York clergy acts as a group in the scene) abuse of institutional power and Latin learning. Most clerics at York use it to compel a laywoman to abandon the practice of fraternal correction, even though it is an essential element in the pastoral movement of reform.[61]

The *Book of Margery Kempe* constructs Kempe as an exemplary figure, making a case for her as a holy woman, perhaps, some have argued, even a saint who should be recognized officially.[62] Pastoral discourse on deviant speech and on fraternal correction recurrently directs this rhetorical shaping, as it does that of the truth-teller in *Mum and the Sothsegger*. In *Mum* Jesus' precept authorizes a life of truth-telling that reveals abuse of power to those in power. The *Book* invokes clerical norms on correction to refute slanderous lies; to restore the will, intention, and causes behind Margery Kempe's public acts of affective piety and correction; to retrieve her stolen good name as a holy woman; and to evade clerical authorities who might restrict, punish, or even kill her. The beekeeper's norms for corrective speech in *Mum* should ensure a hearing for the office-holding truth-teller, so that he, retailing the grievances of the commons, may move King Henry IV, his Council, and others holding authority in state and Church, to reform political practices. Margery Kempe's ostentatious obedience to some constraints is exemplary in itself and manifests a charity and an exemplary readiness to engage in what André Vauchez calls "the church's exaltation of apostolic action."[63] When she exposes vice, pastoral catechesis so informs her speech that she differentiates herself from the *Book*'s deviant speakers even as she turns the tables on her slanderers and accusers, whether envious lay people or powerful clerics who betray the pastoral movement by attempting to silence a woman who is manifestly its apostle.

Postscript

Feminist theory has so shaped literary analysis of *The Book of Margery Kempe* over several decades that it has largely escaped the fate of many medieval narratives since the linguistic turn of the late 1960s: to be read mainly, for some years, in terms of self-reflexive worries about authority, language, and status. By focusing on gender, feminist reading has sharpened our sense of the strategies by which men in the *Book* consolidate, preserve, and manifest their institutionalized power and of the strategies by which Margery Kempe resists, critiques, and (in more recent readings) negotiates male assertions of power. That is, it has accomplished what Foucauldian analysis of confession does, but more subtly and comprehensively. Women's history, literary and social especially, has informed and enriched these readings by recovering discourses that women employed, among themselves and in conflict with male authorities, like that of the unruly female body (Lochrie), the visionary (Voaden), and the preacher (Gertz-Robinson). As a result, readers have reckoned seriously with the *Book*'s claims for Margery Kempe's exemplarity, its authors' attempts to affect the religious and social practices of medieval women – and men as well. They have considered what the text suggests it can do, the ways it might be practiced by readers and auditors (I echo J. Allan Mitchell's fine introduction to *Ethics and Exemplary Narrative in Chaucer and Gower*).

In reading *The Book of Margery Kempe* in the light of pastoral discourse on fraternal correction, I have paid attention to how Margery Kempe uses that discourse and the practice it constructs to negotiate power relations, how they provide her with a social role and with a repertoire of strategies, of rhetorical resources, and norms for speech at once protective and reformist. I have also moved in concert with feminist analysis, but slightly beyond its present bounds, to consider the ends and the goods that she pursues by practicing fraternal correction, what she works for as good for herself as a laywoman aspiring to holiness, for others, and for the Church: amendment of sinning clerics' lives and (to choose a second) space for a woman as a subject of male disciplinary power to admonish anyone, no matter what his or her status or power. To read the *Book* with these bifocals, looking at both power relations and ethics – and, above all, at the way they are intertwined – is to recover some ways in which it is exemplary. The *Book* aims to affect its readers' moral practices and to critique institutions and social groups. It is to read the *Book* as what the historian Andrew Brown calls "a tool of spiritual renewal within a long tradition of pastoral reform."[1]

Taken together with *Mum and the Sothsegger* some thirty years before, with Wycliffite writing of the twenty-five years before *Mum*, and with *Piers Plowman* and John Wyclif's theology of correction in the decade before that, *The Book of Margery Kempe* witnesses to the continued vitality and influence of discourse on fraternal correction as a reformist practice. In *Mum*, as in the *Book*, pastoral discourse licenses reformist speech in a culture more resistant than that of the early-to-mid fourteenth century and of the fermentative years of 1375–1409, presenting in the culturally sanctioned mode of fraternal correction the poet's own satire of abuses in Church and state and the exemplary truth-teller's voicing of the commons' grievances to King Henry IV, his Council, nobles, and prelates. For Wycliffite writers in the two decades just before *Mum*, discourse on fraternal correction provided a way of legitimizing their vehement, often criticized polemics against ecclesiastical communities and institutions. Correction defining them as "true" to scripture and Jesus and as followers of Wyclif, they could use it to discredit the fraternal orders, possessioners' authority to carry out pastoral care, and lay lords' hand in suppressing "true men." For Wyclif just before them, fraternal correction was the practice that could become a potent reformist tool, doing nothing less than providing an ordered, quasi-legal, biblically authorized means of disendowing the clergy, taking tithes out of their hands, and withdrawing obedience from the Pope because he held temporal goods and powers. Even the famously indeterminate *Piers Plowman*, which resists making its dreamer exemplary, advocates fraternal correction as a normative type of speech that tackles known sins, especially abuses of pastoral care by mercenary clerics and their communities.

This study of fraternal correction as a moral practice constructed by the clergy to operate within existing power relations and of reformers' expansion of the practice, seizing on its radical possibilities to help realize what they thought good for themselves and the Church, goes some distance in addressing the central questions raised about pastoral discourse and about the pastoral movement to instruct and reform the laity and clergy alike. How far did pastoral teaching permeate English society? What effects did it have?[2]

Discourse on fraternal correction was so far mastered by lower clerics like Langland and lay people like the Margery Kempe of the *Book* and the author of *Mum* (presumably lay) that it could be critically redeployed. While they could have picked up the pastoral norms and constraints from advanced catechesis with clerics sympathetic to their social, religious, and political concerns, sermons could also have conveyed them and even the canons on reproving bishops who have not corrected the blasphemous speech habits of their retainers or on the culpability of those who witness sin and refuse to reprove it. Even the brief vernacular sermons of the *Northern Homily Cycle* transmit both the four-step practice of correction, carefully marking who does what when, and the need for self-reflection in zealous correctors of others' sins. The many sermons surviving in Latin versions of varying degrees of completeness have been neglected (save for literary historians of preaching, like H. Leith Spencer and Siegfried Wenzel) as a source for knowing what was actually transmitted to people orally.[3] So has been informal and group catechesis, which, of course, leaves only traces like Margery Kempe's conversations with the Carthusian Alan of Lynn in the *Book*.

Fraternal correction witnesses more fully to the effects of pastoral discourse and of the movement of pastoral reform than to its extent. Even though those effects are limited to writers, their works are of considerable variety – dream vision, theological treatise, polemic, life, political satire – and they include figures imagined as practicing correction, like Will (of indeterminate "low" social status), Peres the Plowman, and the lay "sothsegger." Most obviously for those of us raised on methods of reading from the linguistic turn, it authorizes reformist texts themselves. It founds them in evangelical law. How often are Matthew 18:15–17 and other texts like Leviticus 19:17 and Galatians 2 (Paul reproving Peter) cited or even quoted? Pastoral discourse also gives them ethical reasoning, sets of sanctioned norms, even a recognizable rhetoric for demonstrating their pastoral power to critique abuses, not least of all at times when religious writing was under greater surveillance and could lead to severe punishments. Of more importance within these texts – and this has not been recognized even by historical critics, preoccupied as they are with meaning, not rhetorical effect (again, I echo J. Allan Mitchell) – pastoral discourse on correction provides a means to persuade, even to obligate, reform-minded readers to voice criticism of ecclesiastical, economic, social, and political abuses.[4] As a textually constructed practice, fraternal correction becomes a mode of critiquing the conduct of those with disciplinary power in Church and state while at the same time recognizing that power (save for Wyclif and his followers, who would reduce clerical power to admonition alone – and they certainly bow to state powers: of king, of lay magnates, of civil judges).

Recent scholarship on Wycliffism, vernacular religious writing, and Archbishop Arundel's Constitutions has hammered home the limits on pastoral teaching imposed by many, probably most, clerics, who viewed the laity as prone to heresy and puerile, capable only of grasping the literal and fundamentals like the Decalogue or the Creed. Even the historian of lay religious knowledge and practice across Western Europe, André Vauchez, has tended to stress the limited success of pastoral reform due to fear that lay people might "slip into heresy" or discuss religious matters "without proper guidance."⁵ Yet this is only part of the story of the movement of pastoral reform. Pastoral discourse on fraternal correction, as it is built into the texts I have studied, points in another direction. As an agent of pastoral reform of individual lives, it aims first of all, like all pastoral discourse on the virtues and vices, to induce all Christians to become ethically reflective, to examine their wills, their intentions, the likely consequences of corrective speech. In giving them the capacity for ethical reflection, it also gives them moral norms and ethical reasoning (of varying sophistication, certainly, depending on the writer and audience). That is to say, it transmits social ethics, as all discourse on the vices and virtues does. Once Christians can manifest the power to know the hearts of others and to guide them to what is good in terms of religious law, they can actualize pastoral power in specific situations, as pastoral discourse on correction encourages them to do, critiquing individuals' conduct on the basis of pastoral social ethics, no matter how great the sinners' learning and institutionalized power. Through sermon, catechesis, and pastoral texts (for writers who could read them), pastoral discourse, with its exploration of contrary goods and ambiguous texts, also gave reformist writers across the spectrum and, through them, their audiences the rhetorical resources to judge, modify, and expand pastorally advocated practices. Fraternal correction may have been constructed in ways that entrenched clerical power (as I argued in chapter 1), but it contained within itself materials, built into its sacred texts, to scrutinize critically and speak out against clerical and political vices, along with the institutional practices that fed them. Wycliffite polemics against the fraternal orders and Wyclif's procedures for disendowing the whole English clergy, just like Margery Kempe's *exemplum* at York or Will's rebuke of his friar-confessor, were founded on the discourse of pastoral reform itself, not least of all on its requirement that subjects reprove the sins of those who have disciplinary power over them.

Notes

INTRODUCTION

1. Cohen, "The Ethicist," p. 16.
2. The last dissertation I can find is Costello's *The Moral Obligation of Fraternal Correction* of 1949. While Costello cites some medieval moral theologians briefly, his study is less historical than moral.
3. Shogimen, *Ockham*, p. 106. See pp. 107–13 for his general exposition of the theology of fraternal correction from *c.* 1200 to 1350.
4. General and specialist dictionaries of medieval Latin define "correctio" as reproof, discipline, instruction, reformation, amendment, so that its semantic reach takes in the result of corrective speech, as well as the speech itself; they define "correptio" as reproof, correction, chastisement, words for the corrective act of speech alone (e.g., *DML*; Deferrari, *Latin–English Dictionary*). Nevertheless, the terms and their verbal forms are used interchangeably by most pastoral writers (e.g., James le Palmer (attrib.), *Omne bonum*, British Library MS Royal 6.E.VI, f. 435ʳ; William of Nottingham, Commentary, Bodleian Library Oxford MS Laud misc. 165, f. 351ᵛ).
5. In addition to substantial entries, fraternal correction could be treated more briefly under various topics in pastoral texts. Entries on fraternal correction do not appear in most pastoral manuals, like William of Pagula's *Oculus sacerdotis* or Richard of Wetheringsett's *Summa de doctrina sacerdotali*. These manuals were written to instruct the clergy, largely in how to administer the sacraments, rather than to provide material for preaching, as the *distinctiones* and large alphabetical collections did.
6. For these preaching occasions, see chapter 1.
7. Specific texts in all these pastoral genres are described and situated historically as they are introduced, and I give the number of manuscripts extant in British libraries.
8. In the wake of Moore's bold and provocative *The Formation of a Persecuting Society*, many scholars have treated clerical culture as repressive and exclusivistic. One example: avowedly directed by Moore's study, Page characterizes the clerical *literati* who were centralizing the power of the twelfth-century French state as having "a neurotic dread of subversion" and "a desire to tighten the grip of centralised authority on all human relations" (*The Owl and the Nightingale*, p. 6). Behind such ways of seeing clerical culture often

lies Jacques Le Goff's influential binary formulation of an elite, learned clerical culture and a valorized popular culture, often understood by others in Bakhtinian terms: Clerical culture is monolithic (and therefore repressive) and popular culture is polyvalent (and therefore liberating). So, we get narratives of clerical domination and popular resistance. For a skeptical view of Le Goff's dichotomy, see Miller, "Religion."

9. Kerby-Fulton, "Prophecy and Suspicion," pp. 318–41; a revised version appears as chapter four of her *Books Under Suspicion*.

10. Shaw, "Social Selves," p. 3.

11. An excellent (and rare) example of scholarship that places a pastoral writer and his readers in a specific locale at a certain time: Hanna's study of the Middle English translation of Robert of Gretham's *Miroir*, which Hanna thinks may have been done for a London parish guild *c.* 1310–20 (*London Literature*, pp. 177–202).

12. Aers and Staley, *Powers*, pp. 15–58.

13. Strohm, "Afterword," p. 226.

14. Asad argues that monastic practices, like manual labor and public confession of faults, regulated and formed the virtue of humility in twelfth-century monastic life (*Genealogies*, pp. 125–67). While charity in the pastoral tradition I will explore, unlike justice, is a theological virtue infused in the will by God, we learn to exercise charity as we do justice or other virtues: through the example and instruction of others in communities (Sherwin, *By Knowledge*, pp. 204–38).

15. Frazer and Lacey, "MacIntyre, Feminism," pp. 271, 276. MacIntyre's concept of practice is discussed in my first chapter, pp. 26–7.

16. Brown, *Church and Society*, p. 7; see also pp. 16–17.

17. Sandler, *Omne bonum*; the initials are presented on p. 137 of vol. II and the first initial is described on p. 106 of vol. I. Sandler has identified James le Palmer as the scribe, major illuminator, and, probably, compiler.

CHAPTER I

1. The extent to which Margery Kempe of Lynn authored the *Book* and the extent to which her two scribes (the first lay and the second clerical) or someone else did is still unsettled. In 1975, Hirsch argued confidently from internal evidence that the second scribe was closely involved in composition, a position which, while not widely accepted, has not been wholly refuted ("Author and Scribe," pp. 145–50). If accepted, this collaborative authorship would open the way to seeing the cleric's learning and concerns as shaping the text somewhat. Adding more uncertainty, even the traditional position on the roles of the two scribes is not securely founded: that the first scribe wrote all of Part I while the second revised I and wrote II. The question of the scribes' roles in authorship has been taken into new territory by Staley, who, distinguishing between an author (Kempe) and a screen/persona (Margery),

regards the scribes as a trope employed by Kempe to lend authority to the
Book, in the manner of established writing about holy women mediated by
scribes (*Dissenting Fictions*, pp. 1–38). Recently, Watson has made interesting
arguments for the first scribe being Margery Kempe's son, for the revised Part I
being close to the original, and for Kempe collaborating closely with the second
scribe in writing Part II ("Making," pp. 395–435). Given these profoundly unsettled issues, I have adopted the agnostic's dodge, simply referring to "the *Book*"
and taking no position on authorship, a stance appropriate, I believe, to a book
which explores the speech of a holy woman and her adversaries as it is constructed for readers and listeners. As I argue in chapter 6, the *Book*'s Margery
is presented as so thoroughly shaped by pastoral discourse on sin that it would
be well nigh impossible to accomplish what criticism of the Christian Gospels
often attempts: convincingly sifting out the words of the holy person from the
writers' (in this case, scribes' or, perhaps, author's) overlay.

2. Steele, *Theorizing*, p. 1.
3. Vauchez, *Laity*, p. 104.
4. Craun, "*Inordinata Locutio*"; Casagrande and Vecchio, *I Peccati*, pp. 229–40.
   For the punishment of blasphemers in English wall paintings, see Gill,
   "Urban Myth."
5. These dimensions of social power, understood as broadly political, I have
   taken from Aers and Staley's list in *Powers*, p. 3. Some studies, unlike those
   of Aers and Staley, tend to scant or even erase ethics as they exfoliate power
   relations.
6. Steele, *Theorizing*, p. 1. Throughout *Philosophical Chaucer*, Miller makes an
   extended argument for why agency cannot be understood simply in terms
   of the cultural construction of the subject.
7. *Book*, pp. 125–6. All further references are to this edition.
8. I paraphrase loosely Ricoeur's definition of ethical intentionality in *Oneself*,
   p. 172: "aiming at the 'good life' with and for others, in just institutions."
   Ricoeur proceeds to develop how the self which aims to live well takes
   responsibility for others and for the life of institutions (through p. 202).
   I am indebted to Norm Klassen, who pointed out to me the easy passage
   from ethics to politics in this formulation.
9. Steele, *Theorizing*, p. 107.
10. The term "pastoral offensive" is Vauchez's in "Church," p. 183.
11. Foucault, "The Subject," p. 214.
12. Craun, *Lies*, pp. 10–11.
13. Patterson, "The Parson's Tale," p. 341.
14. *Speculum juniorum*, Bodleian Library Oxford MS Bodl. 767, f. 11ᵛ. Fourteen
    manuscripts of the *Speculum* survive, many of the fourteenth century,
    according to the catalogues of the collections containing them. Boyle has
    found evidence indicating that the author was a "Magister Galienus"; he
    dates the *Speculum* 1260–70 ("Three English Pastoral *Summae*," pp. 141–4).
    Many of the same definitions of sin can be found 150 or more years later

in Alexander Carpenter's *Destructorium viciorum* (*c.* 1420), indicating how longlasting and pervasive they are (f. ai^r).

15. Bromyard, *Opus trivium*, unpaged. This compendium for preachers survives in six manuscripts, all of the fourteenth century, found in British libraries (Kaeppeli, *Scriptores*, vol. II, p. 393).

16. Miller, "Religion," pp. 1,096–7; Watt, "Papacy," p. 122.

17. *Constitutiones*, pp. 53, 74–5.

18. Rusconi, "Prédication," p. 71.

19. *Constitutiones*, pp. 58–9.

20. *Constitutiones*, pp. 67–8; Rusconi, "Prédication"; Tentler, *Sin and Confession*, especially pp. xiv and 346.

21. Luke 17:3 also enjoins Christians to rebuke those who sin against them: "Si peccaverit in te frater tuus, increpa illum: et si poenitentiam ergerit, dimitte illi." This text rarely attracts pastoral writers and preachers, probably because Matthew 18:15–17 offers a detailed procedure and because Luke 17:3 was not part of a lection.

22. Ambrose, *Epistulae*, vol. III, pp. 57–8. Ambrose, *Expositio*, p. 195.

23. Augustine's most extended preaching on brotherly rebuke is in his sermon on Matthew 18:15–17 (*Sermones ad populum* 82, cols. 506–14). Some examples of his other writing on the topic: In *De civitate Dei*, he argues that Christians should practice it to avert divine correction (Part 1, pp. 17–18), and he refers to Paul correcting Peter throughout *De correptione et gratia* and in *Contra Faustum* (p. 515).

24. Lawless reviews the evidence on whether the *Regula* was written for men, for women, or for both and on the dating of the *Regula* and the later *Regularis informatio* for nuns (*Augustine*, pp. 135–54).

25. *La règle*, vol. I, pp. 426–7.

26. Verheijen's *La règle* gives a diplomatic text of the MS Rheinau (Zürich) 89 copy of the *Regularis informatio* (vol. I, pp. 53–66). "Soror" replaces "frater" consistently, as in "Magis quippe innocentes non estis, si sorores vestras quas judicando corrigere potestis, tacendo perire permittitis" (p. 59).

27. Hinnebusch, *History*, vol. I, p. 44.

28. The Dominican Constitutions establish a daily chapter of faults, during which the prior ordinarily presided and addressed the friars on anything that might expedite their correction. Friars were to confess their own infractions of the Rule and also accuse other friars, though only on sight or hearsay (with the source named). Novices and *conversi* had their own daily chapters of faults, and it was part of the procedure for both provincial chapters and general chapters. Galbraith explains the procedure in *Constitution*, pp. 41–3; his second appendix provides an edition of the Constitutions from a mid-fourteenth-century British manuscript. The *Constitutiones Narbonenses* of the Franciscan order (1260) mandates that the *guardianus* hold a weekly chapter in which the friars should accuse themselves and each other of infractions of the Rule and statutes (*Statuta*, p. 86). The Benedictines on the Continent had instituted a daily chapter of faults before the tenth century. Thomas

Aquinas and other writers distinguish fraternal correction from accusations in the chapter of faults on two grounds: The latter is public from the outset and it deals only with minor matters (*Summa theologiae*, 2.2.33, 4 and 5).

29. Ailred of Rievaulx, *De spirituali amicitia*, 3.104–8; Peter Damian, "De ferenda," cols. 708–10; Francis of Assisi, *Regula bullata*, 5.5. The Statues of Paris are edited in the *Constitutiones Narbonenses*, in *Statuta*, p. 80.

30. Alexander of Hales, *Quaestiones*, vol. XIX, cols. 497–516, and vol. XXI, cols. 1,510–26; *Glossa*, vol. XV, pp. 342–7; Shogimen, *Ockham*, pp. 107–9. While Alexander treats many of the questions, offers many of the solutions, and writes many of the authoritative *sententiae* that later pastoral writers do, the wording in most pastoral texts is much closer to that of Thomas Aquinas.

31. In the *Summa theologiae* Thomas Aquinas considers fraternal correction an outward act or effect of charity, along with kindness and almsgiving (2.2.31–3). Jordan argues that Thomas's *Summa* should not be regarded simply as academic theology, but that it is "a hybrid genre, at once academic and pastoral." In truth, Thomas's "main effort was directed at expanding the pastoral and practical program of the Dominican houses" (*Cure of Souls*, p. 33). Thomas also treated fraternal correction extensively in a *quaestio disputata* (see chapter 2) and in his commentary on the *Sentences* of Peter Lombard (*Scriptum*, 4.19.2). Thomas's fellow Dominican Hugh Ripelin also takes up fraternal correction in his widely disseminated *Compendium*, but only in a paragraph under evangelical counsels (5.70). Thomas's fellow Dominican Albert the Great does not treat fraternal correction in his theological *summa*, but does at some length in two commentaries on the Gospels.

32. Colish, "Early Scholastics," p. 61.

33. Haren observes that the practical social morality promoted by Pierre le Chantre and his circle, a morality based in the Bible and applied to contemporary social practices and organization, became the concern of canonists in the thirteenth century ("Social Ideas," p. 54). Exact citations of canons, including the abbreviated Latin titles by which they were known, draw them and their commentaries into pastoral texts and sermons, much as citations to theological or biblical texts do. In this way readers were directed to the full canon in the *Decretum* (mid twelfth century), the *Five Books of the Decretals* (1234), or later collections. The titles may also have reminded some clerics of canons that they had memorized while in the schools of law (Brundage, *Canon Law*, pp. 52–3).

34. Colish, "Early Scholastics," p. 61.

35. *Speculum spiritualium*, pp. clxvii^r–clxx^r. Doyle summarizes research on the date, contents, and readership of the *Speculum* in "*Speculum spiritualium*." Johann von Freiburg, *Summa confessorum*, 3.9.3–9 (unpaged).

36. McGrade examines how William of Ockham invokes the traditional distinction between prelatical and fraternal correction, but then dismisses its significance by insisting that the corrected person's cognitive assessment of the validity of rebuke is what matters most in correction. William develops this

position in order to portray Pope John XXII as a heretic because he clung pertinaciously to erroneous teachings even when they were demonstrated to be false (*Political Thought*, pp. 41–77). See also Shogimen, *Ockham*.

37. Higden, *Speculum curatorum*, Balliol College Oxford MS 77, ff. 20ᵛ–1ᵛ. Five copies of all or part of the *Speculum* of 1340 survive (Sharpe, *Handlist*, pp. 454–5), and in 1350 Higden made a second version, which survives only in University of Illinois MS 251/H53.

38. Bromyard, *Summa praedicantium*, c.21.8 and 9 (unpaged). This vast alphabetical compendium for preachers was composed over twenty years and was finished between 1348 and 1352. The *Summa* as a whole (there are several sets of excerpts) survives in four manuscripts, with two more attested (Sharpe, *Handlist*, pp. 220–1); one of the four may be securely placed in the fourteenth century (Kaeppeli, *Scriptores*, vol. II, p. 394). On the *Summa*'s use by preachers, see Wenzel, *Latin Sermon Collections*, pp. 322–5.

39. For Sandler's identification of James le Palmer as the scribe, major illuminator, and, probably, compiler, see *Omne bonum*, vol. I, pp. 16–26.

40. Of the fourteen manuscripts surviving in British libraries, thirteen of them come from the early fourteenth century (Kaeppeli, *Scriptores*, vol. II, pp. 430–2). For Boyle's estimation, see "The *Summa*," p. 258. Johann places his *quaestiones* on fraternal correction under a *titulus* "De doctrina ordinandorum," the first two *quaestiones* of which are devoted to clerical correction, preaching, and clerical teaching. His bridge between the two sets of *quaestiones* suggests that the two are related, but does not specify how: "Quia supra de correctione prelatorum mentio habita est quero etiam his generaliter utrum fraterna correctio sit in precepto" (3.9.3).

41. For the *Summa*'s manuscripts in British libraries, see Kaeppeli, *Scriptores*, vol. I, pp. 158–65. The entry is entitled "correctio ii.scilicet.fraterna"; it follows "correccio primo.scilicet.punicio quam prelatus habet facere." With considerable reluctance, I omit from among the *summae* the *Summa de casibus conscientiae* of the Franciscan Astesano da Asti, with its long, rich entry on fraternal correction, replete with Franciscan theological texts, because the only extant manuscript in British libraries was copied sometime in the fifteenth century (Bodleian Library Oxford MSS Canon Misc. 208 and 209).

42. Wenzel, *Latin Sermon Collections*, pp. 233–4.

43. Matthew 18:15–22 was the lection for the Tuesday after the third Sunday in Quadragesima in parishes following the Sarum, York, and Hereford use, and in Franciscan, Dominican, and Benedictine houses. *Sarum Missal*, p. 75; *Missale Eboracensis*, vol. I, p. 68; *Missale Herefordensis*, p. 62; *Ordo missalis*, p. 228; *Officia varia*, British Library MS Add. 23935, f. 551ᵛ; *Missale Westmonasteriensis*, vol. I, col. 162. I have not included sermons from the *sanctorale* as sources because most saints in the calendar were clerics or Roman martyrs who rebuked pagan officials, not fellow Christians.

44. The original cycle, made up solely of sermons on the Sunday Gospels, was composed in the late thirteenth century; Heffernan has determined from its

pericopes that it was "a product of the Austin canons and was used by them throughout their catechetical ministry in northern England at the end of the 13th century" ("Authorship," p. 292). This expanded version of the cycle, which provides sermons for the entire liturgical year, survives in two manuscripts, dated 1385 and 1392 (Heffernan and Horner, "Sermons," p. 4,258). Sermons for other preaching occasions than Sunday, like the Tuesday in Lent when Matthew 18: 15–22 sermons were preached, were added from the mid fourteenth century. These sermons are largely paraphrases of the Gospel for the occasion, though the Sunday sermons contain *narrationes*.

45. Both the Franciscan Rule and the Dominican constitutions establish visitation as charitable correction (Francis of Assisi, *Regula bullata*, 10.1; Galbraith, *Constitution*, pp. 155 ff.). In his entry "Visitatio" in the *Summa*, Bromyard includes, in his second article, the sketch of a visitation sermon on the *thema* "Si autem peccaverit in te frater tuus" among a number of *collaciones* for visitations to secular priests. Siegfried Wenzel kindly directed me to this passage. In the third article, which deals with visiting religious houses, Bromyard insists that Matthew 18:15–17 should dictate the procedure for the corrector as he makes an *accusatio*, charging someone or a group with an offence (U.8.2, 3). On visitation sermons as models for preaching on other occasions and elsewhere, see Wenzel, *Latin Sermon Collections*, pp. 244–5.

46. Luke 6:36–42 was the lection for the fourth Sunday after Trinity in Sarum, York, and Hereford rite parishes, in Dominican houses, and in at least some Benedictine houses, but for Trinity Sunday itself in Franciscan houses (*Sarum Missal*, p. 177; *Missale Eboracensis*, vol. I, p. 224; *Missale Herefordensis*, p. 184; *Officia varia*, f. 564ʳ; *Missale Westmonasteriensis*, vol. I, cols. 404–5; *Ordo missalis*, p. 261).

47. I have included William's commentary as a source because its indices and abridgments (granted, the surviving ones are of the early fifteenth century) indicate that it was "converted into a homilary." It is worth quoting Spencer more fully as she generalizes about its use: "The proposed audience and destined purpose of a medieval religious text – when these may be ascertained – need by no means circumscribe its use in actuality: for the man casting about for something to preach, or for something to supplement his sermon, religious prose constituted a reservoir of *materia praedicabilia*, a repository of preachable doctrine which was the common property of all" (*English Preaching*, p. 35). For the manuscripts, see Sharpe, *Handlist*, p. 796.

48. Haren, "Interrogatories," pp. 127–31. Bromyard, *Summa*, C.21.8 and 9.

49. Wenzel, *Latin Sermon Collections*, p. 399.

50. Swidler, *Talk of Love*, pp. 178–9, 94–9. It is the ideological cast of discourse on fraternal correction, and the institutional order that sustains both the discourse and fraternal correction, that keep me from conceiving of it as a practice in Bourdieu's terms: a strategy organized logically by unconscious schemes and governed by intuitive skills or tact (*Logic of Practice*, pp. 52–65). Reproof of others' sins during the pastoral offensive may indeed have been,

in part, a practice as conceived by Bourdieu, and it may have been even more so before. At least among the textualized subjects of the clergy like Margery Kempe or English reformist writers of the fourteenth and fifteenth centuries, however, it is overlaid and regulated by a self-conscious, explicit pastoral discourse.

51. This distinction between moral and ethical reasoning has been drawn cogently by Aiken in "Moral Discourse," pp. 235–47.

52. The canon, in the modern style, is c.24 q.3 c.14 (*Corpus*, vol. 1, col. 994). This is apparently the canon to which Bromyard refers inexactly in arguing that all Christians are required to correct the sins of others ("Ideo dicit Canon quod non solum prelatus sed quilibet tenetur peccatorem corripere" [*Summa*, c.16.2]).

53. "'Sacerdotes,' inquit, 'et relique fideles.' Nullum enim excludere voluit a rigore fraterne correpcionis, que pro ejus emendacione sub precepto cadit." British Library MS Royal 7.A.VIII, f. 316ʳ. One of a series of visitation sermons, this (no. 129) is the second to develop the *thema* "Corripe eum inter te et ipsum" (Matthew 18:15). If this was preached at a monastic visitation, which I suspect, the sermon would have been given after the bishop celebrated the office and before he opened the inquiry in the chapter house (Coulet, *Visites pastorales*, p. 29).

54. James le Palmer (attrib.), *Omne bonum*, ff. 435ʳ, 435ᵛ; from Thomas Aquinas, *Summa theologiae* 2.2.33, 3 and 2 (Thomas quotes the canon in full). Augustine's warning ("Si neglexeris [corrigere], pejor es [eo qui peccavit]") comes from *Sermones ad populum* 82.4.7 (col. 508). Hugh Ripelin argues that fraternal correction is only counseled by the Gospel, not commanded, when the evildoing the corrector observes is venial, not mortal, sin (*Compendium*, 5.70); Thomas does not take up venial sin and neither do most pastoral compilers.

55. MacIntyre, *After Virtue*, pp. 52–3.

56. "Sed actus virtutis non quolibet modo fiere debent, sed observatis debitis circumstanciis que requirunter ad hoc quod actus sit virtuosus: scilicet ut fiat ubi debet et secundum quod debet. Et quia disposicio ejus que sit ad bonum finem attenditur secundum rationem finis, in istis circumstanciis virtuosi actus precipue attendenda est ratio finis, quod est bonum virtutis. Si ergo talis aliqua circumstantia omittatur circa actum virtuosum qua totaliter tollit bonum virtutis, hoc contrariatur precepto. Si autem defectus alicuius circumstancie sit que non totaliter tollit virtutem, licet non perfecte attingat ad bonum virtutis, non est contra preceptum domini …¶Correctio autem fraterna ordinatur ad emendacionem fratris et ideo hoc modo cadit sub precepto secundum quod est necesse ad istum finem, non autem quod quolibet modo aut tempore peccator corrigatur" (James le Palmer (attrib.), *Omne bonum*, f. 435ᵛ). See also Higden, *Speculum*, f. 20ᵛ; Johann von Freiburg, *Summa*, 3.9.3; British Library MS Royal 7.A.VIII, f. 315ʳ, from Thomas Aquinas, *Summa*, 2.2.33, 2.

57. "Alio modo pretermittitur fraterna correctio cum peccato mortali, scilicet cum 'formidatur,' ut ibi dicitur, 'judicium vulgi et carnis cruciatio vel

peremptio, dum tamen hoc ita dominentur in animo quod fraterna caritate preponantur'" (Johann von Freiburg, *Summa*, 3.9.3). Also Higden,
Speculum, f. 20ᵛ; James le Palmer (attrib.), *Omne bonum*, f. 435ᵛ; Bartolomeo
da San Concordio, *Summa de casibus*, unpaged under "correctio fraterna."
All four texts then distinguish this total failure to correct, a mortal sin,
from a venial sin, incurred when fear or self-interest makes us slow to correct evildoing, but the charity in our hearts eventually prompts us to do so.
Augustine, *De civitate Dei*, Part i, pp. 17–18.

58. James le Palmer (attrib.), *Omne bonum*, f. 435ʳ, from Thomas Aquinas,
Summa, 2.2.33, 1. In this psychology of human action, derived from Thomas,
charity moves humans to the virtuous end and the acts that realize that
end, while other virtues (prudence in fraternal correction) measure specific
means. Sherwin gives a general account of the relation of other virtues and
knowledge to charity, though he does not treat fraternal correction, where
no virtue other than prudence is involved (*By Knowledge*, pp. 47–203).

59. "quia quilibet tenetur proximo lege charitatis subvenire" (Bromyard,
Summa, A.21.7). Jan Ziolokowski has suggested to me that Bromyard's treatment of fraternal correction in part under *amicitia* points to the monastic origin of the practice. Bishop Brinton's sermon: "*Diliges proximum tuum
sic teipsum. Verbi glossa. Tunc diliges proximum sic teipsum quando eum
diliges ad quod diliges temetipsum, scilicet ad bonum non ad malum. Sic
enim diligendi sunt homines ut non diligantur eorum errores. Hic predico
contra eos, qui licet sciat proximos suos fornicarios, adulteros, et usurarios
manifestos, cicius eligunt suos errores celare instante visitacione quam man-
ifestare ad correctionem animarum. Tales non diligunt … Exempla De sen-
tencia excommunicacionis, Quante, maxime cum teneatur fratri et proximo
peccatum suum denunciare juxta illud Matthei 18, Si peccaverit in te frater
tuus et cetera*" (*Sermons*, vol. ii, p. 297). The canon is x. 5.39.47 (*Corpus*, vol.
ii, col. 909). The Dominican theologian Albert the Great's commentary on
Luke 17:2 also insists that we ought to correct out of love those bound to us
as fellow members of one body. This does not entail offering correction to
infidels, he adds (*In evangelium Lucae*, vol. xxiii, p. 460).

60. "peccat quis in correpcione … per sinistram intencionem, ut si non ex com-
passione et caritate corripiat, sed ex vindicta vel derisione; sic peccavit cham
revelando verenda patris" (Magdalen College Oxford MS 167, f. 176ᵛ). This
early fourteenth-century collection of sermons by Wilhelm von Werda is a
catena constructed of exegesis by prominent Dominican writers. Apparently,
the Magdalen manuscript is a unique copy. I am grateful to Ralph Hanna
for sharing his description of the manuscript from his forthcoming catalogue of the college's medieval manuscripts, to be published by the Oxford
Bibliographical Society.

61. "Sed nonnulli nimis sunt sceleste ad arguendum non in aperto corripiendo
secundum formam caritatis, sed in occulto detrahendo instinctu malignita-
tis, contra quos scribitur Lev. 19:[17–18]: 'Non oderis fratrem tuum, sed publice argue eum ut ne habeas super illum peccatum ne queras ulcionem nec

memor eris injurie.' Tales enim sunt spirituales homicide" (British Library MS Royal 7.A.VIII, f. 321ʳ).

62. Bossy, *Christianity*, pp. 143, 108.

63. Peyraut, *Summa virtutum*, p. 378; *Speculum Christiani*, p. 44; *Summa virtutum de remediis*, p. 265; *Memoriale*, pp. 82, 116; *Distinctiones exemplorum*, Bodleian Library Oxford MS Canon Pat. Lat. 118, f. 11ʳ. The last is typical in expressing the importance of correction (in the first sentence of its entry): "Correctio fraterna est opus misericordie et pietatis spirtualis et est opus magis meritorium quam misericordiam coporalem quia corporalis lucretur vitam corporalem, spiritualis vero vitam anime." This set of *distinctiones* larded with *exempla* survives in the one manuscript, dated fourteenth century in the catalogue of its collection.

64. Roger of Waltham, *Compendium morale*, British Library MS Royal 8.G.VI, f. 96ᵛ; Pierre le Chantre, *Verbum*, British Library MS Add. 30056, f. 53ᵛ; James le Palmer (attrib.), *Omne bonum*, f. 463ʳ; second "Corripe eum" sermon in British Library MS Royal 7.A.VIII, f. 316ᵛ.

65. Spencer quotes a lament about ignorance that places the seven works of spiritual mercy among the fundamentals: "Who knowith the sevene dedly sinnis and her braunchis, the sevene dedis of mercy bodily and goostly ...?" (*English Preaching*, p. 210).

66. On confessing failure to observe the works of spiritual mercy, see *Clensing*, Bodleian Library Oxford MS Bodl. 923, f. 71ʳ; "Confessor," British Library MS Add. 15237, f. 92ʳ; the form for confession in *Disce mori*, Jesus College Oxford MS 39, p. 373; "Whan thow thenkest," British Library MS Royal 18.A.X, f. 60ʳ. The last of these formulates the failure this way: "I have noght ... chastised hem that weren agens god." Nicolas de Byard: "ne similiter sic malorum particeps ut qui vidit homicidam et non clamavit alicubi 'Reus, homicida.' Levit xix. [Leviticus 19:17]: 'Non oderis fratrem tuum in corde tuo sed publice arguas eum ne habeas super eum peccatum.' Unde super illud ro. i. [Romans 1:32]: 'Qui talia agunt digni sunt morte.' Dicit glossa 'consentire est tacere ut possis arguere'" (*Distinctiones*, Bodleian Library Oxford MS Bodl. 563, f. 29ʳ). The gloss on Romans 1:32 in Nicolas de Lyre's commentary identifies those who consent to sin: "isti sunt faventes & prestantes auxilium & illi qui tenentur corrigere et tacent" (*Postilla*, vol. IV, f. aa iiiiʳ). Bataillon lists five British manuscripts of the *Distinctiones*, three from the turn from the thirteenth century to the fourteenth century and two from the latter ("Tradition," p. 245). See chapter three below for pastoral exegesis of Leviticus 19 and its place in the B-version of *Piers Plowman*, and chapter six for how the maxim "consentire est tacere," as developed in canon law and pastoral texts, authorizes reformist literature in the tradition of *Piers*. The sin of those who keep silent became a homiletic commonplace: "peccat qui videt fratrem peccantem et tacet sicut qui peccanti non indulget" (a late-thirteenth-century sermon on "Si autem peccaverit in te" owned by Cistercians, Bodleian Library Oxford MS Hatton 101, p. 511). The maxim's ubiquity may be due to the standard marginal gloss on Matthew

18:15 and Luke 17:3: "peccat qui videns fratrem peccare tacet" (*Biblia latina cum glossu*, vol. IV, unpaged).

67. Bartolomeo, *Summa*, from Thomas Aquinas, *Summa*, 2.2.33, 3. See also Higden, *Speculum*, f. 20ᵛ; Johann von Freiburg, *Summa*, 3.9.5; Nicolas de Lyre, *Postilla*, vol. IV, f. eviiʳ; William of Nottingham, Commentary, f. 352ᵛ. It might seem that Bartolomeo is distinguishing between the terms "correctio" (fraternal correction) and "correptio" (prelatical correction), but later in the same entry "correpcio" designates reproof delivered to a *praélatus* by a *subditus*. Thomas and Johann, in passages similar to this, use the term "correctio" for both types. Shogimen believes that Thomas, like Alexander of Hales before him, presented both types of correction as fraternal since prelates correct *ex caritate* as well as *ex officio* (*Ockham*, pp. 107–9). Even public punishment for the common good, he claims, is fraternal correction in Thomas's *Summa*. However, Alexander, like Thomas and pastoral writers, is very clear that "duplex est correctio" (not "duplex est correctio fraterna"), only one kind springing from "caritate fraterna" and involving admonition alone (Alexander, *Quaestiones*, vol. XIX, pp. 499–500, and vol. XXI, p. 1,513). This is not to deny that the two kinds overlap in many ways (I will point out some shortly and in chapter 2) nor that a few pastoral writers consider both that generated by love and that generated by justice as fraternal correction, though François de Meyronnes, who does so as he focuses on *praelates*, insists that only the former is properly fraternal ("proprie fraterna correptio") (sermon on the *thema* "Respiciens Jesus in discipulos tuos" in *Sermones*, f. 28ᵛ). I have not included his sermon as a major source because, although individual sermons of his circulated in England in the fourteenth century, the surviving two manuscripts of the collection are of the fifteenth century.

68. James le Palmer (attrib.), *Omne bonum*, f. 435ʳ.

69. "Alia est correctio que est actus dilectionis, que est per amicabilem instructionem et boni exhortacionem et mali reprehensionem" (William of Nottingham, Commentary, f. 352ᵛ).

70. Here I draw on how Ricoeur distinguishes morality from ethics (*Oneself*, p. 170).

71. MacIntyre, *After Virtue*, p. 187.

72. "Sic in corpore mistico oportet esse suo modo nam ad bonam ecclesie unitatem et disposicionem et ad spritiualis vite seu gratie conservacionem requiritur necessario quod membra sibi invicem subveniant non solum quantum ad indigencias corporales, sed multo magis quantum ad indigencias spirituales pro sibi invicem orando, delinquentibus parcendo et remittendo, delinquentes corripiendo, ad bonum monenedo, et corrigendo." Because fraternal correction works to meet the spiritual needs of those to whom we are bound in the mystical body, William goes on to reason, it is commanded by Christ in Matthew 18, and to keep silent when a fellow member of the body sins is sin itself (Commentary, f. 352ʳ).

73. Higden, *Speculum*, f. 21ᵛ. William of Nottingham's commentary on Matthew 18:15b develops the effects of reproof in terms of the goods

achieved: "Sequitur de effectu correctionis: *Si te*, id est, tuam correpcionem audierit scilicet penitendo, vitam corrigendo, culpam deferendo, et a culpa cessando; *lucratus es fratrum tuum*, in animam fratris tui, quasi diceret, eius diligens revocacio cadet tibi in lucrum spirituale, quia, ut dicit interlineara, 'per salutum alterius salus tibi adquiritur'" (f. 352ʳ). This spiritual profit for the doer is not widely developed in pastoral texts, but arises when exegetes and preachers must deal with the phrase "lucratus eris fratrem tuum." For example, a fourteenth-century sermon on Matthew 18:15, which draws on Dominican exegesis, glosses the phrase almost exactly as William of Nottingham does (Magdalen College Oxford MS 167, f. 176ʳ). Both incorporate the standard interlinear gloss: "per alterius salutem salus tibi acquiritur" (*Biblia latina cum glossa*, vol. IV, unpaged). Forgiveness and reconciliation often follow successful fraternal correction in pastoral texts and are associated with it generally because the Gospel lection beginning with "Si autem peccaverit in te" ends with Christ's injunction to forgive one's brother seventy times seven (21–2). The Hatton 101 sermon, for example, begins its running commentary by linking the two, "leccio ista agit de correpcione culparum et remissione injurium" (p. 511), and Nicolas de Lyre introduces his commentary on "Si" by proclaiming both correction and forgiveness benevolent acts toward fellow Christians: "ostendit quod debemus esse benefici proximo ex parte anime in effectu, et hoc dupliciter, primo de defectus eorum caritative corrigendo, et secundo offensam misericorditer remittendo" (*Postilla*, vol. IV, f. eviiʳ). Also the phrase "in te" suggests that the reprover may have been injured in some way and so is in a position to extend forgiveness and initiate reconciliation when the sinner repents (see chapter 2 for various readings of the phrase).

74. MacIntyre, *After Virtue*, pp. 190–1.
75. *Ibid.*, p. 222.
76. Bromyard, *Summa*, c.16.2.
77. Bromyard, *Summa*, c.16.3. The *Distinctiones exemplorum* also exemplifies discrete correction with Nathan, contrasting his similitude with blunt language ("You have acted in the worst way"), which would not have been efficacious: "Non cum furore arguit nathan david de adulterio et homicidio, dicens 'Pessime fecisti,' sed cum discretione assumpta similitudine illaque autem illum verbis omnibus ejus et convertur" (f. 11ᵛ). Similarly, the *Distinctiones pro sermonibus* contrasts the direct speech Nathan might have employed ("'O, inique. O, immunde. O, omicida'") with his actual veiled speech ("sub velamine"); like the wise physician he hides the scalpel with which he is about to cut the sick man's body (Bodleian Library MS Rawlinson c.899, f. 144ʳ). These *distinctiones* survive in ten manuscripts in British libraries, two of the late thirteenth century and four of the fourteenth century, according to the catalogues of the collections containing them. Sharpe attributes them to John of Wales (*Handlist*, p. 339, where he entitles them *Tractatus exemplorum alphabeti*).
78. Bartolomeo, *Summa*; Johann von Freiburg, *Summa*, 3.9.6; James le Palmer (attrib.), *Omne bonum*, f. 436ʳ, from Thomas Aquinas, *Summa*, 2.2.33, 4.

79. Second sermon on "Corripe eum" in British Library MS 7.A.VIII, f. 316ʳ, from Thomas Aquinas, *Summa*, 2.2.33, 4.

80. *Distinctiones exemplorum*, ff. 11ᵛ–12ʳ. Judith's speech could also be seen as prophecy or instruction *ex necessitate* (Minnis, *Fallible Authors*, pp. 208, 230).

81. Kienzle explains the different views of what it meant to preach in the late twelfth and early thirteenth centuries, views developed in part in response to Waldensian lay preaching ("Preaching"). Blamires takes a long view, right down to a response to Wycliffite assertions that women may preach, in "Women and Preaching." Blamires and C. W. Marx discuss Henry of Ghent and post-Wycliffite arguments in their edition of a disputation on the topic, "Woman Not to Preach," pp. 34–63. Two recent discussions take in more writers on women and preaching: Gertz-Robinson, "Stepping," and Kerby-Fulton, "When Women Preached." Kerby-Fulton presents an "impressive array" of women preachers and spiritual leaders in the tradition of reformist apocalypticism; she stresses the circumstances when female preaching was allowed. Minnis supplies the most comprehensive analysis of the theological *quaestiones* on gender and preaching in *Fallible Authors*, pp. 170–99.

82. Thomas Aquinas, *Summa*, 2.2.177, 2. For other versions of these arguments, see Blamires, and Blamires and Marx, as in note 81 above.

83. Johann von Erfürt, *Summa de poenitentia*, Oriel College Oxford MS 38, f. 23ʳ; this manuscript of the fourteenth century is the only one extant in British libraries. The passage comes from one of several entries on "correctio." The canon, attributed to Pope Nicolaus, is D.21 c.5 (*Corpus*, vol. I, pp. 70–1).

84. James le Palmer (attrib.), *Omne bonum*, f. 436ʳ. A sermon on the *thema* "Caritas fraternitatis maneat in vobis" in British Library MS. Royal 7.A.VIII grants that while *subditi* may sometimes ignore the precept of Matthew 18:15, *praelati* may never do so (f. 314ʳ). However, this sermon may very well be intended for monks only; see note 53 above on this sermon collection.

85. Johann von Freiburg, *Summa*, 3.9.6; Bartolomeo, *Summa*; James le Palmer (attrib.), *Omne bonum*, f. 436ʳ; second sermon on "Corripe eum" in British Library MS Royal 7.A.VIII, f. 316ᵛ, from Thomas Aquinas, *Summa*, 2.2.33, 4.

86. "Correctio publica et manifesta pertinet solummodo ad prelatos qui subidtos suos tam publice quam private corrigere possunt, sicut pater filios suos. Subditi vero non debent publice corrigere suos prelatos, sicut nec filii patrem suum" (Monaldo da Capo d'Istria, *Summa generalis*, Lincoln College Oxford MS Lat. 74, f. 36ʳ). Monaldo's unusual restriction might be due to the fact that his *summa* was compiled before Johann von Freiburg and others popularized Thomas Aquinas's moral theology of correction, with its conditions under which superiors may be corrected publicly. His *summa* survives in five manuscripts in British libraries, at least one of which is from the late thirteenth century and three of which are from the fourteenth century, according to the catalogues of the collections containing them.

87. "Item ex statu persone que corrigenda est. Quia prelati sunt cum reverentia monendi. Et idem dico etiam de aliis nobilibus et magnis personis. Quia aliter ad impatientiam provocati indociles efficerentur" (*Summa*, 3.9.9).

88. "Inter omnes virtutes prelatorum sola misericordia tenet principatum propter excellencie sue modum, quo aliene misericordie compaciens atque ipsum in se assumens per amoris unionem se extendit ad alterum ... Licet enim caritas sublimior existat in subdito propter suam unionem qua suo superiori per vim amoris ipsum conjungit. Misericordia tamen quodammodo precellentior est in prelato propter suam compassionem, qua suo inferiori attrahari dulcoris coaptatur, sed ejus supprema perfectio est peccatorum correctio quia remocio peccati magis pertinet ad caritatem quam remocio exterioris dampni vel corporalis nocumenti quia magis est ei a fine bonum virtutis quam exteriorum rerum vel proprii corporis. Nichil igitur gloriosius in prelato quam eam subditis exhibere vel convenientius in subdito quam ejus effectum a prelato suscipere" (second sermon on "Corripe eum" in British Library MS Royal 7.A.VIII, ff. 314^v–15^r).

89. "Quia sepe fit peccatorum commissio, ideo sepe debet fieri fraterna correpcio. Eccl. 19:15: 'Corripe amicum sepe.' Ne autem istorum prelatorum correpcio despiciatur, ostenditur quante sit auctoritatis cum dicitur 'Quecumque ligaveritis super terram.' Ex hiis ergo secundo habentur scilicet quod prelati debent subditos corripere et quod subditi debent eorum correpcionem in reverentia magna habere" (Jacopo da Varazze's second of two sermons on "Si autem peccaverit" in University College Oxford MS 109, ff. 34^v–5^r). Fifteen manuscripts of his *Sermones quadragesimales* survive in British libraries (Schneyer, *Repertorium*, vol. III, p. 245), with at least six of them dated to the fourteenth century by the manuscript catalogues of their collections.

90. *Distinctiones exemplorum*, f. 11^v; see also the early-fifteenth-century *Tabula super Bibliam*, Bodleian Library Oxford MS Bodl 688, f. 19^v. (The *Tabula* survives in three manuscripts, two of the early fifteenth century, according to the catalogues of the collections in which they are lodged.) The Dominican sermon in Magdalen College Oxford MS 167 identifies the whole of Matthew 18:15–22 as spoken to Peter (f. 175^v). *Northern Homily Cycle*, vol. II, lines 7,804–11.

91. *Book of Vices*, p. 200. See also *A Myrour to Lewde Men*, p. 146; "*Speculum vitae*," lines 7,942–85; *The Mirroure of the Worlde*, Bodleian Library Oxford MS Bodl. 283, ff. 148^v–9^r.

92. Insisting that all Christians have the responsibility to correct sin, Bromyard acknowledges that some people think that only the institutional Church, charged with the care of souls, should do so. He counters that the Church needs their assistance because sinners have so many confederates: "sed forte dicunt vel cogitant quid nobis ecclesia que habet animas custodire peccatores corrigat, sed irrationalibitur dicitur prima quia quomodo posset ecclesia corrigere illos qui tot habent supportatores" (*Summa*, A.21.7).

CHAPTER 2

1. "Sed contra supra quod 'Si percusserit te in unam maxillam, prebe et aliam.' Ergo pati non loqui est. Respondeo prebes maxillam cum paciencier corripis,

unde et paciencia est adhibenda et correctio non pretermittenda" (Magdalen College Oxford MS 167, f. 176ʳ).

2. William of Nottingham, *Commentary*, f. 351ᵛ.
3. Brown, *Contrary Things*, p. 88.
4. *Ibid.*, p. 3.
5. Harpham, *Shadows*, pp. 27–8.
6. The practice of fraternal correction generated disputed questions on almost the whole range of issues that this chapter and the last consider. Glorieux lists a number of extant quodlibetal questions about fraternal correction debated by prominent Parisian theologians between 1265 and 1310 (*La Littérature quodlibétique*, vol I, pp. 106, 116, 121, 125, 184, 231, 287, 314–17). I have not included these questions as sources for this study because I have not found evidence that they are incorporated directly into pastoral discourse. They may stand behind the moral theology that is incorporated, however. Thomas Aquinas's "Quaestio disputata de correctione fraterna," for example, is closely related to his articles on the precept of fraternal correction and its procedure in the *Summa theologiae*, the major source for the entries on fraternal correction in the pastoral *summae* of Bartolomeo da San Concordio and Johann von Freiburg, as well as James le Palmer's *Omne bonum* and texts to be considered in later chapters (Thomas Aquinas, *Quaestiones disputatae*, vol. II, pp. 793–802; translated in *Disputed Questions*, pp. 195–217).
7. Costello, *Moral Obligation*, p. 58.
8. Augustine, *Sermones ad populum* 82, col. 510.
9. Jacopo da Varazze, first sermon on "Si autem peccaverit," f. 34ʳ.
10. Sermon on "Si autem peccaverit" in Magdalen College Oxford MS 167, f. 176ʳ; William of Nottingham, *Commentary*, f. 351ᵛ.
11. "Sed illa beneficia que non debentur certe persone sed communiter omnibus proximis, sive sint corporalia sive spritualia, non oportet nos querere quibus impendamus, sed sufficit quod impendamus eis qui nobis incurrunt" (Johann von Freiburg, *Summa*, 3.9.4). See also Bartolomeo, *Summa*. They follow Thomas Aquinas in the *Summa theologiae*, 2.2.33, 2.
12. Higden, *Speculum*, f. 21ʳ; Bartolomeo, *Summa*; Johann von Freiburg, *Summa*, 3.9.4; James le Palmer (attrib.), *Omne bonum*, f. 436ʳ. Using this principle, they all argue that the religious should not leave their cloisters to reprove wrongdoers. Prying into the lives of others under the pretext of correcting sin is also forbidden by Augustine, note Johann and James, as well as the second sermon on "Corripe eum" in British Library MS Royal 7.A.VIII, f. 315ʳ (from Augustine's *Sermones ad populum* 82, col. 506).
13. Bartolomeo, *Summa*; Johann von Erfürt, *Summa*, f. 24ʳ; William of Nottingham, *Commentary*, f. 352ʳ.
14. *Distinctiones exemplorum*, f. 11ᵛ.
15. *Northern Homily Cycle*, vol. II, lines 15,598–605.
16. *Ibid.*, lines 15,608–10, 15,613–21.
17. The first version is from Johann von Freiburg, *Summa*, 3.9.7, and Bartolomeo, *Summa*; the second, from James le Palmer (attrib.), *Omne bonum*, f. 436ʳ.

18. *Northern Homily Cycle*, vol. II, line 15,614; James le Palmer (attrib.), *Omne bonum*, f. 436ʳ. William of Nottingham's commentary on Matthew 7 uses the same dialectical move as the preacher in the *Cycle* and comes to the same resolution as he and James do. "¶Ex predictis [his explication of the beam as grave sin] videtur quod peccator non posset corripere.¶Sed contra peccator non absolvitur a precepto divino, ergo nec a correctione nec per consequens a correpcione fraterna cum cadat autem sub precepto" (f. 174ᵛ).

19. Sermon on the *thema* "Estote misericordes" in British Library MS Royal 2.D.VI, f. 190ᵛ; this sermon comes from the thirteenth century and is extant in eight British manuscripts (Schneyer, *Repertorium*, vol. VIII, p. 452). Nicolas de Lyre (on Matthew 7), *Postilla*, vol. IV, f. ciiiʳ. Johann von Freiburg ends his Thomistic analysis of the question of sinners correcting with Romans 2:1: "For, wherein you judge another, you condemn yourself. For you do the same things which you judge" (*Summa*, 3.9.7; also James le Palmer (attrib.), *Omne bonum*, f. 436ʳ).

20. *Mirror*, Bodelian Library Oxford MS Holkam Misc. 40, f. 67ʳ. Six manucripts of these sixty old-fashioned homilies survive (Heffernan and Horner, "Sermons," p. 4,260); Hanna has dated the earliest manuscript *c.* 1340 and the translation *c.* 1310–20 (*London Literature*, pp. 16–17, 20–2). This homily is one of the fifty-three translated from Robert of Gretham's Anglo-Norman verse cycle, *Mirour ou Les évangiles des domnées* (mid thirteenth century). I have not scrupled to use the later Holkam manuscript, despite its many additions, because Hanna's quotation from an earlier manuscript is almost verbatim that in Holkam in note 34 below.

21. Bromyard: "quia aliter corrector derideretur a dicentibus tineosus reprehendit tineosum" (*Summa*, C.16.3). William of Nottingham, Commentary, f. 174ᵛ.

22. Johann von Freiburg, *Summa*, 3.9.7; also Higden, *Speculum*, f. 21ʳ; James le Palmer (attrib.), *Omne bonum*, f. 436ʳ; and the first sermon on "Corripe eum" in British Library MS Royal 7.A.VIII, f. 314ᵛ. From Pseudo-Chrysostom, *Opus*, British Library MS Harley 3235, f. 51ᵛ.

23. Higden, *Speculum*, f. 21ʳ; Johann von Freiburg, *Summa*, 3.9.7; James le Palmer (attrib.), *Omne bonum*, f. 436ʳ, from Thomas Aquinas, *Summa*, 2.2.33, 5.

24. "Et *ejice trabes*: id est, magnum et grave peccatum. *In oculo tuo*: id est, in intencione tua et sic per consequens alium accusas ut te extollas" (William of Nottingham, Commentary, f. 174ᵛ). This manuscript reads "excusas," but British Library MS Royal 4.E.II reads "accusas," a clearly preferable reading. In commenting on Luke 6, William has Christ gloss his own metaphor: "Quasi diceret Xristus, 'Iniquum est proximum tuum pro modico judicare vel condempnare, temetipsum vero magis reum justificare'" (f. 184ʳ).

25. Bromyard, *Opus*, C.24 and A.8, and *Summa*, C.16.3 and A.11.2; the canon is C.3 q.7 c.3 (*Corpus*, vol. I, cols. 526–7). Bromyard is not quoting the canon, but summarizing it.

26. *Northern Homily Cycle*, vol. II, lines 15,549–55, 15,574–9, 15,584–5, 15,594–7; the source of the *narracio* is the *Vitae patrum (Cycle*, vol. II, p. 256). The beam is glossed as hate and envy in the *Glossa ordinaria, Biblia latina cum glossa*, vol. IV, unpaged (on Luke 6).
27. *Nothern Homily Cycle*, vol. II, lines 15,471, 15,527, 15,505–6, 15,539.
28. As Kent explains, Thomas always sees virtuous acts as springing from charity given by God to the human will (*Virtues of the Will*, pp. 23–34).
29. Nicolas is commenting on Christ's command to eject the beam from the eye: "quia est ordo charitatis quod a seipso incipiat" (*Postilla*, vol. IV, f. ciii^r). Bromyard, *Summa*, C.14.3. *Northern Homily Cycle*, vol. II, line 15,614.
30. Johann von Freiburg, *Summa*, 3.9.7; see also Higden, *Speculum*, f. 21^r; James le Palmer (attrib.), *Omne bonum*, f. 436^r. See the sermon on "Estote misericordes" in British Library MS Royal 2.D.VI for the same three stages, worded slightly differently.
31. A paraphrase of the other four considerations: "If you have not committed the same or a graver sin, then consider if you have been like him or her; if so, show mercy, not despising the other person. If you have not been, consider if you might be, given that all must be constantly vigilant against sin. So, you should treat the other person at his or her own level, without acting superior. Fourthly, even if you think you might never be like the sinner, consider if the sinner also has some good qualities and then encourage those even as you rebuke him or her for sin. Finally, consider whether, even though the sinner seems wholly evil, as Saul did in stoning Stephen, that in God's timeless sight he or she might be excellent, like Paul the Apostle." Jacopo da Varazze, second sermon on "Estote misericordes," Bodleian Library Oxford MS Bodl. 320, f. 115^v.
32. Bartolomeo, *Summa*; also Higden, *Speculum*, f. 21^r (an abbreviated version).
33. Nicolas de Byard, *Distinctiones*, f. 28^v.
34. The *Mirror* is expounding the metaphor of the blind leading the blind together with that of the "straw" and the "bem": "For thi they owen to holden hem clene that schal chastise othere and nameliche men of ordre, for if a prest have likinge to don a sinne and therefore he alegeth him that cometh to him for to make his sinne lasse, and in as mychel they ben bothe disceived and fallen bothe in the diche. And also if that he wot that the prest is other coveitous other proud other leccherous and he be usand therinne othre in eny other sinne that he hath in usage and he schrive him to him, he doth dedliche sinne, for if the prest ben in eny of thes sinnes, he may do no sacrement – schrifte ne non of the sevene sacramentes – but if he do dedliche sinne" (f. 68^r).
35. *Northern Homily Cycle*, vol. II, lines 7,810–39.
36. *Magna vita*, vol. I, pp. 19–21. I came upon this story in Spencer's *English Preaching*, pp. 69–70.
37. Higden, *Speculum*, f. 21^r; Bartolomeo, *Summa*; Johann von Freiburg, *Summa*, 3.9.9; James le Palmer (attrib.), *Omne bonum*, f. 436^r; Nicolas de Lyre, *Postilla*, vol. IV, f. evii^r; the principle is used prominently in discourse

on disciplinary correction (e.g., Peyraut, *Summa virtutum*, p. 353, and *Omne bonum*'s article on "correctio," f. 433^r).

38. "Cuius ratio est [for correcting in secret first as an act of charity] sicut enim medicus coporalis, si debito modo procedat nititur inducere sanitatem cum minori dispendio corporis, ut sine membri abscisione, et, si non possit, tunc abscindit membrorum minus nobile, ut conservetur magis nobile vel totum corpus, sic ille qui fratrem peccantem occulte corripit caritative debet tentare si possit fratrem emendare absque detrimento sue fame quia fama computatur inter majora bona hominis circa virtutes" (Nicolas de Lyre, *Postilla*, vol. IV, f. evii^r). Higden also develops this analogy (f. 20^r), as does the second sermon on "Corripe eum" in British Library MS Royal 7.A.VIII, f. 315^r.

39. Johann von Freiburg, *Summa*, 3.9.9; James le Palmer (attrib.), *Omne bonum*, f. 436^v; the second sermon on "Corripe eum" in British Library MS Royal 7.A.VIII, f. 315^v. These interwoven arguments about the value of preserving a sinner's reputation may best be taken from *Omne bonum*: "Nam quilibet debet sic corrigere, si potest, ut illius fama non ledatur, que est utilis ipsi peccanti non solum in temporalibus, in quibus homo quantum ad multa patitur detrimentum amissa fama ... sed etiam quantum ad spiritualia, quia pre timore infamie multi retrahunter a peccato, cum autem sentiunt se esse infamatos, libentius et licentius peccant ... Secundo debet conservari fama peccantis quia uno infamato, alii infamantur, quia dicendum est clerici vel religiosi hoc faciunt." These claims about the value of reputation are less fully argued by Higden and Bartolomeo. Pastoral writers often repeat the interlinear gloss on Matthew. 18:15: "ne publice correptus verecundiam perdat; qua perdita in peccato permaneat" (*Biblia latina cum glossa*, vol. IV, unpaged; see William of Nottingham, Commentary, f. 351^v; the catechetical material with the incipit "Sunt plura per que adquiritur humilitas" in British Library MS Royal 5.A.VIII, f. 131^v; *Summa virtutum de remediis*, p. 265). The argument that the sinner, if shamed by public correction, will be less likely to be drawn back from sin is also voiced by Higden, *Speculum*, f. 21^r; by Nicolas de Lyre, *Postilla*, vol. IV, f. evii^r; and by the sermon on "Si autem peccaverit" in Bodleian Library Oxford MS Hatton 101, p. 511. The British Library MS Royal 7.A.VIII sermon develops that argument most comprehensively: "salvanda est fama correpti ne pejor efficiatur. Multi enim pre timore fame a peccato retrahuntur, sed cum se infamatos conscipiunt, irrefrenate peccant. Unde Jeronimus: 'corripiendus est seorsum frater ne si semel pudorem aut verecundiam amiserit, in peccato permaneat' ... De quo loquens Augustinus de verbis domini exponendo id, 'Corripe ipsum inter te et ipsum solum,' dicit 'studens correcioni, parcens pudori. Forte enim pre verecundia incipit peccatum suum defendere, et quem vis facere meliorem, facis pejorem'" (f. 315$^{r–v}$). The *sententia* of Jerome is taken from his commentary on Matthew 18:15 (*Commentariorum in Mattheum*, p. 161); that of Augustine, from *Sermones ad populum* 82, col. 509. Hanawalt, "*Of Good and Ill Repute*," p. ix and throughout. Kuehn, "*Fama*," pp. 27–46, and Akehurst, "Good Name," pp. 75–94.

40. Higden, *Speculum*, f. 21ʳ; Johann von Freiburg, *Summa*, 3.9.9; James le Palmer (attrib.), *Omne bonum*, f. 436ᵛ. The second sermon on "Corripe eum" in British Library MS Royal 7.A.VIII, a visitation sermon to what is surely a religious community, develops this argument for preserving *fama* out of concern for the reputation of the community of which the sinner is a member: "Tertio, inquam, salvanda est fama correpti ne scandalum communitatis inducatur, quia uno infamato alii faciliter infamantur. Secundum Augustinum ad plebem yponensem, 'Cum de aliquibus,' inquit, 'qui sanctum nomen profitentur aliquid criminis vel falsi sonuerit vel veri patuerit, instant, satagunt, ambiunt ut de omnibus hoc credatur.' Sic ergo ut fama fratris conservetur" (f. 315ᵛ). The Augustinian *sententia* is taken from *Epistulae*, CSEL XXXIV, p. 341.

41. Augustine, *Sermones ad populum* 82, col. 510. The *sententia* on treachery alone is quoted in Johann von Freiburg, *Summa*, 3.9.9; the second sermon on "Corripe eum" in British Library MS Royal 7.A.VIII, f. 315ʳ; *Speculum Christiani*, p. 235. The *Speculum* places the *sententia* last in a series of authoritative sayings on "correptio," just before it develops slander as a vicious perversion of reproof. Simon of Boraston, *Distinctiones*, Bodleian Library Oxford MS Bodl. 216, f. 32ʳ. Von Nolcken dates the *Distinctiones c.* 1327–36 ("Some Alphabetical Compendia," p. 284). Nine manuscripts are extant in British libraries, seven of them from the fourteenth century, and three more are attested to (Sharpe, *Handlist*, p. 610). The canon is c.2 q.1 c.19 (*Corpus*, vol. I, col. 447).

42. One exception to the principle that private admonition ought to precede public accusation is made by several pastoral writers: In religious communities, religious are permitted to accuse their fellows, though only in minor matters (the "chapter of faults"). These do no harm to anyone's reputation, supposedly. British Library MS Royal 7.A.VIII, f. 315ʳ; Johann von Freiburg, *Summa*, 3.9.9; Bartolomeo, *Summa*; James le Palmer (attrib.), *Omne bonum*, f. 436ᵛ, from Thomas Aquinas, *Summa theologiae*, 2.2.33, 7.

43. Johann von Freiburg, *Summa*, 3.9.9; James le Palmer (attrib.), *Omne bonum*, f. 436ᵛ, from Thomas Aquinas, *Summa theologiae*, 2.2.33, 7 and 43, 7 (the latter on scandal). The second sermon on "Corripe eum" in British Library MS Royal 7.A.VIII argues that when someone sins against others, not just the corrector, the imperative of Matthew 18:15 ("go and rebuke him, between him and thee alone") does not apply (f. 315ʳ). Isidore's *sententia* is quoted from the *Speculum Christiani*, p. 235 (*Sententiarum libri tres*, col. 66); it is commonly cited to guide disciplinary correctors (e.g., Peyraut, *Summa virtutum*, p. 353).

44. Bartolomeo, *Summa*; Johann von Freiburg, *Summa*, 3.9.9; James le Palmer (attrib.), *Omne bonum*, f. 436ᵛ. Shogimen roots this concern with the common good in the thirteenth-century language of criminal law, where deviant behavior is regarded as a danger to society that must be punished publicly so it does not infect others (*Ockham*, pp. 110–11).

45. Bartolomeo, *Summa*; Johann von Freiburg, *Summa*, 3.9.9; James le Palmer (attrib.), *Omne bonum*, f. 436ᵛ.

46. "Et in lege precepit deus adulteros et blasphemos et hujusmodi non solum a sacerdotibus sed a toto populo lapidari. Et christus in evangelio precepit fratrem corripere, quod si te non audierit, dic ecclesie, quod si nec eam audierit, sit tibi sicut publicanus: id est, retrahas et fugias ejus societatem" (Bromyard, *Summa*, A.21.7).

47. William of Nottingham, Commentary, f. 352ʳ.

48. James le Palmer (attrib.), *Omne bonum*, f. 436ᵛ.

49. For example, Bartolomeo, *Summa*, and Johann von Freiburg, *Summa*, 3.9.9. The second visitation sermon on "Corripe eum" in British Library MS Royal 7.A.VIII follows Thomas Aquinas in marking firmly three stages of fraternal correction: private admonition, bringing in witnesses, and denouncing the sinner to the Church (with the last still aimed at amending the sinner) (f. 316ʳ). Commentaries on canon law treat admonition briefly in their entries on *denunciatio*, but they share with moral theologians and pastoral writers concern with what conditions legitimate, even demand, denouncing sins to a confessor and/or judge. They add and develop some conditions not central in *pastoralia*. For example: Durant, *Speculum judiciale*, vol. III, unpaged; Henricus de Segusio, *Summa aurea*, pp. 280–1.

50. Jacopo begins by outlining five "documenta" (examples or patterns) that Christ has left his people; the last four "documenta" have to do with verses after 17. "Primum documentum est per quod ostendit qualiter facienda est fraterna correpcio … Quidam [ms: "quidem"] enim sunt corripiendi cum amore, sicut humiles et mansueti; quando enim aliquod offendunt, statim recognoscunt. Et ille modus intelligitur cum dicitur 'inter te et ipsum solum,' id est, dulciter et discrete, tales enim emendantur levi admonicione … ¶Quidam sunt corripiendi cum ratione, sicut astuti. Ille modus tangitur cum subditur 'Si te non audierit, adhibe tecum unum ut in ore duorum vel trium stet omne verbum.' ¶Multi enim astuti sunt qui peccata sua custodunt, abscondunt, et defendunt nec se corrigere volunt. Prelatus enim et judex debet esse astutus cum astutis et debet eos corrigere et per testes et per omnes alios modos quibus possit … ¶Alii autem sunt cohercendi cum timore, sicut superbi et presumptuosi. Ille modus tangitur cum subditur 'Quod si non audierit eos, dic ecclesie,' id est, prelato ecclesie ad quem spectat duros et presumptuosos corrigere. Talis debet esse prelatus et judex qui possit superbos comprimere et domare" (First sermon on "Si autem peccaverit" in University College Oxford MS 109, f. 34ᵛ). Here Jacopo adds to a set of three stages of correction envisioned by Alexander of Hales and restated by some pastoral writers: "correctio amoris" (private reproof), "correctio pudoris" (before witnesses), and "correctio timoris" (when sin is revealed to the Church) (*Quaestiones*, vol. XIX, cols. 501–2, and vol. XXI, col. 1,514).

51. Second sermon on "Corripe eum," British Library MS Royal 7.A.VIII, f. 316ᵛ.

52. William of Nottingham, Commentary, f. 351ᵛ.

53. "Vani sunt," British Library MS Lansdowne 385, f. 79ᵛ; the treatise survives in five manuscripts, four of them from the second half of the fourteenth

century (Sharpe, *Handlist*, p. 761). "Duplex est," British Library MS Royal 8.c.viii, f. 59ʳ; at least fifteen manuscripts survive, one of the late thirteenth century and at least four from throughout the fourteenth, according to catalogues of the collections in which they are lodged.

54. Bromyard, *Summa,* c.16.3.
55. "falsa laus adulatoris mentes hominum a rigore veritatis emollit ad noxia. Et Jeromus: 'Nichil est quod tam facile corrumpat mentes hominum quam adulacio, in tam quod plus nocet lingua adulatoris quam gladius persecutoris'" (British Library MS Royal 7.a.viii, f. 316ᵛ).
56. *Biblia latina cum glossa*, vol. iv, unpaged. In a mini-treatise on the Sins of the Tongue, the Parson couples chiding with uncharitable reproof, reproof generated by wrath and akin to chiding in its open and boorish assault on others (*Canterbury Tales*, 10.622–34). For a fuller definition of chiding as a type of speech, see chapter 3, "Branding reproof as deviant"; also Craun, *Lies*, pp. 190–3.
57. The story of the monk comes from *Narrationes miraculorum*, British Library MS Add. 15833, f. 83ᵛ (the manuscript catalogue dates the manuscript as early fourteenth century): "Item est autem ut aliquando quemdam de amicis suis pro culpa sua objurgaret et juste correctionis modum excederet, cumque pacificam hostiam nec dum pacificato fratre perciperet, visum est ei quod amarissimum absinthii poculum faucibus injecisset, unde primam solitam meruit gratiam experiri."
58. Bartolomeo, *Summa*. Fraternal correction, Johann argues, "debet esse cum benignitate et rationabili persuasione ut conservetur moderamen sumptum ex quatuor. Scilicet ex quantitate culpe: aliter enim in levibus peccatis, aliter in gravibus, debet se corrector habere. Item ex spe correctionis: quia forte opportunius tempus expectat. Item ex statu persone que corrigenda est: quia prelati sunt cum reverentia monendi. Et idem dico etiam de aliis nobilibus et magnis personis, quia aliter ad impatientiam provocati indociles efficerentur. Item ex zelo movente corripientem: si enim ille est zelus amarus invidie vel rancoris non debet corripere" (*Summa*, 3.9.9). Bromyard's entry on "correctio" in *Opus trivium* (unpaged) begins by affirming that love (*amor*) ought to govern all decisions about how to correct differently according to different circumstances; most of his material is taken from the canon he cites: c.12. q.2. c.11 (*Corpus*, vol. i, cols. 689–90).
59. My thinking about the moral authority pastoral discourse confers is much indebted to Ober, "Precedent." Ober has reworked this paper, in ways less useful to me here, as "Historical Legacies," in *Athenian Legacies*, pp. 43–68.

CHAPTER 3

1. On Latin satire, see: Yunck, *Lineage*. On pastoral rhetoric of reform: Craun, *Lies*; Wenzel, *Sin of Sloth*. On new reformist appropriations of discourses directed by one clerical group against another, see Scase, *New Anticlericalism*; for reasons to read them as interclerical, see Kerby-Fulton,

"*Piers Plowman*," pp. 530–3. On the influence of reformist Franciscan thought: Clopper, *"Songes."* On apocalyptic thought: Bloomfield, *"Piers Plowman"*; Kerby-Fulton, *Reformist Apocalypticism*. On the dreamer as an open subject: Lawton, "Subject."

2. Aers, "Visionary Eschatology," p. 6.

3. Lawton, *Chaucer's Narrators*, p. 13.

4. I have chosen to examine the B-version of *Piers* because the last conversation the dreamer has in the twelve *passūs* of the A-version is with Clergie, who does not even mention correction of sin. I treat the C-text revisions of passages on fraternal correction in the next chapter.

5. Harpham writing on the relation of narrative to ethics in *Shadows*, pp. 33, 35.

6. Donaldson explains what being a married clerk might have involved and presents the textual evidence for seeing the dreamer as a clerk in minor orders in *"Piers Plowman"*, pp. 199–226. (I do not mean to endorse Donaldson's ready conflation of dreamer and poet.) Somerset, *Clerical Discourse,* pp. 23–32.

7. Fletcher takes the traditional view that many manuscript sermons preserved in Latin were "likely to have been originally delivered in whole or in part in English" (*Preaching*, p. 17).

8. See Spencer, *English Preaching*, pp. 44–5.

9. Watson, "English Mystics," p. 551, and "Politics," p. 340.

10. Hanna summarizes evidence and thinking for dating the three versions in *William Langland*, supplemented in 2000 by "Emendations," pp. 188–90. More recently, Hanna has re-examined manuscript evidence, especially scribal habits of production in London; he concludes that the B-version (in some form) was known in London in 1376 (*London Literature*, pp. 243–52). Justice has argued cogently that the rebels of 1381 referred to the B-text (*Writing*, pp. 102–39).

11. Burrow, "Audience"; Middleton, "Audience," pp. 104–8. After establishing that a secular cleric with connections to the regular clergy copied *Piers* in the early fifteenth century, Horobin surveys the evidence that other manuscripts were copied and owned by religious houses ("Scribe").

12. Kerby-Fulton, "*Piers Plowman*," pp. 527–8.

13. Middleton, "Audience," pp. 104, 109.

14. For a summary of the evidence on the poet's life, see Hanna's *Langland*, supplemented by his "Emendations," pp. 185–7. Benson has recently written a skeptical review of attempts to outline a life for William Langland and to embrace too easily his authorship of *Piers* (*Public "Piers Plowman,"* pp. 3–42, 77–89).

15. For example, see Craun, *Lies*, pp. 157–86, on how Langland builds into the poem pastoral discourse on the deviant speech of minstrels. Judson Allen and John Alford pioneered the study of Langland's use of pastoral materials, especially *distinctiones*, for poetic invention and development.

16. Lawton is summarizing Anne Middleton's characterization of the public voice of late-fourteenth-century poetry in his *Chaucer's Narrators*, p. 13.

17. For these overlapping conceptions of truth in late medieval English culture, especially its law and literature, see Green, *Crisis of Truth*.

18. Although scholars have focused for more than three decades on the dreamer's problematical reproofs of others, especially in the third dream, and on the poet's struggles to justify his reformist writing, they have neglected how Meed's flyting with Conscience introduces many of the questions that vex the dreamer's speech and writing later in the poem. To take an important example, Simpson does not consider their exchange either in his *"Piers Plowman"* or in his "Constraints."

19. Meed's bribing of the friar, like her counteraccusations against Conscience, are substantially the same in the A-version of the poem, probably dated about 1362 (*Piers Plowman: The A Version*, 3.34–52, 109–214).

20. All quotations are taken from *Piers Plowman: The B-Version*. I have chosen this edition in part because it records manuscript variants, which I will discuss when they are significant.

21. For Meed's excuses for her sin, see my essay "'Freletee.'"

22. Bromyard claims in his entry on "correctio" that bribes (*munera*), not justice, are the object of desire among officials of ecclesiastical and secular courts (*Summa*, c.16.3); also Étienne de Bourbon, *Tractatus*, Oriel College Oxford MS 68, f. 369ᵛ; and Haren, "Interrogatories," p. 128.

23. Conscience's speech has affinities with *accusatio*, the Roman legal procedure by which individuals initiated criminal charges in a court by formally divulging a crime and naming the perpetrator. However, *accusatio* demanded a written statement (*inscriptio*) and sufficient proof in the form of at least two credible witnesses. Pastoral writing and sermons distinguish fraternal correction from *accusatio* on the grounds of the accuser's concern to preserve the common good, not correct the sinner. See, for example, the second sermon on "Corripe eum" in British Library MS Royal 7.A.VIII.

24. For example, Envy confesses to slandering merchants and lying about their goods as part of finding fault with ("lakking") his rivals' wares (5.130–4).

25. Bartolomeo, *Summa*, "contencio," unpaged; Johann von Freiburg, *Summa*, 3.33.226, from Thomas Aquinas, *Summa*, 2.2.38; *Book of Vices*, p. 63; Chaucer, *Canterbury Tales*, 10.622–34.

26. Hanna unfolds how, to the poem's contemporaries, Conscience might very well have been tainted by association, as the king's knight, with the military failures in France (*London Literature*, pp. 258–67).

27. The king's declaration of Meed's immediate victory forces Conscience to change tack altogether, abandoning reproof for scholastic analysis of legitimate and illegitimate profit or reward (3.231 ff.).

28. "Sed heu multi assimilantur equo infirmo in dorso, qui recalcitrat quando locus ille tangitur. Ita isti correctores maledictionibus et asperis verbis pungunt et contra sanitatem propriam recalcitrant" (Bromyard, *Summa*, c.16.5; see also general comments on slander as a response in c.16.8). The metaphor of the galled horse is used similarly in the collection of *distinctiones* entitled "Duplex est," although the horse bites as well: "Tales sunt sicut equus

scabiosus, qui, tactus in loco doloris, pedibus ferit et dentibus mordet. Sed vulgariter dicitur qui semel recalcitrat bis se pungit. Sic multi corripientes dentibus detraccionis lacerunt" (f. 60ʳ). Jacopo da Varazze, preaching on the stoning of St. Stephen, says that some people, when corrected, immediately turn to good works (they are like wax), but that others need frequent correction (they are like stones) or respond with "aspera verba" to any reproof (they are like hedgehogs). Among the latter are those who chide (University College Oxford MS 109, f. 55ʳ).

29. Zeeman surveys medieval conceptions of the powers of knowing and desiring, then examines how they characterize Will, in *Discourse of Desire*, pp. 64–108.

30. Kent's *Virtues of the Will* analyzes comprehensively how scholastic moral theologians all located virtues and vices in the will as they struggled, with their different views of the extent of the will's freedom, to revise Aristotle's definition of moral virtue as a habit involving choice. Several major studies of the third dream concentrate on the education of the will. Wittig traces its stages as he argues that, in this section of *Piers*, all reform is rooted in the reform of the will ("*Piers Plowman*"). Bowers focuses on Will's tendency to paralysis of the will (*Crisis of Will*). Simpson argues for an unfolding affective theology in the third and fourth dreams in "*Piers Plowman*" and "Reason."

31. I am echoing Smith, *Incipit*, p. 80.

32. Zeeman, *Discourse of Desire*, pp. 132–43. In reconceptualizing Clergie, Zeeman shies away too much from an earlier scholarly tendency to see him as clerical learning and so, to some degree, as a social caste invested in maintaining its powers.

33. Bromyard, *Summa*, c.16; Nicolas de Byard, *Distinctiones*, ff. 28ᵛ–9ʳ. See chapter 2, "The dangers of hypocrisy," on sinful correctors.

34. Scase sees Clergie's use of the term "prelates" as pejorative, a satirical recasting of a traditional term in a new, anticlerical way. Her reading aligns the passage with Wyclif's and lollard uses that "connote misused institutional power and, increasingly, wealth" (*New Anticlericalism*, p. 22). This textual version, with its linking of prelates to abbots and priors, certainly does focus on the responsibilities of higher, more powerful disciplinary authorities, but the phrase "all manere prelates" is wholly inclusive, taking in, for example, the parish priests of the other textual version. So, "prelates" definitely carries the traditional meaning of all those who have care of souls. With Scase, I hear the tone of Clergie's address to his fellow clerics as satirical; after all, he is exposing hypocrisy and violations of scriptural precepts. But so is his tone at the outset, when he uses Jesus' satirical image of the mote and beam to mock hypocrisy in all sinful correctors of others. So, it is difficult to see Clergie's satire as anticlerical in Scase's sense: committed to divesting clerics of their institutional power and wealth.

35. The sermon on the *thema* "Nolite judicare" (Matthew 7:1), in Bodleian Library Oxford MS Hatton 101, interprets the mote and beam as clerics

wrongfully reprehending lay people while they leave themselves uncorrected: "*Quid vides festucam et cetera* ¶Sic si dicat melius est nec docere nec reprehendere laicos quam docere et teipsum in reprehensione consistere." Such hypocrisy ensures that the clergy's reproof and teaching of the laity will be mocked: "talis doctrina doctoris non est audibilis sed derisibilis propter quod omnis sacerdos, si vult docere populum, prius seipsum doceat." If a cleric is unwilling to teach and reprove himself, he should cease to teach and reprove lay people so that he does not incur the judgment of God and the opprobrium of men (p. 182). Like Clergie, the Hatton 101 preacher is addressing an imagined audience of clerics, in this case very likely Cistercians. The preacher takes this whole passage almost verbatim from the widespread sermons of Pseudo-Chrysostom (*Opus*, f. 51ᵛ). See also Nicolas de Lyre, *Postilla*, f. ciiiʳ, and Nicolas de Byard, *Distinctiones*, f. 28ᵛ. On the blind as ignorant priests misdirecting the laity, see the *distinctio* on *correctio* in "Duplex est" (f. 24ᵛ) and that on *prelati* in Lathbury's *Distinctiones*, British Library MS Royal 11.A.XIII, f. 190ᵛ. William of Nottingham's commentary on Luke 6 interprets the blind as the "prelatus" ignorant of the truth and so incapable of carrying out his pastoral responsibilities ("presidens sive prelatus qui nescit scripturas intelligere, nec intellectus proponere, nec inter culpas discutere"). So, he leads those in his care into the ditch of error: vices, heresy, scandalous conduct, and hell (f. 183ᵛ).

36. Wenzel establishes that the *exemplum* was used to warn clerics both against greed (the sons) and against correcting those in their care too mildly ("Eli").

37. Kellogg establishes that dumb dogs are glossed as priests from Gregory the Great to the late fourteenth century, when Bromyard attributes their silence to greed ("Langland," pp. 25–36). Gregory's gloss is included in the decretals attributed to Gratian, D.43 c.1 (*Corpus*, vol. 1, col. 153). Like Clergie, Nicolas de Byard associates the "canes muti" with Eli, but he sees greed as the root of excessive leniency (*Distinctiones*, f. 29ᵛ). Étienne de Bourbon laments that clerics' desire for bribes makes them "canes muti," overriding the charity that should direct them to correct firmly the sins of *subditi* (*Tractatus*, f. 369ᵛ).

38. *Corpus*, c.3 q.7 c.2 (vol. 1, col. 526); this whole *quaestio* deals, over many sections, with priests' responsibility to correct their own sins before those of others. *Caput* 2 quotes only the beginning of the section of Psalm 49 ("Peccatori autem dixit Deus: quare te enarras justicias meas?" verse 16), but the "etc." which follows designates that the whole section should be pulled into the decretal. Bromyard, *Summa*, c.16.3.

39. I have been influenced by Simpson's developmental reading of this *passus* ("*Piers Plowman*," pp. 110–18), but also by Zeeman's incisive explication of the disputation, which focuses on Will's tendency to moral inaction and indifference and Scripture's push toward personal moral effort (*Discourse of Desire*, pp. 216–26).

40. Wittig discusses this influential, initially monastic saying in "*Piers Plowman*" throughout.

41. Will's complaint that friars prefer the more lucrative kinds of pastoral care was a common charge made by Richard FitzRalph, the reformist Archbishop of Armagh (d. 1360), whose antimendicant positions were adopted by many monks and secular clerics in the decades after his death. See Scase, *New Anticlericalism*, and Kerby-Fulton, *Reformist Apocalypticism*.

42. Kean traces Lewte's role throughout the poem in "Love."

43. Among the lowerers in *Piers* is Envy, whose lowering is linked to "lakking" understood as illegitimate fault-finding (5.130).

44. Clopper writes compellingly about Will's lack of moral authority, though he sees Will in more biographical terms than I do, as a character with a more sustained, developing life, and though he conflates Will more fully with William Langland than I believe we can (*"Songes"*, pp. 305–7, 332; his "Response" to my "ʒe, by Peter and by Poul!' ").

45. *Sarum Missal*, vol. i, p. 89; "Ordo missalis," vol. ii, p. 233; *Missale Herefordensis*, p. 76; *Missale Eboracensis*, vol. i, p. 81; *Missale Westmonasteriensis*, vol. i, cols. 215–16; *Officia varia*, f. 533ʳ.

46. British Library MS Royal 7.A.viii, f. 321ʳ (quoted in chapter 1, as is Nicolas de Byard on Leviticus 19:17 authorizing fraternal correction). Simon of Boraston also cites Leviticus 19:17 to support his claim that it is good to reprove those who err (*Distinctiones*, f. 12ʳ). Scase notes that the mid-fourteenth-century monastic polemicist Uthred of Bolden cites Leviticus 19:17, along with many other passages of scripture, to justify his reproof of the Dominicans as false brothers (*New Anticlericalism*, p. 162). Alford, "Quotations." Alford argues that the incomplete quotations, often the product of scribal practice, serve as "tags" for the larger biblical context. Lewte's Levitical precept comes from a cluster about proper treatment of one's neighbor that, in recasting the last seven of the Ten Commandments, prohibits various forms of deceptive and destructive speech: lying, calumny, unjust judgment, and detraction. The following verse (19:18) begins by forbidding vengeance and ends with the injunction to love your neighbor as yourself. A Dominican sermon on the reading treats these two verses together, arguing that 17 forbids secret slander while 18 demands that we counsel those who commit evil instead of being seized by the desire for vengeance when we reprove (Magdalen College Oxford MS 167, f. 231ʳ⁻ᵛ).

47. I have not found Leviticus altered in these three ways in any pastoral text, although it may very well have been in an antimendicant text that I have not discovered. "Altering quotations to make them fit a new context," as Kerby-Fulton reminds us, "was a skill taught in *ars dictaminis*" ("*Piers Plowman*," p. 528).

48. Pastoral writers and biblical commentators differed on what Leviticus 19:17's richly ambiguous "publice" meant in light of Matthew 18's four-part structure. It could simply mean "in speech," "voce expressa," writes Nicolas de Lyre, and so refer to all four stages of correction (*Postilla*, vol. i, f. Tviiᵛ). Simon of Boraston, however, insists that Leviticus 19 deals only with people who sin publicly, having nothing to do with private admonition

(*Distinctiones*, f. 12ʳ). And Albert the Great argues that it refers only to the second stage of correction: bringing in witnesses (*In evangelium Lucae*, vol. XXIII, p. 461).

49. Augustine, *Epistulae*, epistles 40, 75, 82. Froehlich gives a reading of the exchange between Jerome and Augustine in a context of early patristic exegesis of Galatians 2 ("Fallibility," pp. 259–69, 351–7). Ian Christopher Levy kindly gave me this reference.

50. *Biblia Latina cum glossa*, vol. I, unpaged; Peter Lombard, *Collectanea,* cols. 110–12; Peter of Tarantasia, *Galatas*, Bodleian Library Oxford MS Laud misc. 467, f. 112ᵛ.

51. Johann von Freiburg, *Summa*, 3.9.6. Also James le Palmer (attrib.), *Omne bonum*, f. 434ʳ; Thomas Aquinas, *Summa*, 2.2.33, 4. In a shortened form, Higden, *Speculum*, f. 20ᵛ. James and Thomas even cite Augustine's reading of Peter as an example to *praelates* not to disdain correction by their subjects when they have gone astray. Bromyard uses the biblical precedent similarly: "Correctus ergo vel reprehensus contra correctorem non murmuret, licet minorem statum teneat qui reprehendit" (*Summa*, c.16.5). From the twelfth century, the incident was cited as "the major biblical proof text for the ethical topos 'that evil prelates must be accused and corrected by their subordinates'" (Froehlich, "Fallibility," p. 264).

52. Apostolic writing, as well as apostolic practice, witnesses to the Levitical precept. Paul's command "Rebuke sinners before all" (Peccantes coram omnibus argue [I Timothy 5:20]) is a central text in the debate over proper procedures for fraternal correction (see chapter 2, "Good repute"). Peter's textual witness is less familiar: His epistle writes of Balaam's miraculous correction by his ass, "a dumb beast used to the yoke" (2 Peter 2:15–16). The epistle refers to an incident in Numbers 22, in which the soothsayer Balaam, hounded by Moabites, goes to curse the emigrating Israelites, but is stopped and rebuked by his ass when the beast sees an angel bearing a sword in the path. Balaam's correction by his ass is an occasional *exemplum*, variously interpreted, in pastoral discourse on correction (James le Palmer (attib.), *Omne bonum*, f. 435ᵛ; Simon of Boraston, *Distinctiones*, f. 32ᵛ). A thirteenth-century commentary on Paul's reproof even resolves its to-and-fro debate over whether subjects (*minores*) may rebuke superiors (*majores*) by quoting the passage from Peter's epistle. Then it turns to the Levitical precept to develop its reasoning: "*restiti* [Galatians 2:11] … si sit manifestum peccatum, et non sit alius qui reprehendat, solunt minores reprehendere majores. [2 Peter 2]: 'Correptionem habuit vesanie sue subjugale mutum animal hominis voce loquens' … *coram omnibus* [Leviticus 19:17]: 'ne [sic] oderis fratrum tuum in corde tuo sed publice argue illum ne habeas super illo peccatum.' Hoc autem ideo fecit quia peccatum suum in omnes redundabat, and ideo coram omnibus argue debebat" (*Notule super epistolas Pauli*, Bodleian Library Oxford MS Auct D.4.19, f. 105ʳ). The gloss cited is that of Peter Lombard, *Collectanea*, col. 108. The *Notule*, placed among other commentaries on the Pauline epistles, survives in only one manuscript (thirteenth century) (Stegmüller, *Repertorium*, vol. VI, pp. 507–12).

53. Nicolas de Lyre, *Postilla*, vol. IV, f. ciii^r; William of Nottingham, Commentary, ff. 182^v–3^r.
54. Pseudo-Chrysostom, *Opus*, f. 50^v.
55. *Book to a Mother*, p. 72. Like Lewte, the *Book* counters the imperative not to judge with our responsibility to uphold God's law. Properly understood, "Wolle not ye jugge" means "not foliliche, withouten certein evidences – and this is the undurstondinge of Crist and of alle holy doctoures that forbeden jugginges. For Crist juggede and cursede muche in this world, and taughte forto jugge to destruye sinne ther as hit is opene agenus his hestis."
56. "for somwhat the Apostle seide / *Non oderis fratrem*." As far as I know, no one has identified this biblical imperative as Pauline, and Alford's *Guide* (p. 72) refers back to the full quotation of Leviticus 19:17. So, I think it best to construe the lines as a shorthand reference back to Paul's correction of Peter and the following precept from Leviticus, here quoted exactly rather than altered to fit Will's anger at the friars: That is, Paul did not hate his brother, but, instead, rebuked him publicly.
57. Ambrosius Autpertus, *Libellus de conflictu*, vol. III, pp. 914–15. The *Libellus* survives in forty-five manuscripts in British libraries, according to Bloomfield's *Incipits*, no. 0455. It was ascribed to Pope Leo I in the fourteenth century.
58. To expand note 6 above, Donaldson, followed by many others, argued that the text presents Will as a clerk in minor orders, perhaps, Donaldson conjectured, an acolyte, the minor order before subdeacon. After marriage (Will refers to a wife and daughter in 18.426), he could not have advanced beyond minor orders or served at the altar in any capacity (*"Piers Plowman,"* pp. 202–20). Scase, however, believes that Langland treats Will as a layman when Lewte refers to "lewed men," but that phrase, of course, can mean "relatively unlearned, less learned" (than the disciplinary superior) (*New Anticlericalism*, p. 66). Certainly Scase is right to indicate throughout *New Anticlericalism* that Will's status is often uncertain and even seems to fluctuate (see also Somerset, *Clerical Discourse*, pp. 22–61). The question of the dreamer's lay or clerical identity in this exchange, however, does not alter my basic argument below: that Lewte draws on discourse on fraternal correction in order to authorize all Christians, particularly those "less" in status than priests, to rebuke publicly manifest sins.
59. Hugo de Saint Cher, for example: "Si manifestus sit excessus prelati omnibus, si majores non reprehendant eum, tunc minores possint eum reprehendere" (*Opera omnia*, vol. VI, f. cxxvii^r).
60. Some manuscripts read "leveful" instead of "*licitum*," a vernacular term which also indicates formal permission or dispensation.
61. Jacopo da Varazze, Bodleian Library Oxford MS Bodl. 320, f. 116^r.
62. Similarly, Mannyng authorizes the *exempla* in his *Handlyng Synne* by claiming that everything he reports has already been written or spoken about so that his book "toucheth no privite" (lines 131–40). I am grateful to Andy Galloway for this reference.

63. Simpson reads this proviso in terms of traditional constraints on writing literary satire as developed in academic commentaries on classical satirists ("Constraints," pp. 25–6, and *"Piers Plowman,"* pp. 129–32). Literary satire, as understood by the academic commentaries, shares with pastoral discourse on fraternal correction vice as a target, amendment as a goal, and worries about committing slander. But in *Piers*, as in other reformist texts, post-Lateran-IV materials on sin and satire interpenetrate each other, and to see Lewte's discourse entirely in terms of the latter is to scant its biblical texts and pastoral rhetoric. Reading the Lewte episode in light of fourteenth-century documentary culture and the poem's own fictive documents, Steiner concludes that only the documents offer an alternative to "the dreamer's uncharitable satire by depicting a public writing that goes beyond satire, that simultaneously confesses the life of the universal subject and acts on the subject's behalf" (*Documentary Culture*, p. 170). While she grants parenthetically that "Lewte appears to authorize moral satire" (p. 166), she develops only Lewte's qualifications, scanting the biblical texts as revealed law and precept that, I think, validate correction; she also sees the episode in terms of writing, not primarily in terms of corrective speech (on this critical tendency see the final section of this chapter).

64. The speaker has been variously identified as Trajan (continuing his speech), Scripture, Lewte, and even Will, but the evidence for any of them is less than overwhelming.

65. Simpson, *Reform*, pp. 479–82.

66. For discourse on charity forbidding harshness, see chapter 2.

67. Twice later in *Piers* figures voice how charity curbs capricious, hostile fault-finding ("lakking," again): Anima at 15.249 and 252 and Grace at 19.254.

68. James le Palmer (attrib.), *Omne bonum*, f. 435ʳ; Thomas Aquinas, *Summa*, 2.2.33, 1. The *Summa virtutum de remediis* links the various modes of spiritual mercy manifested in speech, like rebuking, consoling, and praying for others, to the injunction "Alter alterius onera portate" (p. 145).

69. Chaucer, *Canterbury Tales*, 10.626, from Peyraut, *Summa de vitiis*, ff. H5ᵛ–6ᵛ. On the distinction between *penae* and *culpae* as objects of reproof, see also the widespread English treatise *De lingua*, Oriel College Oxford MS 20, ff. 173ʳ–4ʳ.

70. For the prudential strain in pastoral discourse on deviant speech, which counsels verbal self-control for the speaker's own benefit, as well as that of others, see Craun, *Lies*, pp. 47–56.

71. This is Wittig's argument throughout *"Piers Plowman."*

72. Smith, *Incipit*, p. 16.

73. My argument has been influenced here by Middleton's thoughtful work on the relation of instrumental discourses to Langland's fiction, especially in "Audience." But Middleton tends to see pastoral and other didactic discourses as monological, whereas I see them as containing – and to various extents embracing – seemingly conflicting texts, arguments, and goods.

74. Polemical correction of groups and individuals continues in the next dream. As Simpson writes of Will's whispered invective against the Doctor of Divinity in *passus* 13, "Langland as a poet, as distinct from Will, does not restrain himself from satire of the Doctor here" ("Constraints," p. 29n.). Sometimes even Will delivers fraternal correction effectively, as in his address to lordly patrons of salacious Minstrels (13.421–56, treated in Craun, *Lies*, pp. 157–86). This reproof hews carefully to the constraints laid down by Will's interlocutors in the third dream: Minstrels' lies and lewd tales are Lewte's "Thing that all the world woot" and so hardly slander; they are pastorally designated sins, not Reason's "defautis"; Will is not complicit in the salaciousness he denounces; above all, his focus on the minstrels' amendment (by performing biblical narrative) indicates that his speech is driven by charity, not envy or hatred. In the fourth dream, too, Will's dubious or even undelivered reproofs function as polemical correction. In questioning whether *Piers* as a whole contains acts of fraternal correction, Clopper notes that the poem contains tirades, accusations, and uncharitable speech ("Response," p. 32). I do not argue here that the figures in *Piers* always voice impeccable correction of sin, but rather that Langland explores what constitutes valid correction through a range not only of speakers but also of speech acts, of which this rebuke of minstrels and their patrons is one of the less contestable.

75. This formulation of the biographical/autobiographical approach is Clopper's in *"Songes,"* p. 332. See also Kirk, *Dream Thought*, p. 129.

CHAPTER 4

1. The C-version was likely still in revision in 1388, given the evidence for its response to the Statute of Laborers, promulgated in 1388 (Middleton, "Acts of Vagrancy").

2. Clergie's *exemplum* of Eli and his sons is transported to the C-version prologue, where Conscience develops it to illustrate how God punishes avaricious priests and the disciplinary superiors who fail to rebuke and punish them. *Piers Plowman: The C-Version*, Prologue 95–124.

3. 12.23–41. The unnamed speaker's warnings against uncharitable correction are excised, along with much of the rest of his speech. At the end of the B-version sequence on correction, speech acts are relabeled to make them more injudicious prodding than improper correction. Will's complaint to Reason is labeled "reasoning," not reproof, as is Reason's reply, though Reason's caution against "lakking" others while sinning remains (13.183–212). Meed's earlier (first vision) labeling of Conscience's accusations as chiding and slander, however, remains the same in the C-version.

4. Kerby-Fulton, "Bibliographic Ego," p. 81.

5. Justice, *Writing*, p. 137, and, for the letters and Ball, chapters 1 and 3. The letters, printed on pp. 13–14, speak generally of "blam[ing]" or "chastis[ing]" social evils, but they contain nothing specific to the practice of fraternal

correction. Hudson points out ("Peasants' Revolt," pp. 91–9) that the traceable participants (often the leaders) in the revolt were of the same classes as those later associated with manuscripts of *Piers*: the lesser clergy, often in parishes; minor office-holders; and tradespeople. They could have read *Piers* aloud to the illiterate among the rebels in the secret gatherings before the Uprising, where both the political world it envisions and its passionate critique of Church and state would have been congruent with the rebels' aims and language. (Hudson, however, thinks that it is possible, given the uncertainties involved in dating all three versions, that only the A-version circulated before the revolt.) Earlier scholarship had tended to dissociate *Piers* from the Uprising.

6. Justice, *Writing*, pp. 231–51.
7. Kerby-Fulton, "*Piers Plowman*," p. 522.
8. See Workman's account of the Blackfriars Council in *John Wyclif*, vol. II, pp. 246–93; also Dahmus, *William Courtenay*, pp. 79–83. The original of the proposition: "Item quod domini temporales possunt ad arbitrium eorum auferre bona temporalia ab viris ecclesiasticis delinquentibus, vel quod populares possint ad eorum arbitrium dominos delinquentes corrigere" (*Fasciculi zizaniorum*, pp. 495–6). The Council pronounced this thesis erroneous, not heretical. Kerby-Fulton has argued that the C revisions show, in part, Langland's responses to the Council; for example, Langland repressed the role lords might play in correcting corrupt monasteries (B.10.322–85) in response to the Council's condemnation of the seventeenth thesis ("Bibliographic Ego," p. 75). Bowers has written more generally about the C revisions as reaction to the Uprising and the Blackfriars Council ("Police," pp. 11–15).
9. Kerby-Fulton has argued that the Ilchester manuscript of *Piers*, which contains an unfinished revision of what became the expanded story of Eli and his sons in C Prologue 95–124, shows Langland responding to topical issues raised by Wyclif and the Uprising and readers so interested in his responses that they snapped them up before they were finished ("Bibliographic Ego," pp. 101–3).
10. Justice, *Writing*, p. 233.
11. Walsingham, *Chronicon*, p. 116.
12. Wyclif's closely related defenses of the propositions, the *Protestacio* and the *Libellus*, both contain only eighteen, but Archbishop Sudbury's register refers to nineteen, as does Thomas Netter, the opponent of the Wycliffites. Dahmus argues that Wyclif withdrew the seventh, on unlicensed lay action to disendow the Church, because he found it difficult to defend (*Prosecution*, pp. 50–2).
13. "quod nonnullas Propositiones et Conclusiones erroneas ac falsas, et male in fide sonantes, quae statum totius Ecclesiae subvertere et enervare nituntur" (Walsingham, *Historia*, vol. I, p. 348). Walsingham includes the five papal bulls on pp. 346–53; he also includes them in the *Chronicon*.
14. *Ibid.*, p. 348.

15. Wyclif, *De condemnacione*, in *Fasciculi zizaniorum*, p. 484. The *Fasciculi*, probably put together from Carmelite sources in the later 1430s, contains a number of documents relevant to the opposition between Wyclif (and his followers) and the ecclesiastical hierarchy. Documents covering Wyclif's lifetime may have been gathered between 1393 and 1399 (Hudson, *Premature Reformation*, p. 44).

16. Walsingham, *Historia*, vol. I, p. 355; verbatim in *Chronicon*, p. 183.

17. Walsingham's text of Wyclif's *Protestacio* (*Historia*, vol. I, p. 362); the *Chronicon* (p. 189) has exactly the same wording.

18. Dahmus proposes that Wyclif may have drawn up and circulated the *Libellus* among members of Parliament during the fall session of 1377, when, he believes, Bishop Brinton of Rochester told him that his theses had been condemned at Rome (*Prosecution*, p. 57). Wyclif's bibliographer, Thomson, proposes as another possible audience the continual Council during the regency of Richard II (*Latin Writings*, pp. 254–5). Wyclif himself later claimed that both the *Libellus* and *Protestacio* were widely disseminated in England (*ibid.*, p. 255).

19. Wyclif, *Libellus*, p. 256; for the related statement in the *Protestacio*, Walsingham, *Historia*, vol. I, p. 362, and *Chronicon*, p. 189. We cannot take Walsingham's text as a "faithful rendition" of what Wyclif said because it is a transcription by a third party, but neither "do we have warrant to doubt that the text as we have it is *substantially* what Wyclyf did then declare and assert" (Thomson, *Latin Writings*, p. 253).

20. Walsingham, *Historia*, vol. I, p. 362, and *Chronicon*, p. 189.

21. Wyclif, *Libellus*, p. 256. For peril to the faith as a reason to correct publicly, see chapter 2, "Good repute."

22. Farr, *Legal Reformer*, pp. 124–5.

23. Farr traces carefully Wyclif's arguments for transferring cases on appeal from ecclesiastical courts to secular ones (*ibid.*, pp. 95–138). *Libellus*, p. 256; the language in the *Protestacio* is vaguer (Walsingham, *Historia*, vol. I, p. 362, and *Chronicon*, p. 189). The latter, however, bolsters its defense with canon law, citing D.40, c.6 ("Si Papae"), which binds all faithful Christians to pray for popes who are obdurate in deviating from the faith and then to turn their minds to their own salvation under God (*Corpus*, vol. I, col. 146). Wyclif reasons that such concern may lead to a legal case when the sinful pope will not accept the remedy God, as his superior, proposes.

24. Wyclif, *Protestacio*, in Walsingham, *Historia*, vol. I, pp. 361–2, and *Chronicon*, pp. 188–9. See chapter I for almsgiving as a work of spiritual mercy.

25. Wyclif, *De mandatis divinis*, pp. 413–14. *Postilla*, Bodelian Library Oxford MS Bodl. 716, f. 38^v, ff. 102^{r-v} (a manuscript containing only the *postilla* on the New Testament). Wyclif shows no particular interest in fraternal correction when he treats Matthew 18, focusing on remission of sins in the chapter as a whole.

26. On Grosseteste's influence, see Brown, *Church and Society*, p. 161. On the Oxford debates over FitzRalph's theories, see Catto, "Wyclif," pp. 195–261.

Hughes presents the evidence for Thoresby's patronage of the Wycliffites in *Pastors*, pp. 162–8.

27. Wyclif, *De civili dominio*, vol. i, pp. 331–5. Wyclif also sets forth the stages in a 1377 or 1378 sermon devoted largely to fraternal correction: Its *thema*, "Oportuit et te misereri conservi tui," comes from the latter part of Matthew 18. In this sermon, he advocates a more traditional three-part schema: "correpcio ex amore" (a mild private rebuke), "correpcio ex timore" (drawing in witnesses), and "correpcio ex rigore" (punitive action), but firmly includes excommunication within the latter (*Sermones*, vol. iv, pp. 454–5). For the schema (save that the last stage is labeled "correptio pudoris"), see Ripelin, *Compendium*, 5.70. For the stages of fraternal correction, see chapter 2 above.

28. Wyclif, *De civili dominio*, vol. i, pp. 1–2, 76, and chapters 1–14 *passim*. Dahmus notes that the *Fasciculi* lists, as two of Wyclif's heresies bruited about in Oxford in the early 1370s, that priests did not have civil dominion and that temporal lords had the authority to seize the temporalities of ecclesiastics. So, he concludes, Wyclif had "long pondered over the theses he was in time to set down in his treatises on civil and divine dominion" (*Prosecution*, p. 20).

29. Wyclif, *De civili dominio*, vol. i, pp. 265–6 and, on tithes, see p. 340. Kenny sums up the arguments on grace and dominion in *Wyclif*, pp. 42–52, while Wilks explains the relationship between Wyclif's theory of dominion and the role of kingship in *Wyclif*, pp. 16–32. I am most indebted to Lahey's lucid, patient exposition of the manifold arguments of *De civili dominio* in *Philosophy*, especially chapters 4 and 5. Lahey does not, however, deal with correction, let alone recognize fraternal correction as an ethical and political practice.

30. Farr, *Legal Reformer*, p. 62.

31. Wyclif, *De civili dominio*, vol. ii, p. 11.

32. Thomson, *Latin Writings*, p. 50. On Wyclif's concept of evangelical law, see Farr, *Legal Reformer*, pp. 42–7.

33. Wyclif insists on proper order in correction: The laity should correct clerics only when the clerical order fails to do so. See *Conclusiones*, p. 48. As Farr explains, Wyclif's theocratic king, guardian of evangelical law in his realm, has "a divine mandate to intervene coercively in the conduct of ecclesiastical affairs when the spiritual branch is found wanting" (*Legal Reformer*, p. 83).

34. "Ideo domini temporales debent prepositis cleri in nomine Christi precipere, quod visitent clerum subjectum ne contra legem Christi innitantur possessioni temporalium. ¶Simili modo, positio quod clerus subditus remaneat in peccato, debet adhibere testes idoneos, ut clericos vel dominos seculares qui non corrumpantur muneribus, et iterum sub pena subtraccionis temporalium sunt monendi; quod si tercio in suis prevaricacionibus perseverent, nunciandum est ecclesie, id est, toti congregacioni fidelium tam clericis quam laicis regni dati. In cujus consilio provideri debet discrescius de multitudine ac ministerio presbiterorum ac clericorum proporcionabilium tali

regno et limitari sibi bona fortune necessaria ac suum ministerium exequen-
dum subtrahendo superflua" (Wyclif, *De civili dominio*, vol. ii, pp. 11–12).
The fourth step is described more fully on pp. 12–13. Wyclif also used fraternal correction to disarm clerical authorities who would excommunicate lay
lords attempting to take away the temporal goods of ecclesiastics. In chapters 40 and 41 of Book i, Wyclif argues extensively that Matthew 18:15–17, as
the foundation of excommunication (the Church declaring someone "sicut
ethnicus et publicanus"), permits it only when a person is an obstinate sinner, as the fourth step in a process directed at every point by charity for the
sinner. Furthermore, all of Matthew 18 binds all Christians to forgive injuries against themselves (vol. i, pp. 299–335).

35. On the responsibilities of lay people, especially the king, for the Church, see
Lahey, *Philosophy*, chapter 6. Dahmus argues that the *Protestacio* modifies
De civili dominio somewhat by adding the qualification that civil authorities
may deprive a delinquent Church of temporalities only "with the authoriza-
tion of the church and in cases and form dictated by justice," not on their
authority alone and by what method they choose (*Prosecution*, p. 69). But
the Church, of course, is coterminous with the realm, and secular courts
were an appropriate place for the laity to recover endowments because, as
Wyclif argues, the laity gave them on the condition that they would be used
properly as alms.

36. Aers has traced how Wyclif developed an *imitatio Christi* rooted in the
Gospels and extricated from the usual Eucharistic meditations on the Christ
of the Passion (Aers and Staley, *Powers*, pp. 44–8).

37. Wilks, *Wyclif*, pp. 208–21.

38. Wyclif, *De civili dominio*, vol. ii, pp. 70–2.

39. Farr, *Legal Reformer*, p. 120.

40. Wilks, *Wyclif*, p. 210. In chapter 9 of Book ii, Wyclif calls attention to the
force of quotations from canon law in proving his arguments for coercive
disciplinary action by the laity (*De civili dominio*, vol. ii, p. 95).

41. The main decretal cited is c.2 q.7 c.27; the Jerome is incorporated into c.29
(*Corpus*, vol. i, col. 491). For reservations on disciples reprehending teachers,
see chapter 1 above.

42. Here Wyclif quotes the whole of c.2. q.7. c.28 (*Corpus*, vol. i, col. 491), which
cites a Pauline text entertained in pastoral writing as a potential objection to
subditi reproving *praelati*: "Seniorem te non increpaveris" (1 Timothy 5:1; see
Johann von Freiburg, *Summa*, 3.9.6; James le Palmer (attrib.), *Omne bonum*,
f. 436ʳ). The canon insists that this rule ought never to be observed when a
senior's sinful example might draw a junior to destruction. From his words,
Wyclif concludes "quod non licet subditum superiorem corrigere, nisi dum
fuerit in gracia, superiori peccante mortaliter, et per consequens correptore
existente gracia et dignitate seniore" (*De civili dominio*, vol. ii, p. 94). Paul reprehending Peter comes from c.33 of the same *quaestio* (*Corpus*, vol. i, col. 493).

43. *Ibid.*, vol. ii, p. 94.

44. *De condemnacione*, p. 484.

45. "nullus dominus temporalis debet corripere, nisi prius teneatur esse in gracia, quia juxta mandatum apostoli *omnia nostra in caritate fiant,* et per consequences omnis correpcio fraterna debet sic fieri" (*De civili dominio*, vol. II, p. 69). *Caritas,* as Lahey observes, is associated with grace in Wyclif's writing and springs from "obedience and willing acceptance of Christ's law" (*Philosophy*, p. 126) – including, I would add, the precept of fraternal correction. See also Levy, "Christian Life," pp. 357–9.

46. Wyclif, *De civili dominio*, vol. II, pp. 63–4. Wyclif also argues from Balaam's ass's reproof of his master that inferiors should correct disciplinary superiors. See chapter 2, and chapter 3 (the Lewte episode), above, for imprudent correction.

47. From the sermon on "Oportuit," *Sermones*, vol. IV, pp. 454–5. There is no extant ferial cycle of Wyclif's sermons, so we do not have a sermon on Matthew 18:15–22. In this sermon Wyclif preaches on Matthew 18:33, but turns to fraternal correction after just a few pages on the *thema* itself. For the pastoral prohibition, see chapter 2 above.

48. Lahey, *Philosophy*, pp. 133–46, expounding Book III of *De civili dominio*.

49. Wyclif, *Sermones*, vol. IV, pp. 459, 456; *De civili dominio*, vol. I, p. 311; *De veritate*, vol. III, pp. 6–7. Chapter 25 of *De veritate* argues that it is permissible for lay people to judge clerics, while chapter 27 insists that temporal lords must protect the Church as the community of the faithful, especially by punishing sinful clerics of all orders.

50. Wyclif, *Sermones*, vol. IV, pp. 456–8. See chapter 1, "Fraternal correction as moral practice," for silence in the face of sin.

51. Bromyard, c.16.6, for example.

52. Wyclif, *De potestate pape*, p. 59; *Cruciata* (of late 1382), pp. 611–12. A few years later, near the end of his life, Wyclif was still using the incident from Galatians to present Peter as a humble companion of the other Apostles, thus countering papal pride, greed for power, and persecution of true practitioners of the Gospel (*Responsiones*, pp. 267–8).

53. "Ex istis manifeste sequitur, cum papa ex lege domini tantum astringitur in moribus sequi Christum, et tam manifeste vadit viam contrariam, totus christianismus debet ipsum reprehendere et specialter superiores domini seculares ... Sic Paulus in facie Petro restitit, quia reprehensibilis erat ad Gal. 2, cuius reprehensionis causa fuit, quia Petrus non fovebat generaliter ecclesiam, sed personas aliquas acceptavit" (Wyclif, *Cruciata*, p. 609). Wyclif, *De potestate pape*, pp. 133–4.

54. Wyclif, *De simonia*, pp. 62–3. Levy places Wyclif's thinking on papal correction in the traditions of canon law and theology in "John Wyclif."

55. Wyclif, *De potestate pape*, pp. 159–60. On peril to the Church, see chapter 2 above.

56. Brown, *Church and Society*, p. 163.

57. Wilks, *Wyclif*, p. 197.

58. Dahmus, *Prosecution*, treats the accusations on pp. 82–5 and the Council on pp. 90–100. See also Catto, "Wyclif," p. 215.

59. This proposition is quoted in note 8 above. Dahmus notes that it develops the implications of Wyclif's doctrine of dominion for sinful lay lords: they, as well as ecclesiastical lords, forfeit authority and power if they sin mortally, and so they may be disciplined by the people (*Prosecution*, p. 96).

60. "docentes doctrinas et mandata hominum" (Wyclif, *De fundacione sectorum*, vol. i, p. 49); this concludes chapter 9, devoted largely to failures in correction. Also Wyclif, *Trialogus*, p. 371. Wyclif develops more fully how religious communities fear loss of reputation and fortune in his attack on monks who fail to correct their brothers in *De civili dominio*, vol. iii, p. 16.

61. Thomson, *Latin Writings*, p. 221.

62. Wyclif, *Opus evangelicum*, vol. i, pp. 371–3.

63. Cole, *Literature and Hersey*, pp. 38–45, 60–71.

CHAPTER 5

1. Especially in *Premature Reformation*.

2. Hudson reviews the evidence for the earliest documentary usage of "lollard" to designate a Wycliffite in "Langland and Lollardy," pp. 93–106. She concludes that the term begins to occur in 1387–90. For Cole's distinctions between Wycliffism and lollardy, see "William Langland's Lollardy," pp. 25–54.

3. Lambert defines heresy in these terms in *Medieval Heresy*.

4. Dahmus gives an account of the events at Oxford in *Prosecution*, pp. 104–28, while Catto describes the constantly shifting status of Wyclif and his disciples within the University, in "Wyclif," pp. 213–21. Cole, *Literature and Heresy*, p. 19.

5. *Of Pseudo-Friars*, p. 82. Lindberg argues on linguistic grounds that this tract is probably by Wyclif, but these grounds (a Northern dialect) are highly unreliable and the *MED* dates it around 1400. So, it is best to regard it as late-fourteenth-century and Wycliffite.

6. Although the Wycliffite sermons argue that no one may know with certainty whether he or she is predestined to salvation, they exhort believers to do good in hopes that they are (*English Wycliffite Sermons*, vol. iv, pp. 58–60).

7. *Of Dominion*, pp. 104–6.

8. See, for example, the Wycliffite tract *Hou Sathanas*, which attacks three heresies, the last of which is claiming that "it is agenst charite to crye opynly agens prelatis sinnes & other mightty mennys." This heresy, it claims, reigns "among prelatis, feined religious & lordis & comyns for the more part" (pp. 264–5).

9. Justice notes references in Wyclif's Latin writings to issuing writings in the vernacular, as well as in Latin (*Writing*, pp. 77–9).

10. Simpson, *Reform*, pp. 345–6. Copeland explains how the *Glossed Gospels* were introduced and set up so that they provided "the technical materials

of exegetical 'user's guides.'" Their prologues "assume an audience that is at once textually untrained and textually hyperconscious" (that is, characterized by "hermeneutical aptitude and astuteness") (*Pedagogy*, pp. 136–7).

11. Pitard, "Sowing Difficulty," p. 320.

12. Somerset, *Clerical Discourse*, pp. 12–13.

13. *Pierce the Ploughman's Crede*, lines 43–4. All subsequent references within the text are to this edition.

14. For pastoral definitions of slander, including its subtypes, see Craun, *Lies*, pp. 136–42. Barr notes that the narrator questions Peres's speech in the legal terms of defamation (*Signes*, p. 156).

15. For example, reprovers of sin are subject to slanderous lies in *Of the Leaven of the Pharisees* (p. 9), while they are accused of slander in *Of Prelates* (p. 101) and *How the Office of Curates* (p. 155). The final chapters of the accompanying tract, *Of Clerkis Possessioneris*, generalize this retaliatory tactic: Possessioners project their own sins on "cristene men" just as the Pharisees and scribes accused Jesus of their own sins of blasphemy and heresy (pp. 137–9). All are extant in the same two manuscripts, the first of the late fourteenth century (Talbert and Thomson, "Wyclif," pp. 374, 530–1).

16. *Hou Sathanas*, pp. 271, 273. It survives in the same two manuscripts as the tracts in note 15 above.

17. On lying as a form of deception, see Craun, *Lies*, pp. 37–47; on flattery, pp. 121–9.

18. *Of Clerkis Possessioneris*, p. 138.

19. *Hou Sathanas*, p. 274. The tractate *Of Prelates* attributes both possessioners' accusations of slander against reprovers and their arrogant refusal to let anyone reprove them in their presence to their fears about losing *temporalia*: "but alle here care is last here ypocrisye bi knowen to lordis & mighty men, for drede of taking awey of here temporal lordischipis that ben cause of here sinful lif" (p. 101). Lahey sketches out the influence of Wyclif's theory of dominion on Wycliffite writing in the final chapter of *Philosophy*, pp. 200–24.

20. The friars, alleges *Of the Leaven*, "chastisen not here brethren for opyn swering veinly and pride and inpacience and false coveitinge of ther neigheboris goodis, but for litil trespasinge agenst here owne statutis or customis" (p. 17). The sermon on the lection "Si peccaverit" in the English Wycliffite ferial cycle (*c.* 1400) contrasts the Gospel imperative to correct the sinning brother with friars who evade reproof by taking refuge in their orders' disciplinary systems, like the chapter of faults or correction by the master: "And so what time that thou knowist that ony man sinneth in thee, thou shuldust snibbe him by yousilf whanne time and othere thingis wolen suffere … Many newe lawis ben maad to susteine thes newe ordris that letten siche snibbing, as the gospel tellith heere, for it is ofte knowen to men that ther britheren sinnen agens hem. And if men snibben hem of ther sinne, they seyn they han a soverein as a priour or an abbot that shulde knowe in this trespas; and this fallith not to this brother but if he wole reverse this ordre" (*English Wycliffite Sermons*, vol. III, p. 110). The Wycliffite treatise *Of the Church and Her*

Members follows Wyclif in claiming that any friar who would dare to correct openly the sins of his brothers would be imprisoned, if not immediately killed. Such intimidation, it concludes, has destroyed the practice of Jesus' precept in Matthew 18:15–17 that "men shulden snybbe ther bretheren by thre times & aftir-ward forsake ther companye as venym" (p 133). *Of the Church* is extant in four manuscripts, one of the late fourteenth century (Talbert and Thomson, "Wyclif," p. 527).

21. *Of the Church*, p. 134.
22. *English Wycliffite Sermons*, vol. III, p. 109.
23. *Of Pseudo-Friars*, pp. 61–2.
24. *Ibid.*, p. 81. In contrast to polemical tractates like *Of Pseudo-Friars*, Wycliffite *distinctiones*, the *Floretum* (between 1384 and 1396), and its abbreviated form the *Rosarium theologie*, preserve the traditional ethical worries of pastoral discourse before 1380. Because their entries on "correpcio" (*Floretum*, British Library MS Harley 401, ff. 64^v–5^v) and "correpcio fraterna" (*Rosarium*, British Library MS Harley 3226, f. 32^v) are composed largely of *sententiae* from Augustine and other theologians up to Hugh Ripelin, they transmit debates about under what circumstances correction should be made public and the relative severity with which different types of Christians should be rebuked. While Wyclif is quoted 180 times in the *Floretum* (Hudson, *Premature Reformation*, p. 107), he is not in this entry nor in the *Rosarium*'s. For the dating and sources of both compilations, see *Middle English Translation of the "Rosarium Theologie,"* pp. 19–29.
25. *Of Pseudo-Friars*, pp. 62–5.
26. *Ibid.*, p. 63.
27. Compare Jack Upland's penultimate address to his friar-antagonist: "Frere, take hede to my tale and to min entent also, for charite chasith me therto to chalenge youre defautis that ye moun amende to God and to man this mis or ye die" (*Jack Upland*, p. 132). Somerset gives good reasons for dating the various versions between the early 1380s and early 1390s (*Clerical Discourse*, pp. 216–17).
28. *Of Pseudo-Friars*, p. 79.
29. Peres's way of life and deeds in *Crede* often authenticate the details of his polemic, as well. For example, his abject poverty is consistent with his critique of friarly wealth – in contrast to the Franciscan's lavish convent giving the lie to his Rule's prohibition against handling money.
30. Ghosh, *Wycliffite Heresy*, pp. 115–16.
31. *Of Pseudo-Friars*, p. 80.
32. *Ibid.*, p. 75.
33. *Ibid.*, pp. 62, 80.
34. Green, *Crisis of Truth*, pp. 24–31.
35. Matthew 23:29–31 (the tombs of the prophets); Matthew 5:3 (the poor in spirit).
36. For these theological senses of truth, see Green, *Crisis of Truth*, pp. 19–24.
37. *Of Pseudo-Friars*, pp. 62–3.

38. *Jack Upland*, p. 126. In his set of counter-arguments to claims in *Jack Upland* (1395), the Franciscan William Woodford, a frequent opponent of Wyclif and his followers, devotes several folios to explaining why fraternal correction should not be practiced generally – that is, in every case by any Christian whatsoever ("non est servandus generaliter in omni delicto a quolibet bono xhristiano"). In the case of notorious sins, he reasons, we ought to skip admonition and move openly and immediately to public correction, a longstanding pastoral practice. When a large group of sinners is involved, especially the head of an ecclesiastical community, private admonition will do more harm than good. And so on. *Responsiones ad Quaestiones LXV*, Bodleian Library Oxford MS Bodl. 703, ff. 44ᵛ–5ᵛ. These arguments are a direct rebuttal of Jack's claim that the friars violate the Gospel teaching when they imprison, rather than rebuke fraternally, their sinning fellows.

39. *Of Pseudo-Friars*, p. 80.

40. Green explains the ethical sense of truth and its roots in legal practice in *Crisis of Truth*, pp. 10–19.

41. Hudson, "Lollard Sect Vocabulary?" pp. 16–17.

42. *Of Pseudo-Friars*, p. 62.

43. Ghosh, *Wycliffite Heresy*, p. 114.

44. *Of Pseudo-Friars*, p. 83. See Krug's incisive interpretation of the records about Hawisia Moon, a Norfolk lollard accused of heresy. Moon rejects priestly law-making for a "lived spiritual experience" in which the believer desires to hear, embrace, live out, and cleave to scripture (*Reading Families*, pp. 133–7).

45. Barr, *Signes*, p. 49.

46. Swidler, *Talk of Love*, p. 131. She characterizes ideological religion on pp. 43–110.

47. Steiner, "Inventing Legality," p. 200.

48. Hudson, *Premature Reformation*, p. 248.

49. Ghosh, *Wycliffite Heresy*, pp. 12–15; Copeland, *Pedagogy*, Part 1.

50. The Wycliffite long commentary on Luke survives only in Cambridge University Library MS ᴋᴋ.2.9 (here ff. 61ᵛ–2ʳ).

51. *Ibid.*

52. The Wycliffite short commentary on Matthew, British Library MS Add. 41175, f. 24ʳ. See Pseudo-Chrysostom, *Opus*, ff. 50ʳ–1ᵛ. Wyclif includes large chunks of this commentary in his *Opus evangelicum*, as do the *Floretum* and the *Rosarium*. In contrast to its exegesis of Matthew 7, "short Matthew" clings to patristic exegesis of Matthew 18 itself (ff. 60ᵛ–1ʳ), a chapter not reached by Pseudo-Chrysostom.

53. On the dating, readership, and authorship, see *English Wycliffite Sermons*, vol. IV, pp. 20–37. On the manuscripts, see vol. I, pp. 8–97. An astonishingly full cycle, *EWS* includes sermons on Sunday Epistles as well as Gospels, sermons on the saints (the *sacerdotale*), and ferial sermons – 274 altogether.

54. The Sidney Sussex 74 sermon hews to the *EWS* fairly closely, abbreviating some material. The compilation in this manuscript and its later version in

Bodleian Library Oxford MS Bodl. 95 are described by Spencer, *English Preaching*, pp. 298–302; Hudson also describes the manuscript in *English Wycliffite Sermons*, vol. I, pp. 70–1. The scribal hands are of the late fourteenth and early fifteenth centuries.

55. From the *Speculum vitae Christiani*, a Wycliffite tract from the end of the fourteenth century (Bodleian Library Oxford MS Douce 274, ff. 11ᵛ–12ʳ). See chapter 1 above on correction as a work of spiritual mercy.

56. On payments to priests in the English parish, see Swanson, *Church and Society*, pp. 210–17.

57. Little, *Confession*, pp. 36–7. She compares the *EWS* sermon with the exegesis of Luke 6 in the *Glossa ordinaria*, but, without knowing pastoral discourse on fraternal correction and without reading widely in sermons on this lection, she concludes erroneously that the orthodox writing on the mote and beam does not allow "reformation of the other" (p. 35).

58. *English Wycliffite Sermons*, vol. I, p. 237. The derivative sermon in Sidney Sussex MS 74 develops clerics' lack of mercy into a general contrast of those who live by man's law and those who live by God's: "soche loken al amisse aftur godes lawe, & so unethes is any abouten to see his oune defaute. Aftur mannes law men loken wurcipes to winne, hou they may geten money by sleightes & by wiles, & godes law is left bihinde that techeth hem the contrarye" (f. 13ᵛ).

59. The Sidney Sussex sermon on "Nolite judicare" develops the opacity of the human heart and the folly of judging except by the Gospel: "folye it is to deme a man of thing that he knoweth not, of the privete of monnes herte, or elles of dome that falleth to god, for ofte men demen hem for ivel that ben in auntre ful dere to god or elles demen hem for goode that ben ful foule in godes sight for no mon here in erthe con knowe hou sone thorw grace a mon is turned or elles is bicomen ivele thorw counseile of the fend" (f. 79ᵛ).

60. *Floretum*, f. 65ᵛ.

61. *English Wycliffite Sermons*, vol. I, p. 238.

62. *Ibid.*, pp. 239, 237.

63. *Ibid.*, p. 237.

64. Ghosh, *Wycliffite Heresy*, p. 138.

65. Wyclif, *Sermones*, vol. I, pp. 241–3.

66. *Ibid.*, pp. 243–4. In Wyclif's sermon on "Cum turbe," the lection for the following Sunday, he argues that clerics who neglect to reprove others fail to carry out the third work of spiritual mercy and that lay lords are bound, then, to correct them (p. 250).

67. *English Wycliffite Sermons*, vol. III, p. 110.

CHAPTER 6

1. Some examples. The second Durham Cathedral manuscript (B.IV.36) of Higden's *Speculum curatorum* comes from the turn of the century (Sharpe, *Handlist*, p. 454), as do Peterhouse College Cambridge MSS 24 and 25, a

copy of Bromyard's *Summa praedicantium* in a two-volume set (*ibid.*, p. 221), and Durham Cathedral MS A.I.i., a copy of William of Nottingham's Commentary on the Gospel. Two other copies of the latter appear in 1381 and around the beginning of the fifteenth century (*ibid.*, p. 796). The two extant manuscripts of the first expanded recension of the *Northern Homily Cycle* were copied in 1385 and 1392 (Heffernan and Horner, "Sermons," p. 4,258).

2. John of Mirfield, *Florarium Bartholomaei*, British Library MS Royal 7.F.XI, ff. 35ʳ–6ʳ; the entry runs from 35ʳ to 37ʳ. John was a canon of St. Bartholomew's, Smithfield, in London; his collection of *distinctiones* is dated broadly late fourteenth century (Hartley and Aldridge, *Johannes de Mirfeld*). Ten copies of the whole or of extracts survive, one of the late fourteenth century; five copies are attested to (Sharpe, *Handlist*, p. 284).

3. The vernacular commentary on Matthew from about 1400, which survives in two manuscripts, promotes the practice of fraternal correction in vigorous traditional terms, insisting that "sojettes" may correct and amend "hor prelates" "when nede askes" and that anyone who sees his brother sin and chooses not to correct him sins as much as someone who will not forgive the sins of others (British Library MS Egerton 842, ff. 50ʳ⁻ᵛ and 146ʳ⁻ᵛ). Also Philip Repingdon's expansive traditional sermon on "Estote misericordes," which makes extensive use of Matthew 18:15–17 (Bodleian Library Oxford MS Laud Misc. 635, ff. 267ᵛ–73ᵛ). Repingdon, Wyclif's defender at Oxford in 1382 who abjured Wyclif's teaching later that year, probably wrote this dominical cycle during his Oxford years, 1382–94. His model dominical sermons, designed to make biblical scholarship available to the educated, had a wide readership (Wenzel, *Latin Sermon Collections*, pp. 50–3). No non-Wycliffite sermon on "Si autem peccaverit" survives from these years, which is not surprising because quadragesimal cycles were rare at any time in England in the late Middle Ages.

4. Citing the traditional circumstances when correction should be omitted (when there is no hope of amendment, when admonition may harm a sinner), this *quaestio* advances the conventional argument that beautiful women preachers would arouse the sexual desires of male listeners and so harm them spiritually ("Woman not to Preach," pp. 62–3). Minnis analyzes the final argument of the *quaestio* in *Fallible Authors*, p. 228.

5. The vernacular commentary on Matthew, f. 147ʳ; *Book for a Simple and Devout Woman,* pp. 285–6; John of Mirfield, *Florarium*, ff. 35ʳ–7ʳ.

6. The statute as quoted by Simpson, *Reform*, p. 335.

7. Forrest traces the process by which heresy was investigated by both Church and state in *Detection*, pp. 28–59. Strohm explicates the ecclesiastical and political rhetoric that led up to and justified Sawtry's burning (*England's Empty Throne*, pp. 32–62).

8. Watson, "Censorship," p. 828. Although scholars are qualifying some of his sweeping conclusions, his bold and fresh essay reoriented scholarly thinking about late medieval orthodox religious writing, especially in the vernacular, refusing to divorce it "from the ideological and political struggles that Lollardy precipitated" (p. 825).

9. *Councils*, Part II, p. 904.

10. Preaching of catechetica such as the seven works of spiritual mercy could be brief and formulaic in the hands of the less well-educated, as Wenzel observes (*Latin Sermon Collections*, pp. 352–3).

11. Spencer, *English Preaching*, p. 210; Wenzel, *Latin Sermon Collections*, p. 397. I have not found a surviving sermon on Matthew 18:15–22 that can be dated securely between 1409 and 1440, though there is a Latin one that may have been written before 1440 in a collection given to Merton College in 1468 by its warden Henry Sever (Merton College Oxford MS 236, ff. 155ᵛ–7ʳ). Sermons on "Estote misericordes" appear in an early-fifteenth-century preachers' handbook and a set of University sermons from 1414 and 1424–5 (Wenzel, *Latin Sermons Collections*, pp. 182–8, 81–3). I have not examined these because preaching on this lection does not bear closely on the texts at the center of this chapter. The author of *Dives et Pauper*, a friar, wrote a long vernacular sermon on that lection, but he confines his treatment of correcting sin largely to confessors and judges (Longleat House MS 4, ff. 72ʳ–74ʳ).

12. Manuscripts of the original *Northern Homily Cycle*, which includes the sermon on "Estote misericordes" discussed in chapter 2, were copied in 1425 (two), 1400–25, and 1400–50, while manuscripts of the second expanded recension, which includes as well the "Si autem peccaverit" sermon discussed in chapters 1 and 2, are dated 1400–25 and 1400–15 (Heffernan and Horner, "Sermons," p. 4,258). Several manuscripts of Jacopo's sermons belong to the early fifteenth century, according to the manuscript catalogues of the collections in which they are now housed: British Library MS Royal 8.c.xii, Bodleian Library Oxford MS. Canon Pat. Lat. 35, and, perhaps, Lambeth Palace MS 23. Other manuscripts loosely dated to the fifteenth century may have been copied before 1440.

13. *Concilia*, vol. iii, p. 317. Somerset argues that the Constitutions were meant to regulate the entire system of advanced Latin education and writing, that is, scholastic argumentation that entertains propositions it later dismisses or modifies ("Expanding," pp. 78–92).

14. Spencer, *English Preaching*, p. 432, n. 162. Two manuscripts of the *Destructorium* survive, and one more is attested to (Sharpe, *Handlist*, p. 49). For the *Speculum*, see chapter 1, "Major Sources." I am grateful to Vincent Gillespie for saving me from repeating printed errors about the *Speculum*.

15. Carpenter, *Destructorium*, pp. kiᵛ–kiiʳ. The distinction between slander and detraction comes much later, in the entry on *detractio* (Dviiᵛ). Nine manuscripts of the *Florarium* or excerpts from it survive from the fifteenth century, though no one has attempted to date them exactly (Sharpe, *Handlist*, p. 284).

16. See the discussion of this constitution by Watson, "Censorship," pp. 828–9, which relies on conclusions drawn by Hudson.

17. Watson, "Censorship," p. 825.

18. I accept Barr's dating based on several topical allusions, the most important of which is to Archbishop Arundel's March 1409 letter to the provincial clergy

declaring that friars were exempted from the constitutions stipulating that preachers must be licensed on the basis of examinations ("Dates," pp. 272–5). Horobin has traced the writer to Bristol on the basis of relict spellings and alliterative techniques ("Dialect and Authorship"). I do not consider in this chapter Sir John Audelay's poems (1420s), filled though they are with denunciations of clerical and social vices, because Audelay does not cast them as fraternal correction in any specific way. For the same reason I pass over the early-fifteenth-century "advice to princes" narrative, *Richard the Redeless*.

19. In framing what a life involves I am indebted generally to Middleton, "Langland's Lives." In contrast to *Mum* and the *Book*, *Piers Plowman* leaves different discourses about the proper ethical and religious life still competing, still often discontinuous.

20. Mitchell, *Ethics*, pp. 14–15.

21. *Mum and the Sothsegger*, lines 523–7. All references are to the Barr edition.

22. For a detailed narrative of how these political matters developed and played out, see Kirby, *Henry IV*, pp. 60–225. Several scholars have spelled out the ways of thinking and the social/religious concerns that the poem shares with Wycliffites: Barr in her excellent notes to the edition, in *Socioliterary Practice*, pp. 158–75, and in *Signes*, pp. 113–15, 125–32; Lawton in "Lollardy," pp. 785–93. Nevertheless, as Hudson observes, *Mum* "appears to be without unequivocal sign of unorthodoxy" (*Premature Reformation*, p. 400).

23. *"Piers Plowman" Tradition*, p. 7.

24. To qualify "outset": *Mum* is a fragment, albeit a long one (1,751 lines, plus some Latin lines not numbered); its beginning and ending are missing from the single manuscript.

25. "Tale" here has the sense of a plaintiff's complaint in a legal suit, as Barr notes in her edition, p. 295. I am indebted to her keen sense of the poem's legal diction.

26. Barr's editorial procedure is to incorporate into the main text the Latin quotations written in the margins of the manuscript in the same hand. They are, she notes, "clearly designed to authorise the argument of the main text," in the manner of the Latin lines in *Piers Plowman* (*"Piers Plowman" Tradition*, p. 42).

27. In contrast to the explicit biblical authority here, Thomas Hoccleve, a clerk of the Privy Seal, states more generally the obligation to correct, as one of the duties involved in Justice, in his *Regement of Princes*:

> Of counceill & of helpe we be dettoures
>   Eche to other, by right of bretherhede;
> For whan a man y-falle in-to errour is,
>   His brother ought him counceille & rede
>   To correcte & amende his wikked dede;
>   And if he be vexed with maladye
>   Ministre him helpe, his greef to remedye. (lines 2,486–92)

28. For example, Simpson in "Constraints" and Barr in *Signes*. Barr analyzes usefully the legal vocabulary of these two passages and others, concluding

that the author presents the writing of corrective poetry as a legal activity "analogous to prosecuting a suit at law and passing judgement on those
found guilty of the charges against them" (p. 164). All well and good, but
I cannot agree that, in a poem where the Gospel "ground is of lore" and is
"grounde of all lawes" (lines 140 and 1,622), legal authority "provides the
ultimate poetic authority" (p. 169).

29. For the pastoral metaphor of oil as false praise and the consequences of flattery, see Craun, *Lies*, pp. 126–8. The second sermon on "Si autem peccaverit"
in British Library MS Royal 7.A.VIII constructs the antithesis between fraternal correction and flattery in representative ways (and does so just after setting forth how *subditi* should word rebukes of their *praelati*): "Glossa: 'falsa
laus adulatoris mentes a rigore veritatis emollit ad noxia.' Et Jeromus: 'Nichil
est quod tam facile corrumpat mentes hominum quam adulacio in tam
quod plus nocet lingua adulatoris quam gladius persecutoris'" (f. 316ᵛ). For
other contrasts: John of Mirfield, *Florarium*, f. 36ʳ. See chapter 2, "Moral
authority," for the pastoral contrast between flattery and *objurgatio* (scolding, chiding) in corrective speech.

30. The catechetical treatise with the incipit "Vani sunt" presents in a typical
way a much cited gloss on Romans 1:32 attributed to Ambrose: "Bene agere
et illicita non prohibere consensus erroris est. Consentire est tacere cum possis redarguere. Dicit apostolus ad rom. [Rom. 1:32]: 'Non solum qui faciunt
ea sed qui consenciunt facientibus digni sunt morte.' Gregorius: 'Facientis
culpam habet qui quod possit corrigere negligit emendare'" (f. 80ʳ). See also
chapter 1 and Bromyard, *Summa*, c.16.9, which contains references to several canons.

31. In order to silence the narrator, Mum threatens him with punishment if
he criticizes the clergy in front of an audience that includes lay people,
speech which would defy Archbishop Arundel's third constitution (697–
700; p. 325 n.).

32. Steiner argues persuasively that, by using documents, the *Mum* poet "repre-
sents the means by which society confesses to or witnesses its own corruption; thus, he avoids the agency of the self-interested speaker" (*Documentary
Culture*, p. 182).

33. Craun, *Lies*, pp. 76–86; Peyraut, *Summa de vitiis*, ff. F5ᵛ–G3ʳ; Étienne de
Bourbon, *Tractatus*, ff. 251ᵛ–3ᵛ; *De lingua*, ff. 180ʳ–2ʳ.

34. See Simpson, *Reform*, pp. 217–18, on the contractual political vision of
Mum.

35. Ferguson, "Problem of Counsel," p. 78.

36. Unwise silence (*indiscreta taciturnitas*) was a Sin of the Tongue in pastoral
treatises, which present it as especially reprehensible in priests (e.g., Peyraut,
Summa de vitiis, 13ʳ). On the failure of the clergy to practice correction in
any form, see Bromyard, *Summa*, c.16.9.

37. For male, particularly clerical, readings of the female body and female
speech, see Lochrie, *Margery Kempe*, especially the first chapter.

38. Hughes, *Pastors*, pp. 127–250.

39. For several decades scholars have attributed – often convincingly – Margery Kempe's authoritative criticism of clerics and others to a variety of religious and social forces. For the mystic's voicing of a divine utterance that answers her desire, see Lochrie, *Margery Kempe*. For a culturally constructed female disruptiveness, see Wilson, "Margery"; also McAvoy, "'Aftyr hyr owyn tunge.'" For the influences of Continental holy women, see Dickman, "Margery Kempe"; for the speech of "Marthas" in houses of the Beguines and the *Devotio Moderna*, see Kerby-Fulton, *Books Under Suspicion*, pp. 252–6. For the tradition of female prophecy, see Watt, *Secretaries,* pp. 15–50. For the conflict between clerical codes and those of bourgeois life, see Staley, *Dissenting Fictions*. For the dissenting strategies of Wycliffites and other reformist groups, see Shklar, "Cobham's Daughter"; also Wilson, "Communities," pp. 155–85.

40. Carpenter, *Destructorium*, f. ki^v. *Tabula super Bibliam*, f. 19^v. Also the Wycliffite *Floretum*, f. 64^v.

41. Virtually all of the female saints in the *Gilte Legende* (version of 1438), a translation and adaptation of Jacopo da Varazze's *Legenda Aurea*, and in Osbern Bokenham's *Legendys of Hooly Wummen* (about 1445).

42. Rees Jones, "'A peler'"; Kerby-Fulton, "When Women Preached"; Vauchez, *Laity*, pp. 220–53. For a survey of the lives read in England, see Barratt, "Continental Women Mystics."

43. Brewer, *Tradition and Innovation*, p. 90.

44. For gossip as speech that transforms, see Phillips, *Transforming Talk*.

45. The *Book for a Simple and Devout Woman*, from Margery Kempe's lifetime (*c.* 1400), sees angry slander as the opposite of loving correction. It quotes Matthew 18:15 to insist on private reproof (pp. 285–6).

46. On *convicium* as a Sin of the Tongue, see Craun, *Lies*, pp. 189–93. For honor as its target, Bartolomeo, *Summa*, unpaged under *contumelia sive convitium*.

47. For an account of the battle over Margery Kempe's will and intention in her public displays of affective piety, see Craun, "*Fama*," pp. 195–8. Arnold observes that what got Margery Kempe into trouble with others, sometimes leading to official interrogation, was "the spectre of heresy … framed as feigned piety," which made it difficult for people to decide "how to 'read' the interior person from the exterior shell" ("Margery's Trials," p. 90).

48. For the comparison of slanderers to thieves, see Peyraut, *Summa de vitiis*, f. G10^r; Bromyard, *Summa*, D.6.4.

49. See chapter 3 for pastoral texts on "contentio."

50. Bromyard, *Summa*, C.16.2 and 3; *Corpus* C.22 q.1 c.10 (vol. 1, col. 863). Middle English derivatives of the *Somme le roi* insist, as Margery Kempe does, on the great lord's accountability for the sins of his servants and his retinue (*Book of Vices*, p. 200; *Mirroure of the Worlde*, ff. 148^v–9^r). See also John of Mirfield, who singles out *praelati* (*Florarium*, f. 35^v).

51. Cohen, *Medieval Identity Machines*, p. 158.

52. For the *Book*'s contemporaries it would have been clear that Margery Kempe acquired knowledge of the ethics of fraternal correction not just

from listening to sermons but from clerical catechesis. Spencer notes that she gives a "model answer" to her York inquisitors' question about the verse "Be fruitful" because, in all probability, she had received instruction on the text. Catechesis leaves almost no historical record and so has been undervalued as a source of Margery Kempe's learning, even though the *Book* states that "Masityr Aleyn," a Carmelite doctor of divinity at Lynn, "enformyd hir in qwestions of Scriptur whan sche wolde any askyn him" (p. 168). Even diverse, controverted interpretations could be conveyed in such catechesis, Spencer argues, as "a reflex in the vernacular of scholastic disputations and commentary," though such advanced catechesis might fall under suspicion after Arundel's Constitutions (Spencer, *English Preaching*, pp. 44–6).

53. *Liber Celestis*, p. 197. See also Christ's injunction transmitted through Birgitta: No bishop should have a retainer who does not amend his life (p. 476). We do not know which translation or adaptation of Birgitta's revelations was read to Margery Kempe.

54. Arnold examines carefully the circumstances and legal mechanisms that may very well have brought Margery Kempe to trial at York in "Margery's Trials," pp. 85–93.

55. Margery Kempe uses an *exemplum* earlier in the *Book* in another situation where she is threatened by clerics in an alien place: to counter the chiding of the Canterbury monks. That time, however, her aim is to make herself exemplary by turning chiding to good (*Book*, p. 24).

56. *Liber Celestis*, p. 293.

57. Margery Kempe's subject position has been defined most recently by Gertz-Robinson, "Stepping," pp. 459–68.

58. Staley notes that the *exemplum* also serves to demonstrate Margery Kempe's orthodoxy because of Wycliffite objections to fables of all kinds (*Dissenting Fictions*, pp. 7, 120).

59. Rees Jones argues that minor clerics at York, as throughout the *Book*, are the object of Margery Kempe's correction, thus solidifying episcopal authority and objectives (chiefly to reform the conduct of the lower clergy) (" 'A peler' "). This is certainly an important strain in the *Book*, but in the Canterbury and York episodes she neglects the complicity of the Archbishops in the conduct of their retinues, households, and clerics subject to them, and at York she neglects the Archbishop's own moves to silence Margery Kempe.

60. Gertz-Robinson, "Stepping," pp. 464–8. Voaden has shown how Margery Kempe at once observes some strictures on women visionaries and manages to assert her authority, even in ways contrary to the discourse on *discretio spirituum* (*God's Words*, pp. 109–46).

61. In transforming constraints on speaking into opportunity, Margery Kempe is akin to the women Cannon has studied in legal records, who manage to get their voices into the legal record by using their limited legal rights, in spite of restrictions on their speech in courts of law ("Rights").

62. Wilson, "Communities," pp. 159–64; Ashley, "Historicizing Margery," p. 371; Dickman, "A Showing," p. 176; Lewis, "Margery Kempe."

63. Vauchez, *Laity*, pp. 99, 104.

POSTSCRIPT

1. Brown, *Church and Society*, p. 179.
2. Fiona Somerset, then a graduate student, asked these penetrating questions of me when I gave a paper on pastoral discourse on deviant speech and *Patience* back in 1989.
3. Spencer observes throughout *English Preaching*, but especially in chapter 5, "The Preaching of *Pastoralia*," that most Middle English sermon collections presented "knowledge over and above" the minimal pastoral standard, largely by including basic exegesis of the Bible in English.
4. Mitchell, *Ethics*, p. 13.
5. On puerility, see especially Copeland, *Pedagogy*, and Ghosh, *Wycliffite Heresy*; on fundamentals, Watson's analysis of Arundel's Constitutions in "Censorship." Vauchez, "Church," p. 194.

Bibliography

PRIMARY SOURCES

MANUSCRIPTS

Cambridge, Cambridge University Library Gg.1.1: *Miroir ou Les évangiles des domnées* of Robert of Gretham
    Kk.2.9: Wycliffite long commentary on Luke
Cambridge, Sidney Sussex College 74: Wycliffite sermons
London, British Library Additional 15237: *forma confessionis* ("Confessor venientem")
    Additional 15833: *Narrationes miraculorum*
    Additional 23935: *Officia varia ad usum fratrum praedicatorum*
    Additional 30056: *Verbum abbreviatum* of Pierre le Chantre
    Additional 41175: Wycliffite shorter commentary on Matthew
    Egerton 842: vernacular commentary on Matthew
    Harley 401: *Floretum*
    Harley 3226: *Rosarium theologie*
    Harley 3235: *Opus imperfectum in Matthaeum* of Pseudo-Chrysostom
    Lansdowne 385: catechetica ("Vani sunt")
    Royal 2.D.VI: dominical sermons
    Royal 5.A.VIII: catechetica ("Sunt plura")
    Royal 6.E.VI and VII: *Omne bonum* attributed to James le Palmer
    Royal 7.A.VIII: sermon collection
    Royal 7.F.XI: *Florarium Bartholomaei* of John of Mirfield
    Royal 8.C.VIII: *distinctiones* ("Duplex est")
    Royal 8.G.VI: *Compendium morale de virtutibus* of Roger of Waltham
    Royal 11.A.XIII: *Distinctiones* of John Lathbury
    Royal 18.A.X: *modus confitendi* ("Whan thow thenkest")
Longleat House, Longleat 4: dominical sermons by the author of *Dives et Pauper*
Oxford, Balliol College 77: Ranulph Higden, *Speculum curatorum*
Oxford, Bodleian Library Auct. D.4.19: anonymous commentary on Galatians
    Bodleian 216: *Distinctiones* of Simon of Boraston
    Bodleian 283: *The Mirroure of the Worlde*
    Bodleian 320: *Sermones de tempore* of Jacopo da Varazze

194

Bodleian 563: *Distinctiones theologicae* of Nicolas de Byard
Bodleian 583: *Tabula super historias Bibliae* ("Abstinentia caro domatur")
Bodleian 688: *Tabula super Bibliam* ("Abstinentia. Precepit Deus")
Bodleian 703: *Responsiones* of William of Woodford
Bodleian 716: *Postilla* of John Wyclif (New Testament only)
Bodleian 767: *Speculum juniorum*
Bodleian 923: *The Clensing of Manes Sawle*
Canon Misc. 208 and 209: the *Summa de casibus conscientie* of Astesano da Asti
Canon Pat. Lat. 118: *Distinctiones exemplorum* ("Abstinentia et jejunio")
Digby 103: *Summa de doctrinas sacerdotali* of Richard of Wetheringsett
Douce 274: *Speculum vitae Christiani*
Hatton 101: sermons on Matthew
Holkam Misc. 40: Middle English *Mirror*, translation of Robert of Gretham
Laud Misc. 165: William of Nottingham's Commentary on *Unum ex quatuor*
Laud Misc. 200: Wycliffite sermons
Laud Misc. 467: *Galatas secundum litteram* of Peter of Tarantasia
Laud Misc. 635: dominical sermons of Philip Repingdon
Rawlinson A.361: *Oculus sacerdotum* of William of Pagula
Rawlinson C.899: *Distinctiones pro sermonibus* of John of Wales
Oxford, Jesus College 39: *Disce mori*
Oxford, Lincoln College Lat. 74: *Summa* of Monaldo da Capo d'Istria
Oxford, Magdalen College 167: sermon collection
Oxford, Merton College 236: sermon collection
Oxford, Oriel College 20: *De lingua*
   38: *Summa confessorum* of Johann von Erfürt
   68: *Tractatus de diversis materiis predicabilibus* of Étienne de Bourbon
Oxford, University College 109: *Sermones quadragesimales* of Jacopo da Varazze

EDITIONS

Ailred of Rievaulx. *De spirituali amicitia*. Anselm Hoste (ed). CCCM I.
Albert the Great. *Enarrationes in evangelium Lucae*. In *Opera omnia*, A. Borgnet (ed.), vols. XXII and XXIII. Paris: Vives, 1894–5.
   Enarrationes in evangelium Matthaei. In *Opera omnia*, A. Borgnet (ed.), vols. XX and XXI. Paris: Vives, 1893–4.
Alexander of Hales. *Quaestiones disputatae*. Bibliotheca Franciscana Medii Aevi, vols. XIX–XXI. Quaracchi: Collegium S. Bonaventurae, 1960.
   Glossa in librum IV Sententiarum Petri Lombardi. Bibliotheca Franciscana Medii Aevi, vols. XII–XV. Quaracchi: Collegium S. Bonaventurae, 1951–7.
Ambrose. *Epistulae*. M. Zelzer (ed.), 4 vols. CSEL LXXXII.
   Expositio psalmi cxviii. M. Petschenig (ed.). CSEL LXII.
Ambrosius Autpertus. *Libellus de conflictu vitiorum atque virtutum*. *Ambrosi Autperti opera*. Robert Weber (ed.), 3 vols. CCCM XXVIIB. pp. 909–31.

Audelay, John. *The Poems of Sir John Audelay*. Ella K. Whiting (ed). EETS o.s. CLXXXIV. London: Oxford University Press, 1931.

Augustine, Aurelius. *Contra Faustum*. J. Zycha (ed.). CSEL xxv.
De civitate Dei. E. Hoffmann (ed.). CSEL XL.
Epistulae. A. Goldbacher (ed.). CSEL XXXIV, XLIV, LVII, LXVIII.
Sermones ad populum. PL XXXVIII.

Bartolomeo da San Concordio. *Summa de casibus conscientie*. Cologne: Hurnen, 1474.

Biblia latina cum glossa ordinaria. 4 vols. Strasbourg: Rusch, 1480–1. Rpt. Turnhout: Brepols, 1992.

Biblia vulgata. Alberto Colunga and Laurentino Turrado (eds.). Madrid: Biblioteca de Auctores Christianos, 1977.

Book for a Simple and Devout Woman: A Late Middle English Adaptation of Peraldus's "Summa de Vitiis et Virtutibus" and Friar Laurent's "Somme le Roi". F. N. M. Diekstra (ed.). Mediaevalia Groningana XXIV. Groningen: Forsten, 1998.

The Book of Margery Kempe. Sanford Meech and Hope Emily Allen (eds.). EETS o.s. CCXII. London: Oxford University Press, 1940.

The Book of Vices and Virtues. W. Nelson Francis (ed.). EETS o.s. CCXVII. London: Oxford University Press, 1942.

Book to a Mother: An Edition with Commentary. Adrian T. McCarthy (ed.). Salzburg Studies in English: Elizabethan and Renaissance Studies XCII. Salzburg: Institut für Anglistik und Amerikanistik, 1981.

Brinton, Thomas. *Sermons*. Mary Aquinas Devlin (ed.). 2 vols. Camden Society, Third Series, vols. LXXXV and LXXXVI. London: Royal Historical Society, 1954.

Bromyard, John. *Opus trivium*. Cologne: Zel, not after 1473.
Summa praedicantium. Nuremberg: Koburger, 1485.

Carpenter, Alexander. *Destructorium viciorum*. Paris: n.p., 1516.

Chaucer, Geoffrey. *The Riverside Chaucer*, 3rd edn. L. Benson *et alia* (eds.). New York: Houghton Mifflin, 1987.

Concilia Magnae Britanniae et Hiberniae. David Wilkins (ed.). 4 vols. London: R. Gosling, 1737.

Constitutiones concilii quarti Lateranensis una cum commentariis glossatorum. Antonius Garcia y Garcia (ed.). Monumenta Juris Canonici, Series A, vol. II. Vatican City: Biblioteca Apostolica Vaticana, 1981.

Corpus iuris canonici. A. Friedberg (ed.). 2 vols. Leipzig: Tauchnitz, 1879 and 1881.

Councils and Synods with other Documents Relating to the English Church II. F. M. Powicke and C. R. Cheney (eds.). 2 parts. Cambridge University Press, 1964.

Durant, Guillaume I. *Speculum judiciale cum additionibus Johannis Andree*. 3 vols. Rome: L. Pflugel and G. Lauer, 1471.

The English Works of Wycliff. F. D. Matthew (ed.). EETS o.s. LXXIV. London: Kegan Paul, Trench, and Trübner, 1880.

English Wycliffite Sermons. Anne Hudson and Pamela Gradon (eds.). 5 vols. Oxford: Clarendon, 1983–96.

Fasciculi zizaniorum. W. W. Shirley (ed.). Rolls Series v. London: Longman, 1858.

Francis of Assisi. *Regula bullata.* In *Die Opuscula des hl. Franziskus von Assisi.* K. Esse (ed.). Spicilegium Bonaventurianum, 1976.

François de Meyronnes. *Sermones.* Brussels: n.p., 1481.

Henricus de Segusio. *Summa aurea.* Lyon: Gueynard, 1517.

Hoccleve, Thomas. *The Regement of Princes and Fourteen Minor Poems.* Frederick J. Furnivall (ed.). EETS e.s. LXXII. London: Kegan Paul, Trench, and Trübner, 1897.

Hou Sathanas & His Prestis & His Feined Religious Casten by Thre Cursed Heresies to Distroye Alle Good Livinge & Maintene Alle Manere of Sinne. In *The English Works of Wyclif,* pp. 263–74.

How the Office of Curates Is Ordained by God. In *The English Works of Wyclif,* pp. 141–63.

Hugo de Saint Cher. *Opera omnia in Vetus et Novem Testamentum.* Pezzana: n.p., 1732.

Isidore of Seville. *Sententiarum libri tres.* PL LXXXIII.

Jack Upland. In *Six Ecclesiastical Satires,* James Dean (ed.). TEAMS Middle English Text Series. Kalamazoo: Medieval Institute Publications, 1991. pp. 115–44.

Jerome. *Commentariorum in Mattheum libri IV.* D. Hurst and M. Adriaen (eds.). CCSL LXXVII.

Johann von Freiburg. *Summa confessorum.* Augsburg: Zainer, 1476.

Langland, William. *Piers Plowman: The A-Version.* George Kane (ed.), rev. version. London: Athlone, 1988.

    Piers Plowman: The B-Version. George Kane and E. Talbot Donaldson (eds.), rev. version. London: Athlone, 1988.

    Piers Plowman: The C-Version. George Russell and George Kane (eds.). London: Athlone, 1997.

Liber Celestis of St. Bridget of Sweden. Roger Ellis (ed.). EETS o.s. CCXCI. Oxford University Press, 1987.

Magna vita Sancti Hugonis. Decima L. Douie and David Hugh Farmer (eds.), 2 vols. Oxford: Clarendon, 1985.

Mannyng, Robert. *Handlyng Synne.* Idelle Sullens (ed.). Medieval and Renaissance Texts and Studies XIV. Binghamton: Center for Medieval and Early Renaissance Studies, 1983.

Memoriale credencium. J. H. L. Kengen (ed.). Nijmegen: Katholicke Universiteit, 1979.

The Middle English Translation of the "Rosarium theologie": A Selection. Christina von Nolcken (ed.). Heidelberg: Winter, 1979.

Missale ad usum Ecclesiae Westmonasteriensis. John Wickham Legg (ed.), 3 vols. Henry Bradshaw Society I, V, XII. London: Harrison and Sons, 1891, 1893, 1897.

Missale ad usum insignis Ecclesiae Eboracensis. W. Henderson (ed.), 2 vols. Publications of the Surtees Society LIX and LX. Durham: Andrews, 1874.

Missale ad usum percelebris Ecclesiae Herefordensis. W. Henderson (ed.). Leeds: n.p., 1874. Rpt. Farnborough: Gregg, 1969.

Mum and the Sothsegger. In *The "Piers Plowman" Tradition*, pp. 135–202.

A Myrour to Lewde Men and Wymmen. Venetia Nelson (ed.). Heidelberg: Winter, 1981.

Nicolas de Lyre. *Postilla super totam Bibliam.* 4 vols. Strasbourg: n.p., 1492. Rpt Frankfurt am Main: Minerva, 1971.

Northern Homily Cycle. Saara Nevanlinna (ed.). 3 vols. *Mémoires de la Société Néophilologique de Helsinki*, 35 (1972), 41 (1973), 43 (1984).

Of Clerkis Possessioneris. In *The English Works of Wyclif*, pp. 114–40.

Of Dominion. In *English Wyclif Tracts 4–6*, Conrad Lindberg (ed.). Studia Linguistica Norvegica XI. Oslo: Novus Forlag, 2000. pp. 93–106.

Of Prelates. In *The English Works of Wyclif*, pp. 52–107.

Of Pseudo-Friars. In *English Wyclif Tracts 4–6*, Conrad Lindberg (ed.). Studia Linguistica Norvegica XI. Oslo: Novus Forlag, 2000. pp. 61–92.

Of the Church and Her Members. In *English Wyclif Tracts 1–3*, Conrad Lindberg (ed.). Studia Linguistica Norvegica V. Oslo: Novus Forlag, 1991. pp. 106–70.

Of the Leaven of the Pharisees. In *The English Works of Wyclif*, pp. 1–27.

Ordo missalis fratrum minorum. In *Sources of the Modern Roman Liturgy*, S. J. P. Van Rijk (ed.), 2 vols. Leiden: Brill, 1963. Vol. II, pp. 205–331.

Peter Damian. "De ferenda aequanimiter correptione." PL CXLV.

Peter Lombard. *Collectanea in omnes b. Pauli Apostoli epistolas.* PL CXCI and CXCII.

Peyraut, Guillaume. *Summa de vitiis.* Cologne: Quentell, 1479.
  Summa virtutum. Lyons: n.p., 1688.

Pierce the Ploughman's Crede. In *The "Piers Plowman" Tradition*, pp. 61–97.

The "Piers Plowman" Tradition. Helen Barr (ed.). London: Dent, 1993.

The Plowman's Tale. In *Six Ecclesiastical Satires*, James Dean (ed.). TEAMS Middle English Texts Series. Kalamazoo: Medieval Institute Publications, 1991. pp. 51–114.

La règle de saint Augustin. Luc Verheijen, OSA (ed.), 2 vols. Paris: Études Augustiniennes, 1967.

Richard the Redeless. In *The "Piers Plowman" Tradition*, pp. 99–133.

Ripelin, Hugh. *Compendium theologicae veritatis.* Venice: Bevilaqua, 1492.

The Sarum Missal. J. Wickham Legg (ed.), 2 vols. Oxford: Clarendon, 1916.

Speculum Christiani. Gustaf Holmstedt (ed.). EETS o.s. CLXXXII. London: Oxford University Press, 1933.

Speculum spiritualium. Paris: Wolfgang Hopyl, 1510.

"*Speculum vitae:* An Edition of British Museum Manuscript Additional 17. C.VIII." J. W. Smelz (ed.), unpublished Phd thesis, Duquesne University, 1977.

Statuta generalis ordinis. P. M. Biel (ed.). *Archivum Franciscanum Historicum*, 34 (1941), 13–94, 284–358.

Summa virtutum de remediis anime. Siegfried Wenzel (ed.). The Chaucer Library. Athens: University of Georgia Press, 1984.

Thomas Aquinas. *Disputed Questions on the Virtues.* E. M. Atkins and Thomas Williams (trans.). Cambridge Texts in the History of Philosophy. Cambridge University Press, 2005.

Quaestiones disputatae. P. Bazzi *et alia* (eds.), 2 vols. Rome: Marietti, 1949.

Scriptum super Sententiis. M. F. Moos (ed.), 4 vols. Paris: Lethielleux, 1947.

Summa theologiae. Blackfriars (eds. and trans.), 60 vols. London: Eyre and Spottiswoode, 1964–75.

Walsingham, Thomas. *Chronicon Angliae.* Edward M. Thompson (ed.). Rolls Series LXIV. London: Longman, 1874.

Historia Anglicana. H. T. Riley (ed.), 2 vols. Rolls Series XXVIII. London: Longman, 1863.

"Woman not to Preach: A Disputation in BL MS Harley 31." Alcuin Blamires and C. W. Marx (eds.). *Journal of Medieval Latin*, 3 (1993), 34–63.

Wyclif, John. *Conclusiones triginta tres sive de paupertate Christi.* In *Opera minora*, Johann Loserth (ed.). London: C. K. Paul for The Wyclif Society, 1913. pp. 19–73.

Cruciata. In *John Wyclif's Polemical Works in Latin*, R. Buddensieg (ed.), 2 vols. London: Trübner for the Wyclif Society, 1883. Vol. II, pp. 588–632.

De civili dominio. Vol. I, Reginald L. Poole (ed). Vols. II, III, and IV, Johann Loserth (ed.). London: Trübner for the Wyclif Society, 1885–1904.

De condemnacione XIX conclusionum. In *Fasciculi zizaniorum*, pp. 481–92.

De ecclesia. Johann Loserth (ed.). London: Trübner for the Wyclif Society, 1886.

De fundacione sectorum. In *John Wyclif's Polemical Works in Latin*, R. Buddensieg (ed.), 2 vols. London: Trübner for the Wyclif Society, 1883. Vol I, pp. 13–80.

De mandatis divinis. Johann Loserth and F. D. Matthew (eds.). London: C. K. Paul for the Wyclif Society, 1922.

De potestate pape. J. Loserth (ed.). London: Trübner for the Wyclif Society, 1907.

De simonia. S. Herzberg-Fränkel and M. H. Dziewicki (eds.). London: Trübner for the Wyclif Society, 1898.

De veritate sacre scripture. Rudolpf Buddensieg (ed.), 3 vols. London: Trübner for the Wyclif Society, 1905–7.

Libellus. In *Fasciculi zizaniorum*, pp. 245–57.

Opus evangelicum. Johann Loserth (ed.), 2 vols. London: Trübner for the Wyclif Society, 1895 and 1896.

Protestacio. In Walsingham, *Historia*, and Walsingham, *Chronicon Angliae*, pp. 357–63.

Responsiones ad argumenta cuiusdam emuli veritati. In *Opera minora*, Johann Loserth (ed.). London: C. K. Paul for the Wyclif Society, 1913. Vol. I, pp. 259–312.

Sermones. Johann Loserth (ed.), 4 vols. London: Trübner for the Wyclif Society, 1887–90.

Trialogus. G. Lechler (ed.). Oxford: Clarendon, 1869.

SECONDARY SOURCES

Aers, David. "Visionary Eschatology: *Piers Plowman*." *Modern Theology*, 16 (2000), 3–17.

Aers, David, and Lynn Staley. *The Powers of the Holy: Religion, Politics, and Gender in Late Medieval English Culture.* University Park: Pennsylvania State University Press, 1996.

Aiken, Henry David. "The Levels of Moral Discourse." *Ethics,* 62 (1952), 235–47.

Akehurst, F. R. P. "Good Name, Reputation, and Notoriety in French Customary Law." In Fenster and Smail (eds.), pp. 75–94.

Alford, John. *"Piers Plowman": A Guide to the Quotations.* Binghamton: State University of New York Press, 1992.

"The Role of Quotations in *Piers Plowman*." *Speculum,* 52 (1977), 80–99.

Arnold, John H. "Margery's Trials: Heresy, Lollardy and Dissent." In *A Companion to "The Book of Margery Kempe",* Arnold and Katherine J. Lewis (eds.). Cambridge: Brewer, 2004. pp. 75–93.

Asad, Talal. *Genealogies of Religion: Discipline and Reasons of Power in Christianity and Islam.* Baltimore: Johns Hopkins University Press, 1993.

Ashley, Kathleen. "Historicizing Margery: The Book of Margery Kempe." *Journal of Medieval and Early Modern Studies,* 28 (1998), 371–88.

Barr, Helen. "The Dates of 'Richard the Redeless' and 'Mum and the Sothsegger'." *Notes and Queries,* 235 (1990), 270–5.

Signes and Sothe: Language in the "Piers Plowman" Tradition. Cambridge: Brewer, 1994.

Socioliterary Practice in Late Medieval England. Oxford University Press, 2001.

Barratt, Alexandra. "Continental Women Mystics and English Readers." In *The Cambridge Companion to Medieval Women's Writing,* Carolyn Dinshaw and David Wallace (eds.). Cambridge Companions to Literature. Cambridge University Press, 2003. pp. 240–55.

Bataillon, L. J. "The Tradition of Nicholas of Biard's *Distinctiones.*" *Viator,* 25 (1994), 245–88.

Benson, C. David. *Public "Piers Plowman": Modern Scholarship and Late Medieval English Culture.* University Park: Pennsylvania State University Press, 2004.

Blamires, Alcuin. "Women and Preaching in Medieval Orthodoxy, Heresy, and Saints' Lives." *Viator,* 26 (1995), 135–52.

Bloomfield, Morton W., with B.-G. Guyot, D. Howard, and T. Kabealo. *Incipits of Latin Works on the Virtues and Vices, 1100–1500 A.D.* Cambridge, MA: Medieval Academy of America, 1979.

. *"Piers Plowman" as a Fourteenth-Century Apocalypse.* New Brunswick: Rutgers University Press, 1962.

Bossy, John. *Christianity in the West, 1400–1700.* Oxford University Press, 1985.

Bourdieu, Pierre. *The Logic of Practice.* Richard Nice (trans.). Stanford University Press, 1990.

Bowers, John. *The Crisis of Will in "Piers Plowman."* Washington: Catholic University of America Press, 1986.

"*Piers Plowman* and the Police: Notes toward a History of the Wycliffite Langland." *Yearbook of Langland Studies,* 6 (1992), 1–50.

Boyle, Leonard E. "The *Summa confessorum* of John of Freiburg and the Popularization of the Moral Teaching of St. Thomas and Some of His Contemporaries." In *St. Thomas Aquinas, 1274–1974: Commemorative Studies,* Armand A. Maurer *et alia* (eds.), 2 vols. Toronto: Pontifical Institute of Mediaeval Studies, 1974. Vol. II, pp. 245–68. Rpt. *Pastoral Care, Clerical Education, and Canon Law, 1200–1400.* London: Variorum Reprints, 1981.

"Three English Pastoral *Summae* and a 'Magister Galienus'." *Studia Gratiana,* 11 (1967), 133–44.

Brewer, Derek. *Tradition and Innovation in Chaucer.* London: Macmillan, 1982.

Brown, Andrew. *Church and Society in England, 1200–1500.* Basingstoke: Palgrave, 2003.

Brown, Catherine. *Contrary Things: Exegesis, Dialectic, and the Poetics of Contrary Things.* Stanford University Press, 1998.

Brundage, James. *Medieval Canon Law.* New York: Longman, 1995.

Burrow, John A. "The Audience of Piers Plowman." *Anglia,* 75 (1957), 373–84.

Cannon, Christopher. "The Rights of Medieval English Women: Crime and the Issue of Representation." In *Medieval Crime and Social Control,* Barbara Hanawalt and David Wallace (eds.). Medieval Cultures XVI. Minneapolis: University of Minnesota Press, 1999. pp. 156–85.

Casagrande, Carla, and Silvana Vecchio. *I peccati della lingua: disciplina ed etica nella cultura medievale.* Rome: Instituto della Enciclopedia Italiano, 1987.

Catto, J. I. "Wyclif and Wycliffism at Oxford, 1356–1430." In *The History of the University of Oxford: Vol. II: Late Medieval Oxford,* J. I. Catto and Ralph Evans (eds.), 2 vols. Oxford: Clarendon, 1992. pp. 195–262.

Clopper, Lawrence. "Response to '3e, by Peter and by Poul!'" *Yearbook of Langland Studies,* 15 (2001), 30–2.

"Songes of Rechelesnesse": Langland and the Franciscans. Ann Arbor: University of Michigan Press, 1997.

Cohen, Jeffrey. *Medieval Identity Machines.* Medieval Cultures XXXV. Minneapolis: University of Minnesota Press, 2003.

Cohen, Randy. "The Ethicist." *New York Times,* July 11, 1999.

Cole, Andrew. *Literature and Heresy in the Age of Chaucer.* Cambridge Studies in Medieval Literature LXXI. Cambridge University Press, 2008.

"William Langland's Lollardy." *Yearbook of Langland Studies,* 17 (2003), 25–54.

Colish, Marcia. "The Early Scholastics and the Reform of Doctrine and Practice." In *Reforming the Church before Modernity: Patterns, Problems and Approaches,* Christopher M. Bellitto and Louis I. Hamilton (eds.). Aldershot: Ashgate, 2005. pp. 61–8.

Copeland, Rita. *Pedagogy, Intellectuals, and Dissent in the Later Middle Ages: Lollardy and Ideas of Learning.* Cambridge Studies in Medieval Literature XLIV. Cambridge University Press, 2001.

Costello, Joseph A. *The Moral Obligation of Fraternal Correction.* Washington: Catholic University of America Press, 1949.

Coulet, Noël. *Les Visites pastorales.* Typologie des Sources du Moyen Age Occidental XXIII. Turnhout: Brepols, 1977.

Craun, Edwin. "*Fama* and Pastoral Constraints on Rebuking Sinners: *The Book of Margery Kempe*." In Fenster and Smail (eds.), pp. 187–209.

"*Inordinata Locutio*: Blasphemy in Pastoral Literature, 1200–1500." *Traditio*, 39 (1983), 135–62.

"'It is a freletee of flessh': Excuses for Sin, Pastoral Rhetoric, and Moral Agency." In *In the Garden of Evil: The Vices and Culture in the Middle Ages*, Thelma Fenster and Daniel L. Smail (eds.). Toronto: Pontifical Institute of Mediaeval Studies, 2005. pp. 170–92.

Lies, Slander and Obscenity in Medieval English Literature: Pastoral Rhetoric and the Deviant Speaker. Cambridge Studies in Medieval Literature XXXI. Cambridge University Press, 1997.

"'3e, by Peter and by Poul!': Lewte and the Practice of Fraternal Correction." *Yearbook of Langland Studies*, 15 (2001), 15–29.

Dahmus, Joseph H. *The Prosecution of John Wyclif*. New Haven: Yale University Press, 1952.

William Courtenay: Archbishop of Canterbury, 1381–1396. University Park: Pennsylvania State University Press, 1955.

Deferrari, R. J. *A Latin–English Dictionary of St. Thomas Aquinas: Based on the "Summa Theologica" and Selected Passages of His Other Works*. Boston: St. Paul Editions, 1960.

Dickman, Susan. "Margery Kempe and the Continental Tradition of the Pious Woman." In *The Medieval Mystical Tradition in England*, Marion Glasscoe (ed.). Cambridge: Brewer, 1984. pp. 150–68.

"A Showing of God's Grace: *The Book of Margery Kempe*." In *Mysticism and Spirituality in Medieval England*, William F. Pollard and Robert Boenig (eds.). Cambridge: Brewer, 1997. pp. 159–76.

Donaldson, E. Talbot. *"Piers Plowman": The C-Text and Its Poet*. New Haven: Yale University Press, 1949.

Doyle, A. I. "The *Speculum spiritualium* from Manuscript to Print." *Journal of the Early Book Society*, 11 (2008), 145–54.

Farr, William. *John Wyclif as a Legal Reformer*. Leiden: Brill, 1974.

Fenster, Thelma, and Daniel L. Smail (eds.). *"Fama": The Politics of Talk and Reputation in Medieval Europe*. Ithaca: Cornell University Press, 2003.

Ferguson, Arthur B. "The Problem of Counsel in *Mum and the Sothsegger*." *Studies in the Renaissance*, 2 (1955), 67–83.

Fletcher, Alan J. *Preaching, Politics and Poetry in Late-Medieval England*. Dublin: Four Courts, 1998.

Forrest, Ian. *The Detection of Heresy in Late Medieval England*. Oxford: Clarendon, 2005.

Foucault, Michel. "The Subject and Power." In *Michel Foucault: Beyond Structuralism and Hermeneutics*, Hubert Dreyfus and Paul Rabinow (eds.). University of Chicago Press, 1982. pp. 208–26.

Frazer, Elizabeth, and Nicola Lacey. "MacIntyre, Feminism, and the Concept of Practice." In *After MacIntyre: Critical Perspectives on the Work of Alasdair MacIntyre*, John Horton and Susan Mendus (eds.). University of Notre Dame Press, 1994. pp. 265–82.

Froehlich, Karlfried. "Fallibility Instead of Infallibility? A Brief History of the Interpretation of Galatians 2:11–14." In *Teaching Authority and Infallibility in the Church,* Paul Empie, J. Austin Murphy, and Joseph Burgess (eds.). Lutherans and Catholics in Dialogue VI. Minneapolis: Augsburg, 1980. pp. 259–69, 351–57.

Galbraith, G. R. *The Constitution of the Dominican Order, 1216–1360.* Manchester University Press, 1925.

Gertz-Robinson, Genelle. "Stepping into the Pulpit?: Women's Preaching in *The Book of Margery Kempe* and *The Examinations of Anne Askew.*" In Olson and Kerby-Fulton (cds.), pp. 459–82.

Ghosh, Kantik. *The Wycliffite Heresy: Authority and the Interpretation of Texts.* Cambridge Studies in Medieval Literature XLV. Cambridge University Press, 2002.

Gill, Miriam. "From Urban Myth to Didactic Image: The Warning to Swearers." In *The Hands of the Tongue: Essays on Deviant Speech,* Edwin D. Craun (ed.). Kalamazoo: Medieval Institute Publications, 2007. pp. 137–60.

Glorieux, Palémon. *La Littérature quodlibétique de 1260 a 1320.* 2 vols. Vol. I at Le Saulchoir: Kain, 1925, and vol. II at Paris: Vrin, 1935.

Green, Richard F. *A Crisis of Truth: Literature and Law in Ricardian England.* Middle Ages Series. Philadelphia: University of Pennsylvania Press, 1999.

Hanawalt, Barbara. *"Of Good and Ill Repute": Gender and Social Control in Medieval England.* New York: Oxford University Press, 1998.

Hanna, Ralph. "Emendations to a Life of Ne-erdowel." *Yearbook of Langland Studies,* 14 (2000), 183–98.

London Literature: 1300–1380. Cambridge Studies in Medieval Literature LVII. Cambridge University Press, 2005.

William Langland. Aldershot: Variorum, 1996.

Haren, Michael. "The Interrogatories for Officials, Lawyers and Secular Estates of the *Memoriale presbyterorum.*" In *Handling Sin: Confession in the Middle Ages,* Peter Biller and A. J. Minnis (eds.). York Studies in Medieval Theology II. Woodbridge: York Medieval Press, 1998. pp. 123–39.

"Social Ideas in the Pastoral Literature of Fourteenth-Century England." In *Religious Beliefs and Ecclesiastical Careers in Late-Medieval England,* C. Harper-Bill (ed.). Woodbridge: Brewer, 1991. pp. 43–57.

Harpham, Geoffrey Galt. *Shadows of Ethics: Criticism and the Just Society.* Durham, NC: Duke University Press, 1999.

Hartley, Percival and H. R. Aldridge. *Johannes de Mirfeld of St. Bartholmews, Smithfield: His Life and Works.* Cambridge University Press, 1936.

Heffernan, Thomas. "The Authorship of the 'Northern Homily Cycle': The Liturgical Affiliation of the Sunday Gospel Pericopes as a Test." *Traditio,* 41 (1985), 289–309.

Heffernan, Thomas and Patrick J. Horner. "Sermons and Homilies." In *A Manual of the Writings in Middle English, 1050–1100, vol. XI,* Peter Beidler (ed.). New Haven: Connecticut Academy of Arts and Sciences, 2005.

Hinnebusch, William. *The History of the Dominican Order,* 2 vols. New York: Alba House, 1965.

Hirsch, John C. "Author and Scribe in The Book of Margery Kempe." *Medium Aevum*, 44 (1975), 145–50.

Horobin, Simon. "The Dialect and Authorship of 'Richard the Redeless' and 'Mum and the Sothsegger'." *Yearbook of Langland Studies*, 18 (2004), 133–52.

"The Scribe of Rawlinson Poetry 137 and the Copying and Circulation of *Piers Plowman*." *Yearbook of Langland Studies*, 19 (2005), 2–26.

Hudson, Anne. "Langland and Lollardy." *Yearbook of Langland Studies*, 17 (2003), 92–104.

"A Lollard Sect Vocabulary?" In *So meny people longages and tonges: Philological Essays in Scots and Mediaeval English Presented to Angus McIntosh,* Michael Benskin and M.L. Samuels (eds.). Edinburgh: Middle English Dialect Project, 1981. pp.14–30.

"*Piers Plowman* and the Peasants' Revolt: A Problem Revisited." *Yearbook of Langland Studies*, 8 (1994), 85–106.

The Premature Reformation: Wycliffite Texts and Lollard History. Oxford: Clarendon, 1998.

Hughes, Jonathan. *Pastors and Visionaries: Religion and Secular Life in Late Medieval Yorkshire.* Woodbridge: Boydell, 1988.

Jordan, Mark D. *The Cure of Souls and the Rhetoric of Moral Teaching in Bonaventure and Thomas. Spirit and Life* iv. St. Bonaventura, NY: The Franciscan Institute, 1993.

Justice, Stephen. *Writing and Rebellion: England in 1381.* Berkeley: University of California Press, 1994.

Kaeppeli, Thomas, O.P. *Scriptores Ordinis Praedicatorum Medii Aevi,* 4 vols. Rome: ad S. Sabinae, 1970–93.

Kean, P.M. "Love, Law, and *Leute* in *Piers Plowman,*" *Review of English Studies*, n.s. 15 (1964), 241–61. Rpt. in *Style and Symbolism in "Piers Plowman": A Modern Critical Anthology,* Robert Blanch (ed.). Knoxville: University of Tennessee Press, 1969. pp.132–55.

Kellogg, Alfred L. "Langland and the 'Canes Muti.'" In *Essays in Literary History Presented to J. Milton French,* R. Kirk and C.F. Main (eds.). New Brunswick, NJ: Rutgers University Press, 1960. pp.25–36.

Kenny, Anthony. *Wyclif.* Oxford University Press, 1985.

Kent, Bonnie. *Virtues of the Will: The Transformation of Ethics in the Late Fourteenth Century.* Washington: Catholic University of America Press, 1995.

Kerby-Fulton, Kathryn. *Books Under Suspicion: Censorship and Tolerance of Revelatory Writing in Later Medieval England.* Notre Dame University Press, 2006.

"Langland and the Bibliographic Ego." In *Written Work: Langland, Labor, and Authorship,* Stephen Justice and Kathryn Kerby-Fulton (eds.). Middle Ages Series. Philadelphia: University of Pennsylvania Press, 1997. pp.67–143.

"*Piers Plowman.*" In *The Cambridge History of Medieval English Literature,* David Wallace (ed.). Cambridge University Press, 1999. pp.513–38.

"Prophecy and Suspicion: Closet Radicalism, Reformist Politics, and the Vogue for Hildegardiana in Ricardian England." *Speculum*, 75 (2000), 318–41.

Reformist Apocalypticism and "Piers Plowman". Cambridge Studies in Medieval Literature VII. Cambridge University Press, 1990.

"When Women Preached: An Introduction to Female Homiletic, Sacramental, and Liturgical Roles in the Later Middle Ages." In Olson and Kerby-Fulton (eds.), pp. 31–56.

Kienzle, B. M. "Preaching as a Touchstone of Orthodoxy and Dissent in the Middle Ages." *Medieval Sermon Studies*, 43 (1999), 19–53.

Kirby, J. L. *Henry IV of England*. London: Constable, 1970.

Kirk, Elizabeth. *The Dream Thought of "Piers Plowman."* New Haven: Yale University Press, 1972.

Krug, Rebecca. *Reading Families: Women's Literate Practice in Late Medieval England*. Ithaca: Cornell University Press, 2002.

Kuehn, Thomas. "*Fama* as Legal Status in Renaissance Florence." In Fenster and Smail (eds.), pp. 27–46.

Lahey, Stephen E. *Philosophy and Politics in the Thought of John Wyclif*. Cambridge Studies in Medieval Life and Thought, Fourth Series, LIII. Cambridge University Press, 2003.

Lambert, Malcolm. *Medieval Heresy: Popular Movements from the Gregorian Reform to the Reformation,* 3rd edn. Oxford: Blackwell, 2002.

Lawless, George, O. S. A. *Augustine of Hippo and his Monastic Rule*. Oxford: Clarendon, 1987.

Lawton, David. *Chaucer's Narrators*. Chaucer Studies XIII. Cambridge: Brewer, 1985.

"Lollardy and the 'Piers Plowman' Tradition." *Modern Language Review*, 76 (1981), 780–93.

"The Subject of *Piers Plowman*." *Yearbook of Langland Studies*, 1 (1987), 1–39.

Levy, Ian Christopher. "John Wyclif on Papal Election, Correction, and Deposition." *Mediaeval Studies*, 69 (2007), 141–85.

"Wyclif and the Christian Life." In *A Companion to John Wyclif: Late Medieval Theologian,* Ian Christopher Levy (ed.). Leiden: Brill, 2006.

Lewis, Katherine J. "Margery Kempe and Saint Making in Late Medieval England." In *A Companion to the Book of Margery Kempe,* John H. Arnold and Katherine J. Lewis (eds.). Cambridge: Brewer, 2004. pp. 195–205.

Little, Katherine. *Confession and Resistance: Defining the Self in Late Medieval England*. University of Notre Dame Press, 2006.

Lochrie, Karma. *Margery Kempe and the Translations of the Flesh*. Middle Ages Series. Philadelphia: University of Pennsylvania Press, 1991.

MacIntyre, Alasdair. *After Virtue: A Study of Moral Theory,* 2nd edn. Notre Dame University Press, 1984.

McAvoy, Liz Herbert. "'Aftyr hyr owyn tunge': Body, Voice, and Authority in *The Book of Margery Kempe*." *Women's Writings: The Elizabethan to Victorian Period*, 9 (2002), 159–76.

McGrade, A. S. *The Political Thought of William of Ockham: Personal and Institutional Principles*. Cambridge Studies in Medieval Life and Thought, Third Series, VII. Cambridge University Press, 1974.

Middleton, Anne. "Acts of Vagrancy: The C Version 'Autobiography' and the Statute of 1388." In *Written Work: Langland, Labor, and Authorship*, Stephen Justice and Kathryn Kerby-Fulton (eds.). Middle Ages Series. Philadelphia: University of Pennsylvania Press, 1997. pp. 208–317.

"The Audience and Public of *Piers Plowman*." In *Middle English Alliterative Poetry and Its Literary Background: Seven Essays,* David Lawton (ed.). Cambridge: Brewer, 1982. pp. 101–23.

"Langland's Lives: Reflections on Late-Medieval Religious and Literary Vocabulary." In *The Idea of Medieval Literature: New Essays on Chaucer and Medieval Culture in Honor of Donald R. Howard,* James M. Dean and Christian Zacher (eds.). Newark: University of Delaware Press, 1992. pp. 227–42.

Miller, Mark. *Philosophical Chaucer: Love, Sex, and Agency in the "Canterbury Tales"*. Cambridge Studies in Medieval Literature LV. Cambridge University Press, 2004.

Miller, Maureen. "Religion Makes a Difference: Clerical and Lay Cultures in the Courts of Northern Italy, 1000–1300." *American Historical Review,* 105.4 (2000), 1,095–1,130.

Minnis, A. J. *Fallible Authors: Chaucer's Pardoner and Wife of Bath*. Middle Ages Series. Philadelphia: University of Pennsylvania Press, 2008.

Mitchell, J. Allan. *Ethics and Exemplary Narrative in Chaucer and Gower*. Chaucer Studies XXXIII. Cambridge: Brewer, 2004.

Moore, R. I. *The Formation of a Persecuting Society: Power and Deviance in Western Europe, 950–1250*. Oxford: Blackwell, 1987.

Ober, Josiah. *Athenian Legacies: Essays on the Politics of Going on Together*. Princeton University Press, 2005.

"Precedent, Amnesty, and History." Paper at "Does the Past have Moral Authority?," a conference marking Robert Conner's retirement as Director of the National Humanities Center, Research Triangle Park, November 1, 2002.

Olson, Linda, and Kathryn Kerby Fulton (eds.). *Voices in Dialogue: Reading Women in the Middle Ages*. University of Notre Dame Press, 2005.

Page, Christopher. *The Owl and the Nightingale: Musical Life and Ideas in France. 1100–1300*. Berkeley: University of California Press, 1989.

Patterson, Lee. "The Parson's Tale and the Quitting of *The Canterbury Tales*." *Traditio,* 34 (1978), 331–80.

Phillips, Susan. *Transforming Talk: The Problem with Gossip in Late Medieval England*. University Park: Pennsylvania State University Press, 2007.

Pitard, Derrick. "Sowing Difficulty: The 'Parson's Tale', Vernacular Commentary and the Nature of Chaucerian Dissent." *Studies in the Age of Chaucer,* 26 (2004), 299–330.

Rees Jones, Sarah. "'A peler of Holy Cherch': Margery Kempe and the Bishops." In *Medieval Women: Texts and Contexts in Late Medieval Britain: Essays for*

Felicity Riddy, Jocelyn Wogan-Browne *et alia* (eds.). Turnhout: Brepols, 2000. pp. 377–91.

Ricoeur, Paul. *Oneself as Another.* Kathleen Blamey (trans.). University of Chicago Press, 1992.

Rusconi, Roberto. 'De la prédication à la confession: transmission et contrôle des modèles de comportement au XIIIe siècle." In *Faire croire: Modalités de la diffusion et la réception des messages religieux du XIIe au XVe siècle.* Rome: École Française de Rome, 1981. pp. 67–85.

Sandler, Lucy Freeman. *Omne bonum: A Fourteenth-Century Encyclopedia of Universal Knowledge,* 2 vols. London: Harvey Miller, 1996.

Scase, Wendy. *"Piers Plowman" and the New Anticlericalism.* Cambridge Studies in Medieval Literature IV. Cambridge University Press, 1989.

Schneyer, J. B. *Repertorium der lateinischen Sermones des Mittelalters für die Zeit von 1150–1350,* 11 vols. Münster: Aschendorffsche Verlagsbuchhandlung, 1969–90.

Sharpe, Richard. *A Handlist of the Latin Writers of Great Britain and Ireland Before 1540.* Turnhout: Brepols, 1997, reissued 2001.

Shaw, David Gary. "Social Selves in Medieval England: The Worshipful Ferrour and Kempe." In *Writing Medieval History,* Nancy Partner (ed.). London: Hodder Arnold, 2005. pp. 3–21.

Sherwin, Michael, O.P. *By Knowledge and by Love: Charity and Knowledge in the Moral Theology of St. Thomas Aquinas.* Washington: Catholic University of America Press, 2005.

Shklar, Ruth. "Cobham's Daughter: *The Book of Margery Kempe* and the Power of Heterodox Thinking." *Modern Language Quarterly,* 56.3 (1995), 277–304.

Shogimen, Takashi. *Ockham and Political Discourse in the Late Middle Ages.* Cambridge Studies in Medieval Life and Thought, New Series, LXIX. Cambridge University Press, 2007.

Simpson, James. "The Constraints of Satire in 'Piers Plowman' and 'Mum and the Sothsegger'." In *Langland, the Mystics and the Medieval English Religious Tradition: Essays in Honour of S. S. Hussey,* Helen Phillips (ed.). Cambridge: Brewer, 1990. pp. 11–30.

"From Reason to Affective Knowledge: Modes of Thought and Poetic Form in *Piers Plowman*." *Medium Aevum,* 55 (1986), 1–23.

"Piers Plowman": An Introduction to the B-Text. London: Longman, 1990.

Reform and Cultural Revolution: The Oxford Literary History Volume II (1350–1547). Oxford University Press, 2002.

Smith, Vance D. *The Book of the Incipit: Beginnings in the Fourteenth Century.* Medieval Cultures XXVIII. Minneapolis: University of Minnesota Press, 2001.

Somerset, Fiona. *Clerical Discourse and Lay Audience in Late Medieval England.* Cambridge Studies in Medieval Literature XXXVII. Cambridge University Press, 1998.

"Expanding the Langlandian Canon: Radical Latin and the Stylistics of Reform." *Yearbook of Langland Studies,* 17 (2003), 73–92.

Spencer, H. Leith. *English Preaching in the Late Middle Ages.* Oxford: Clarendon, 1993.

Staley, Lynn. *Margery Kempe's Dissenting Fictions.* University Park: Pennsylvania State University Press, 1994.

Steele, Meili. *Theorizing Textual Subjects: Agency and Oppression.* Literature, Culture, Theory, xxi. Cambridge University Press, 1997.

Stegmüller, F. *et alia. Repertorium biblicum medii aevi,* 11 vols. Madrid: Instituto Francisco Suárez, 1950–80.

Steiner, Emily. *Documentary Culture and the Making of English Literature.* Cambridge Studies in Medieval Literature L. Cambridge University Press, 2004.

"Inventing Legality: Documentary Culture and Lollard Preaching." In *The Letter of the Law: Legal Practice and Literary Production in Medieval England,* Emily Steiner and Candace Barrington (eds.). Ithaca, NY: Cornell University Press, 2002. pp. 185–201.

Strohm, Paul. "Afterword: What Happens at Intersections?" In *Bodies and Disciplines: Intersections of Literature and History in Fifteenth-Century England,* Barbara Hanawalt and David Wallace (eds.). Medieval Cultures ix. Minneapolis: University of Minnesota Press, 1996. pp. 223–32.

England's Empty Throne: Usurpation and the Language of Legitimation, 1399–1422. New Haven: Yale University Press, 1998.

Swanson, R. H. *Church and Society in Late Medieval England.* Oxford: Blackwell, 1989.

Swidler, Ann. *Talk of Love: How Culture Matters.* University of Chicago Press, 2001.

Talbert, Ernest and H. Harrison Thomson. "Wyclif and His Followers." In *A Manual of the Writings in Middle English, 1050–1500,* vol. II, J. Burke Severs (ed.). New Haven: Connecticut Academy of Arts and Sciences, 1970. pp. 354–77, 522–33.

Tentler, Thomas. *Sin and Confession on the Eve of the Reformation.* Princeton University Press, 1977.

Thomson, Williel R. *The Latin Writings of John Wyclyf: An Annotated Catalog.* Toronto: Pontifical Institute of Mediaeval Studies, 1983.

Vauchez, André. "The Church and the Laity." In *The New Cambridge Medieval History: Vol. V (1198–1300),* David Abulafia (ed.). Cambridge University Press, 1999. pp. 182–203.

The Laity in the Middle Ages: Religious Beliefs and Devotional Practices, Margery J. Schneider (trans.) and Daniel Bornstein (ed.). Notre Dame University Press, 2000.

Voaden, Rosalynn. *God's Words, Women's Voices: The Discernment of Spirits in the Writing of Late-Medieval Women Visionaries.* Woodbridge: Brewer, 1999.

von Nolcken, Christina. "Some Alphabetical Compendia and How Preachers Used Them in Fourteenth-Century England." *Viator,* 12 (1981), 217–88.

Watson, Nicholas. "Censorship and Cultural Change in Late-Medieval England: Vernacular Theology, the Oxford Translation Debates, and Arundel's Constitutions of 1409." *Speculum,* 70 (1995), 822–64.

"The Making of *The Book of Margery Kempe*." In Olson and Kerby-Fulton (eds.), pp. 395–435.

"The Middle English Mystics." In *The Cambridge History of Medieval English Literature,* David Wallace (ed.). Cambridge University Press, 1999. pp. 539–65.

"The Politics of Middle English Writing." In *The Idea of the Vernacular: An Anthology of Middle English Literary Theory, 1280–1520,* Jocelyn Wogan-Browne *et alia* (eds.). University Park: Pennsylvania State University Press, 1999. pp. 331–52.

Watt, Diane. *Secretaries of God.* Cambridge: Brewer, 1997.

Watt, J. A. "The Papacy." In *The New Cambridge Medieval History: Vol. V (1198–1300),* David Abulafia (ed.). Cambridge University Press, 1999. pp. 107–63.

Wenzel, Siegfried. "Eli and His Sons." *Yearbook of Langland Studies,* 13 (1999), 137–52.

Latin Sermon Collections from Later Medieval England: Orthodox Preaching in the Age of Wyclif. Cambridge Studies in Medieval Literature LIII. Cambridge University Press, 2005.

The Sin of Sloth: "Acedia" in Medieval Thought and Literature. Chapel Hill: University of North Carolina Press, 1967.

Wilks, Michael. *Wyclif: Political Ideas and Practice: Papers by Michael Wilks Selected and Introduced by Anne Hudson.* Oxford: Oxbow Books, 2000.

Wilson, Janet. "Communities of Dissent: The Secular and Ecclesiastical Communities of Margery Kempe's *Book*." In *Medieval Women in Their Communities,* Diane Watt (ed.). University of Toronto Press, 1997. pp. 155–85.

"Margery and Alison: Women on Top." In *Margery Kempe: A Book of Essays,* Sandra J. McEntire (ed.). New York: Garland, 1992. pp. 223–37.

Wittig, Joseph. "*Piers Plowman* B. Passūs IX–XII: Elements of the Inward Journey." *Traditio,* 28 (1972), 211–80.

Workman, H. B. *John Wyclif: A Study of the English Medieval Church,* 2 vols. Oxford University Press, 1926.

Yunck, John A. *The Lineage of Lady Meed: The Development of Mediaeval Venality Satire.* University of Notre Dame Press, 1963.

Zeeman, Nicolette. *"Piers Plowman" and the Medieval Discourse of Desire.* Cambridge Studies in Medieval Literature LIX. Cambridge University Press, 2005.

Index

CAMBRIDGE STUDIES IN MEDIEVAL LITERATURE